Sass and Compass Designer's Cookbook

Over 120 practical and easy-to-understand recipes that explain how to use Sass and Compass to write efficient, maintainable, and reusable CSS code for your web development projects

Bass Jobsen

[PACKT] open source*

PUBLISHING · community experience distilled

BIRMINGHAM - MUMBAI

Sass and Compass Designer's Cookbook

First published: April 2016

Production reference: 1250416

Published by Packt Publishing Ltd.
Livery Place
35 Livery Street
Birmingham B3 2PB, UK.

ISBN 978-1-78328-693-5

www.packtpub.com

Credits

Author
Bass Jobsen

Reviewers
Saeed Afzal

Andrew Koebbe

Mark Reilly

Commissioning Editor
Kevin Colaco

Acquisition Editor
Vinay Argekar

Content Development Editor
Shali Deeraj

Technical Editor
Jayesh Sonawane

Copy Editor
Akshata Lobo

Project Coordinator
Sanchita Mandal

Proofreader
Safis Editing

Indexer
Rekha Nair

Graphics
Jason Monteiro

Production Coordinator
Aparna Bhagat

Cover Work
Aparna Bhagat

About the Author

Bass Jobsen has been programming for the Web since 1995, covering everything from C to PHP and is always on the hunt to find the most accessible interfaces. He is based in Orthen, the Netherlands.

Bass uses Sass in his daily job for web designing tasks and WordPress theme development.

He can be contacted via http://stackoverflow.com/users/1596547/bass-jobsen and he writes a blog that you can find at http://bassjobsen.weblogs.fm/.

Also, check his Bootstrap WordPress Starters Themes (JBST) and other projects at GitHub: https://github.com/bassjobsen.

Information on his current projects and development is available at http://www.streetart.com/, https://menstrualcups.eu/ and https://github.com/bassjobsen/jbst-4-sass.

This book is for Colinda, Kiki, Dries, Wolf, and Leny.

Adrian Raposo and Shali Deeraj were patient and excellent motivators and critical readers. I will thank also the reviewers of this book, Saeed Afzal, Andrew, and Mark, for their critical and valuable suggestions, which make this book even better.

About the Reviewers

Saeed Afzal is a young software engineer with more than 7 years of solid hands-on experience, specializing in solution architecture and the implementation of scalable, high performance applications.

He loves to build beautiful websites with a focus on user problems and providing genuine solutions. He joined IT and started his career at a very early age. Being self-trained, he has been moving forward with a spirit of entrepreneurship in different technologies in a timely manner.

When he's not in the zone coding, you can find him geeking out over comic books, science, football, and most importantly spending quality time with family and friends. Some call him Smac; if you knew him, you would understand. Overall, he's a pretty cool guy. Sit back and feel free to take a look at his latest work.

More detailed information about his skills and experience can be found at `http://saeedafzal.com`. He can be contacted at `sirsmac@gmail.com`.

I would like to thank the Allah Almighty, my parents, my twin brother, and my life partner Hafiza Zara Saeed for their encouragement.

Thank you Packt Publishing for selecting me as one of the technical reviewers for this wonderful book. It is my honor to be a part of it.

Andrew Koebbe is a software architect and a web developer currently focused on PHP and Symfony. He has worked in the digital advertising and medical research fields. He is a Grav CMS contributor and presenter. He enjoys dabbling in Drupal, DevOps, and Raspberry Pi and Arduino hacking. He also enjoys spending time hanging out with his wife and son, sous-vide cooking, personal care hacking, and watching MST3k. This is the first time he has reviewed a book for Packt Publishing.

I would like to give special thanks to my wife and son for their support and encouragement during this endeavor.

Mark Reilly is a senior user experience designer at Spies & Assassins in NYC. He's worked in the Web for the last 20 years as both a web designer and a frontend developer. He's an open source enthusiast and has been active in the Sass, Drupal, and Sakai communities. He's the author of the compass gems *Style Tiles and Compass Pattern Primer* that he hopes one day to port to LibSass and a build tool, possibly Grunt.

www.PacktPub.com

eBooks, discount offers, and more

Did you know that Packt offers eBook versions of every book published, with PDF and ePub files available? You can upgrade to the eBook version at www.PacktPub.com and as a print book customer, you are entitled to a discount on the eBook copy. Get in touch with us at customercare@packtpub.com for more details.

At www.PacktPub.com, you can also read a collection of free technical articles, sign up for a range of free newsletters and receive exclusive discounts and offers on Packt books and eBooks.

https://www2.packtpub.com/books/subscription/packtlib

Do you need instant solutions to your IT questions? PacktLib is Packt's online digital book library. Here, you can search, access, and read Packt's entire library of books.

Why Subscribe?

- ▶ Fully searchable across every book published by Packt
- ▶ Copy and paste, print, and bookmark content
- ▶ On demand and accessible via a web browser

Table of Contents

Preface

Sass (Syntactically Awesome Stylesheets) is a CSS extension language or preprocessor, which means that Sass or SCSS code compiles into static CSS code. Sass changes the way you write and maintain your CSS code; the final CSS code will be the same, although better organized in many situations.

Since the introduction of CSS3 in 2012, the role of CSS in modern web development has become more and more important. Nowadays, CSS3 is not only used to style your HTML documents, but it also plays an important role in the responsibility of your designs too. Last, but not least, CSS3 extends CSS with features such as animations and transitions.

Writing correct functional CSS code will be the first thing; keeping this code readable, working on all major browsers, and maintainable will be the second. CSS files grow and become untidy in the development and maintenance processes. CSS doesn't have the ability to modify existing values or reuse common styles. Also, doing the math or defining variables is not possible in CSS. This is where the Sass language comes into the frame.

The Sass language enables you to write your CSS code DRY (Do not Repeat Yourself) because it extends the CSS syntax with variables, mixins, functions, and many other techniques. Sass makes the CSS language is more maintainable, themeable, and extendable.

Also, others know the power of Sass. Projects such as Bootstrap 4 and the Foundation are built with Sass. These projects create clear and extendable Frameworks with Sass. Bootstrap chose Sass because of the increasingly large community of Sass developers. You can't ignore these proofs. Stop writing cumbersome CSS with bugs and browser defects and learn Sass by reading this book.

In this book, you will learn to write, compile, and understand the Sass language. It helps with faster and more cost-effective web development. You will get practical tips to integrate Sass in your current and new projects. After reading this book, you will write clear and readable CSS3 with Sass. Instead of spending your time debugging your complex CSS code for a specific device or browser, you could pay more attention to your real design tasks.

Your clients will be happy with your advanced and stable designs. Development and maintenance time, and therefore costs, shall decrease.

Sass is available for use and modification under the MIT License. You can use Sass free of charge.

What this book covers

Chapter 1, Getting Started with Sass, gives you an introduction to the Sass language. You will learn how to install and use Sass for your projects on your system, read how to edit your code, and organize your files. It will also tell you why you should use newer SCSS syntax instead of the intended Sass Syntax.

Chapter 2, Debugging Your Code, teaches you how to comment and debug your Sass code. Get introduced to an online tool to test your code and impress with style guides.

Chapter 3, Variables, Mixins, and Functions, showcases the power of Sass. Learn to use variables to define commonly used values at a single place and write reusable code by using mixins and functions.

Chapter 4, Nested Selectors and Modular CSS, explains about the nested selectors and other methodologies to structure your code. Reuse your selectors by extending them and use placeholders to prevent duplicated and unused CSS selectors.

Chapter 5, Built-in Functions, dynamically assigns property values based on your input. Use the built-in functions of Sass, among others, for color values and mathematical operations.

Chapter 6, Using Compass, teaches you to code faster using Compass. Compass contains many useful helper mixins and functions to write clean and reusable CSS code.

Chapter 7, Cross-Browser CSS3 Mixins, helps to write maintainable and cross-browser CSS code. Learn about the CSS3 introduced vendor-specific rules, and read how Sass helps you prefix your code to support different browsers.

Chapter 8, Advanced Sass Coding, uses conditionals and loops to create dynamic code and avoid repeats. Learn how to use prebuilt libraries for vertical rhythms, color contrasts, iconic fonts, and CSS Media Queries.

Chapter 9, Building Layouts with Sass, introduces grid-based layouts, help coders and designers, to work together in a consistent manner. Sass can help you create semantic or responsive grids for your projects.

Chapter 10, Building Grid-based Layouts with Susy and Sass, introduces Susy, which is a Sass add-on for grids; learn how to use it. You can also use Susy to create asymmetric or responsive layouts.

Chapter 11, Foundation and Sass, explores Foundation for Sites 6. Foundation is a responsive frontend framework built with Sass.

Chapter 12, Bootstrap and Sass, explains details about Bootstrap 4. Bootstrap 4 uses Sass now. Learn how to develop mobile first and responsive projects with Bootstrap and Sass.

Chapter 13, Meeting the Bourbon Family, explains about Bourbon, which is a simple and lightweight mixin library for Sass; it helps you write CSS faster and easier without the need of using vendor prefixes.

Chapter 14, Ruby on Rails and Sass, builds web applications with Ruby on Rails (RoR) and Sass. Get to grips with sass-rails to compile the CSS code for your RoR apps.

Chapter 15, Building Mobile Apps, explains that the look and feel of mobile apps may differ from that of other web applications. Get introduced to Frameworks for mobile app development with Sass. Build mobile apps with Foundation for Apps and Ionic.

Chapter 16, Setting up a Build Chain with Grunt, gives introduction to Grunt, a build tool for JavaScript projects. Learn how to create tasks to automatically compile, compress, and prefix your CSS code.

What you need for this book

To understand and fully profit from the contents of this book, we expect you have built a website with CSS before. A basic understanding of CSS will be required. Understanding CSS selectors and CSS precedence will help you get most out of it.

Understanding the basics of using functions and parameters in functional languages such as JavaScript will be valuable, but not required. Don't panic if you know nothing about functions and parameters. This book contains clear examples. Even without any (functional) programmers' knowledge, you can learn Sass and the book will help you do this. The most important skill will be the willingness to learn.

Finally, some experience with the command line for your system is useful too.

All the chapters of this book contain examples and example code. Running and testing these examples will help you develop your Sass skills. Use any preferred text or CSS editor to write your Sass code.

Most code examples are linked with the `scss-lint` tool. This tool helps keep your SCSS files clean and readable. Code examples may include special comments to configure this tool.

Who this book is for

This book is mainly intended for web developers and designers who are comfortable with CSS and HTML. If you are someone with some experience with CSS, you will find the learning curve of learning Sass syntax will be less steep. A basic knowledge of web development is helpful, but you don't have to be a programmer to understand Sass.

Sections

In this book, you will find several headings that appear frequently (Getting ready, How to do it, How it works, There's more, and See also).

To give clear instructions on how to complete a recipe, we use these sections as follows:

Getting ready

This section tells you what to expect in the recipe, and describes how to set up any software or any preliminary settings required for the recipe.

How to do it...

This section contains the steps required to follow the recipe.

How it works...

This section usually consists of a detailed explanation of what happened in the previous section.

There's more...

This section consists of additional information about the recipe in order to make the reader more knowledgeable about the recipe.

See also

This section provides helpful links to other useful information for the recipe.

Conventions

In this book, you will find a number of text styles that distinguish between different kinds of information. Here are some examples of these styles and an explanation of their meaning.

Code words in text, database table names, folder names, filenames, file extensions, pathnames, dummy URLs, user input, and Twitter handles are shown as follows: "We can include other contexts through the use of the `include` directive."

A block of code is set as follows:

```
// scss-lint:disable ColorKeyword
$link-color: green;

@mixin colors {
  color: darken($link-color, 10%);
}

%box {
  display: block;
}
```

When we wish to draw your attention to a particular part of a code block, the relevant lines or items are set in bold:

```
.code {
  @include colors;
  p & {
    @extend %box;
  }
}
```

Any command-line input or output is written as follows:

```
sass --compass code.scss code.css
```

New terms and **important words** are shown in bold. Words that you see on the screen, for example, in menus or dialog boxes, appear in the text like this: "Clicking the **Next** button moves you to the next screen."

Warnings or important notes appear in a box like this.

Tips and tricks appear like this.

Reader feedback

Feedback from our readers is always welcome. Let us know what you think about this book—what you liked or disliked. Reader feedback is important for us as it helps us develop titles that you will really get the most out of.

To send us general feedback, simply e-mail `feedback@packtpub.com`, and mention the book's title in the subject of your message.

If there is a topic that you have expertise in and you are interested in either writing or contributing to a book, see our author guide at `www.packtpub.com/authors`.

Customer support

Now that you are the proud owner of a Packt book, we have a number of things to help you to get the most from your purchase.

Downloading the example code

You can download the example code files for this book from your account at `http://www.packtpub.com`. If you purchased this book elsewhere, you can visit `http://www.packtpub.com/support` and register to have the files e-mailed directly to you.

You can download the code files by following these steps:

1. Log in or register to our website using your e-mail address and password.
2. Hover the mouse pointer on the **SUPPORT** tab at the top.
3. Click on **Code Downloads & Errata**.
4. Enter the name of the book in the **Search** box.
5. Select the book for which you're looking to download the code files.
6. Choose from the drop-down menu where you purchased this book from.
7. Click on **Code Download**.

You can also download the code files by clicking on the **Code Files** button on the book's webpage at the Packt Publishing website. This page can be accessed by entering the book's name in the **Search** box. Please note that you need to be logged in to your Packt account.

Once the file is downloaded, please make sure that you unzip or extract the folder using the latest version of:

- WinRAR / 7-Zip for Windows
- Zipeg / iZip / UnRarX for Mac
- 7-Zip / PeaZip for Linux

Downloading the color images of this book

We also provide you with a PDF file that has color images of the screenshots/diagrams used in this book. The color images will help you better understand the changes in the output. You can download this file from `http://www.packtpub.com/sites/default/files/downloads/SassandCompassDesignersCookbook_ColorImages.pdf`.

Errata

Although we have taken every care to ensure the accuracy of our content, mistakes do happen. If you find a mistake in one of our books—maybe a mistake in the text or the code—we would be grateful if you could report this to us. By doing so, you can save other readers from frustration and help us improve subsequent versions of this book. If you find any errata, please report them by visiting `http://www.packtpub.com/submit-errata`, selecting your book, clicking on the **Errata Submission Form** link, and entering the details of your errata. Once your errata are verified, your submission will be accepted and the errata will be uploaded to our website or added to any list of existing errata under the Errata section of that title.

To view the previously submitted errata, go to `https://www.packtpub.com/books/content/support` and enter the name of the book in the search field. The required information will appear under the **Errata** section.

Piracy

Piracy of copyrighted material on the Internet is an ongoing problem across all media. At Packt, we take the protection of our copyright and licenses very seriously. If you come across any illegal copies of our works in any form on the Internet, please provide us with the location address or website name immediately so that we can pursue a remedy.

Please contact us at `copyright@packtpub.com` with a link to the suspected pirated material.

We appreciate your help in protecting our authors and our ability to bring you valuable content.

Questions

If you have a problem with any aspect of this book, you can contact us at `questions@packtpub.com`, and we will do our best to address the problem.

1
Getting Started with Sass

In this chapter, you will learn how to do the following:

- ▸ Installing Sass for command line usage
- ▸ Installing Compass
- ▸ Using Sass on the command line
- ▸ Using the Sass interactive mode and SassScript
- ▸ Using the sass-gulp plugin with Gulp
- ▸ Using Sass in the browsers
- ▸ Writing Sass or SCSS
- ▸ Choosing your output style
- ▸ Working with partials
- ▸ Writing your code in a text editor

Introduction

This chapter guides you through the installation of Sass and explains the different ways you can compile your Sass code into static **CSS**. You will not only learn how to use Sass using the **command line interface** (**CLI**), but you will also be introduced to **LibSass**. LibSass is a **C/C++** port of the Sass engine.

Based on LibSass, `sass.js` is a pure JavaScript implementation of the Sass engine, which enables you to compile Sass code with JavaScript and run `sass.js` in your browser.

The `sass-node` is an interpreter of LibSass for **Node.js**, and it enables you to compile Sass in a Node.js environment. Together with a task runner, such as **Gulp** or **Grunt**, you can use the `sass-node` to set up a build chain for your projects.

In this book, the **SCSS** syntax for Sass has been used in favor of the original indented Sass, that is, the **Ruby**-like syntax. You can write your SCSS code in your favorite text editor, but at the end of this chapter, you will also be introduced to some **Graphical User Interfaces** (**GUI**) that will help you write and compile your code more easily.

Installing Sass for command line usage

In this recipe, you will learn how to use Sass on the command line.

Getting ready

You can install Sass on Linux, Mac, and Windows. Sass has been written in Ruby. So, installing Sass requires that you install Ruby first. Ruby is a dynamic open source programming language with its focus on simplicity and productivity. You can read more about Ruby in the *Ruby and MongoDB Web Development Beginner's Guide* book by *Gautam Rege*. You will find this book at `https://www.packtpub.com/web-development/ruby-and-mongodb-web-development-beginners-guide`. If you are using Mac, you are lucky because OS X has Ruby preinstalled. Linux users should use a packages manager, such as **Advanced Package Tool** (**APT**), to install Ruby:

```
sudo apt-get install ruby-full
```

Other methods to install Ruby on Linux can be found at `https://www.ruby-lang.org/en/documentation/installation/`.

Finally, if you are on Windows, **RubyInstaller** is available. RubyInstaller is a single-click installer that includes the Ruby language, an execution environment, important documentations, and more. You can find RubyInstaller at `http://rubyinstaller.org/`.

How to do it...

After installing Ruby, you can use the following steps to install Sass on your system:

1. Open a terminal or a command prompt. Mac users should run `Terminal.app` and Window users can use the `cmd` command.

2. Then, enter the following command in your console:

   ```
   gem install sass
   ```

   The preceding command requires administrator rights for some systems. Use the `sudo` command for global installations with administrator rights.

3. Now, you should be able to check your installation by running a command, such as the following one:

```
sass -version
```

4. The preceding command should generate the following output:

```
Sass 3.4.13 (Selective Steve)
```

How it works...

RubyGems is Ruby's package manager. Ruby packages, called **gems**, can easily be installed via the command line and be distributed over the Internet. Many gems are hosted at `https://rubygems.org/` and `https://github.com/`. Also, Sass is distributed as a gem. The Sass gem will not only install Sass, but also install all the dependencies for you. Installing Sass with RubyGems will be easy and straightforward.

The `gem install sass` command in this recipe should install Ruby Sass and all its dependencies.

There's more...

After installing Sass, you can use the `--help` option to get a list of the available options and a short instruction on how to use the command-line compiler:

```
sass --h+elp
```

Besides the Sass compiler tool, the Ruby Sass gem also installs the sass-convert command-line tool. The sass-convert tool can be used to convert files from the indented syntax into the newer SCSS syntax and vice versa. Notice that you can also use `sass-convert` to migrate the CSS code Sass or the SCSS code. This will give you some basic nesting when migrating your CSS code.

In the *Writing Sass or SCSS* recipe of this chapter, you can read about the differences between the original indented syntax and the newer SCSS syntax.

The Ruby on rails apps can also use the Ruby Sass gem to compile the CSS code. Read more about Ruby on rails and Sass in *Chapter 14, Ruby on Rails and Sass*, of this book.

See also

▶ The website of the Ruby community can be found at `https://www.ruby-lang.org/`

▶ You can read more about Ruby gems at `http://guides.rubygems.org/what-is-a-gem/`

Installing Compass

Compass is an open source framework for Sass. Compass helps you write reusable **CSS3** code with Sass by using reusable patterns. In this recipe, you will learn how to install Compass for command-line usage. Compass can easily be extended, and it ships with handy features, such as mixins for creating typographic rhythms and image sprites. Finally, Compass can also help you prefix your properties to handle browser compatibility. Read more about vendor prefixes in the *Using vendor prefixes* recipe of *Chapter 7, Cross-Browser CSS3 Mixins*. You can read more about Compass and its features further on in this book and especially in *Chapter 6, Using Compass*.

Getting ready

You will have to install Ruby before installing Compass. In the *Installing Sass for command line usage* recipe of this chapter, you can read how to install Ruby on your system. Both Compass and Ruby run on Linux, OS X, and Windows. When you install Compass before you have installed Sass, Sass will be installed automatically, since Ruby Sass is a dependency of Compass.

How to do it...

After installing Ruby, you simply have to run the following command in your console to install Compass:

```
gem install compass
```

That's all. You can also try the following steps to get a short impression of how to run Compass on the command line:

1. Create a new compass project with the following command:

    ```
    compass create project
    ```

2. The preceding command will create a new folder called `project`, which will contain the files shown in this image:

    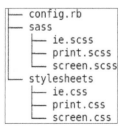

    ```
    ├─ config.rb
    ├─ sass
    │    ├─ ie.scss
    │    ├─ print.scss
    │    └─ screen.scss
    └─ stylesheets
         ├─ ie.css
         ├─ print.css
         └─ screen.css
    ```

3. Now, you can compile your project by running the following command:

`compass compile project`

How it works...

The `config.rb` file contains the configuration for your Compass project. This file is well-commented, and it contains, among others, the path to your project's folders.

Running the compile project command compiles each Sass file from the Sass (`sass_dir`) folder into a CSS file in the stylesheets (`css_dir`) folder. Files having a name starting with an underscore (_) are called partials and are not compiled into a CSS file. You can read more about partials and how to use them in the *Working with partials* recipe of this chapter.

There's more...

You can also directly use the features, mixins, and helper functions of Compass together with the command-line Sass compiler (see the *Using Sass on the command line* recipe of this chapter) by setting the `--compass` option. For more information on integrating compass in your compile process, you can read *Chapter 6, Using Compass*.

Compass is a widely used Sass framework. Many other frameworks for Sass are available too. Susy is a powerful set of Sass mixins for building grid-based layouts. Susy was originally built to be a part of the Compass ecosystem. In *Chapter 9, Building grid-based layouts with Sass*, and *Chapter 10, Susy and Sass*, of this book, you can read about Susy. And in *Chapter 13, Meeting the Bourbon Family*, of this book you will be acquainted with Bourbon. Bourbon is another library of Sass mixins.

This recipe demonstrates how to set up a project with only Compass. In the *Adding Compass to an existing Sass project* recipe of *Chapter 6, Using Compass*, you can read how to integrate Compass into existing projects too.

See also

The official website for the Compass framework can be found at `http://compass-style.org/`.

Using Sass on the command line

You can run Sass on the command line to compile your Sass files directly into the CSS code.

Getting ready

In the *Installing Sass for command line usage* recipe of this chapter, you have already read how to install Sass. Linux users have to open a terminal, while Mac users have to run the `Terminal.app`, and Window users have to use the `cmd` command for command-line usage.

How to do it...

Use the following steps to find out how to compile your Sass code in the command line:

1. Create a Sass template called `first.scss` that contains the following SCSS code:

   ```scss
   $color: orange;


   p {
     color: $color;
   }
   ```

2. Then, run the following command in your console:

   ```
   sass first.scss
   ```

3. You will find that the preceding command outputs the CSS code as it is shown here:

   ```css
   p {
     color: orange;  }
   ```

How it works...

Firstly, notice that the example code in this recipe uses the newer SCSS syntax for Sass. In the *Writing Sass or SCSS* recipe of this chapter, you can read why this book uses the SCSS syntax in favor of the original indented Sass syntax.

The `sass` command directly outputs the compiled CSS code to your console. To save the output in a file, you will have to set a second output argument, as follows:

```
sass first.scss first.css
```

The preceding command creates a new `first.css` CSS file that contains the compiled CSS code.

There's more...

When compiling your Sass templates into CSS files, Sass does not only create CSS files, but also a folder called `.sass-cache`. By default, Sass caches compile templates and partials. In the *Working with partials* recipe of this chapter, you can read what partials are. Caching of the compiled templates and partials makes recompiling after your changes faster.

You can use the `--no-cache` option to disable caching.

The `--compass` option makes Compass imports available and loads the project's configuration. You can read more about this option in the *Extending Sass with Compass helper functions and more* recipe of *Chapter 6, Using Compass*.

Using the Sass interactive mode and SassScript

In the *Using Sass on the command line* recipe of this chapter, you had to create a Sass sample as an input for the Sass compiler. In this recipe, you will be introduced to the interactive Sass mode and SassScript. SassScript is a small set of extensions of the plain CSS property syntax. You can use SassScript to set property values using variables, arithmetic, and extra functions. The interactive mode enables you to enter and test your SassScript code directly in the console. SassScript can also be used to generate selectors and property names via string interpolation. You can read more about interpolation in the *Interpolation of variables* recipe of *Chapter 3, Variables, Mixins, and Functions*.

Getting ready

The interactive mode of Sass comes with the Sass gem. You can use it after installing Sass. In the *Installing Sass for command line usage* recipe of this chapter, you can read how to install Sass.

How to do it...

Take a look at the following steps to understand how to use the Sass interactive mode:

1. You can start the interactive shell by running the following in your console:

   ```
   sass -interactive
   ```

2. Now, you can enter the following code into the shell:

   ```
   >> 1px + 1px
   ```

3. The preceding command will give the following output:

   ```
   2px
   ```

4. Also, notice that you can only enter a valid code. Consider the following code:

   ```
   >> 1px + 2em
   ```

5. Because Sass cannot sum different units, the preceding code will generate the following error:

   ```
   SyntaxError: Incompatible units: 'em' and 'px'.
   ```

6. Also, Sass built-in function can be evaluated. Enter the following code into the shell:

   ```
   change-color(#ff0000, $alpha: 0.5)
   ```

7. You will find that this returns the following output:

   ```
   rgba(255, 0, 0, 0.5)
   ```

How it works...

As it has already been made clear in the introduction of this recipe, you can use the interactive shell to test the property values set by SassScript. The interactive shell does not allow you to use variables or mixins, but you can make use of Sass's built-in functions. *Chapter 5*, *Built-in Functions*, of this book will introduce you to the useful built-in functions of Sass. The function used in the fourth step of this recipe is an example of a built-in function.

To quit once you have entered the interactive mode, just type *Ctrl + D*.

There's more...

The Compass gem has an interactive shell that is available too. You can start Compass's interactive shell by running the following command in your console:

```
compass interactive
```

In the interactive shell, you can run SassScript and you can also test the results of the Compass helper functions. Try the following command to evaluate the `append-selector()` helper function:

```
>> append-selector("p, div, span", ".bar")
```

The preceding command will give the following output:

```
"p.bar, div.bar, span.bar"
```

In your Sass code, you should use the preceding result inside an interpolation escape: #{ }.

Using the sass-gulp plugin with Gulp

As you know, Sass was originally written in Ruby. People wrote a port of Sass in C/C++ called LibSass, which can also be used in a development environment outside of Ruby. LibSass can easily be implemented in other languages and people have reported that LibSass is about 4,000% faster than the original Sass library (http://www.moovweb.com/blog/libsass/).

In fact, LibSass is just a library that needs an implementer. Implementers for the library can be written in any language. Implementers for C (command-line usage), Node, JavaScript, PHP, C#, and many other languages and platforms are available already.

The node-sass can be used in a Grunt/Gulp workflow. Nowadays, many developers use Grunt/Gulp workflows to compile their Sass code. This recipe will give you a short impression on how to compile Sass code with Gulp. *Chapter 3, Variables, Mixins, and Functions*, of this book describes the usage of Gulp to set build chains in more detail.

Getting ready

To use `gulp-sass` (uses `node-sass`), you should install Node.js (`npm`) and Gulp on your system first. Node.js is a platform built on Chrome's JavaScript runtime to easily build fast, scalable network applications. Gulp is a task runner or a build system written for Node.

You also have to install gulp-sass by running the following command in your console:

```
npm install gulp-sass
```

How to do it...

The following step will show you how to use Gulp and `gulp-sass` to compile your Sass code into CSS code:

1. Create an example Sass file called `main.scss` and save this file in the `sass` folder. The content of this file can look as follows:

    ```scss
    $color: orange;

    p {
      color: $color;
    }
    ```

2. Then, create your `Gulpfile.js` file as follows:

    ```js
    var gulp = require('gulp');
    var sass = require('gulp-sass');
    ```

```
gulp.task('sass', function () {
    gulp.src('./sass/*.scss')
        .pipe(sass())
        .pipe(gulp.dest('./css'));
});
```

3. Now, running gulp in your console will output to your console, as follows:

    ```
    [17:22:51] Using gulpfile ~/Gulpfile.js
    [17:22:51] Starting 'sass'...
    [17:22:51] Finished 'sass' after 24 ms
    ```

4. The preceding command creates a new file called `css/main.css`. This CSS file contains the following CSS code now:

    ```
    p {
      color: orange; }
    ```

How it works...

The `gulp-sass` plugin is a plugin for Gulp that enables you to compile your Sass code with `node-sass`. `node-sass` is the node interpreter for LibSass.

As it has been already explained, Gulp is a task runner. The `Gulpfile.js` file defines the task. This file has been written in the **JSON** format.

The `gulp.src('./sass/*.scss')` code reads all the files with the `.scss` extension from the `sass` folder. The content of each file is compiled with the `sass()` command from the `gulp-sass` plugin. And the compiled CSS will finally be saved in the folder set by `gulp.dest()`.

Each SCSS file will be compiled in a new CSS file, but notice that the partial files (see the *Working with partials* recipe of this chapter) are ignored.

There's more...

Gulp is just like Grunt—a task runner for node. Grunt does not use streams like Gulp, but saves results directly in files. Grunt has a longer history and a big community too. On the other hand, people find streams (saving file contents in memory) more intuitive and the number of Gulp plugins grows fast. In this book, Gulp is used for setting up build chains without saying that it's better than Grunt or any other task runner. Bootstrap, as discussed in *Chapter 12, Bootstrap and Sass*, of this book, uses Grunt, while Foundation uses Gulp. You can read more about Foundation in *Chapter 11, Foundation and Sass*. You can read more about Grunt in *Chapter 16, Setting up a Build Chain with Grunt*, of this book.

Also, a gulp version for Ruby Sass is available at `https://github.com/sindresorhus/gulp-ruby-sass`. In the past, the Sass Ruby gem was leading in regards to developing new features. Because LibSass was not directly updated after the releases of Ruby Sass, there were differences between Ruby Sass and LibSass. Recently, LibSass has become part of the Sass community, and Ruby Sass and LibSass are maintained at the same speed as much as possible. Some minor differences between both the versions can be found, but Ruby Sass will usually wait for feature parity with LibSass.

See also

> ► Sass Compatibility is a database that reports incompatibilities between different Sass engines. If you want to be sure about whether a feature differs between Ruby Sass and LibSass, you can look up information about the future in the database at `http://sass-compatibility.github.io/`. The website of Sass Compatibility will also give you the possibility of comparing different versions of the same engine.

> ► Read more about Gulp at `http://gulpjs.com/`.

> ► Read more about Grunt at `http://gruntjs.com/`.

Using Sass in the browsers

LibSass for JavaScript, called sass.js in short, also offers the opportunity to run the Sass compiler in browsers. In this recipe, you will learn how to run Sass in browsers with **sass.js**. sass.js is the only pure JavaScript implementation of LibSass, and it should generate the same output as node-sass does.

You should not use the code in this recipe for production. Besides, JavaScript files are large; you do not want every user of your website having to compile your client-side stylesheets.

Getting ready

Bower is a package manager for the web-optimized for the frontend. You can install bower by running the following command:

```
npm install - bower
```

You can run the following command to install **sass.js** and **jQuery**:

```
bower install sass.js jquery
```

After installing sass.js, you will need a text editor to edit the HTML file and a browser to inspect the results. You can also find the source code of this recipe in the downloaded files of this book.

How to do it...

Here is how you can compile Sass code in your browser:

1. Use your favorite text editor to write down the following HTML code in a file called demo.html:

```html
<!doctype html>
<html lang="en">
  <head>
    <meta charset="utf-8" />
    <meta name="viewport" content="width=device-width, initial-scale=1.0" />
    <title>Sass in browser</title>
    <script src="bower_components/jquery/dist/jquery.min.js"></script>
    <script src="bower_components/sass.js/dist/sass.js"></script>
    <style id="csscode"></style>
    <script>
      Sass.initialize('bower_components/sass.js/dist/sass.worker.js');
      function compileCSS(color) {
      var options = {};
      Sass.compile('$color: ' + color +  '; h1 { color: $color; }', function(result){
          $('#csscode').html(result.text);
      });
      }
      compileCSS('orange');
    </script>
</head>
<body>
<h1>Colored text</h1>
<form>
  Enter color name and hit enter:
  <input type="text" value="orange" name="color" />
  <input type="submit" />
</form>
<script>
      $( 'form' ).submit(function(event) {
      color = $( 'input[name="color"]' ).val();
      compileCSS(color);
      event.preventDefault();
      });
```

```
</script>
</body>
</html>
```

2. Now open `demo.html` in your web browser. It will look like the following screenshot:

3. Test the demo by entering another color name in the input field and pressing submit. You will find that the color of the `colored text` will change according to your input.

How it works...

Every time you hit the submit button, the sass.js compiler will compile the following code:

```
$color: {color};
h1 { color: $color; }
```

With `{color}` depending on your input, your input should be a valid color name. The 147 color names defined by the **Scalable Vector Graphics** (**SVG**) are according to their specifications used by HTML and CSS3 too. See also `http://www.w3.org/TR/css3-color/`. You can use any valid CSS color value in Sass, so `rgb(0,255,255)` or even `rgba(0,255,255,0.5)` can be used too. You can read more about color usage in Sass in the *Color functions* recipe of *Chapter 5, Built-In Functions*.

The demo uses jQuery to insert the compiled CSS into the **DOM** (in line with the tag of the head section). jQuery is a feature-rich JavaScript library that can be used for HTML document traversal and manipulation, and event handling. Neither Sass nor sass.js requires jQuery for compiling.

In the *Editing and debugging your Sass code in browser* recipe of *Chapter 2, Debugging Your Code*, you can read how to debug your Sass code in a browser using the **Google Chrome** browser. Although the code of this recipe runs in a browser, the sass.js compiler is not used here. In browsers, debugging uses the Ruby Sass compiler with the watch function or LibSass with live reload.

There's more...

As it has already been made clear, you should not use sass.js for production in the first place. When you use Sass for a demo proposal as in this recipe, and you need to compile Sass based on user input, you can reduce the total load time leveraging a web worker. A web worker is a JavaScript that runs in the background, independently of other scripts. Sass.js ships with a web worker, which can be invoked as follows:

```
<script src="dist/sass.js"></script>
<script>
  // telling sass.js where it can find the worker,
  // url is relative to document.URL
  Sass.initialize('dist/sass.worker.js');
```

Because sass.js runs in a browser and does not have access to your files' system, you should register individual files before using them with the @import directive. The following is an example code that shows you how to register files:

```
Sass.writeFile('one.scss', '.one { width: 123px; }');
Sass.writeFile('some-dir/two.scss', '.two { width: 123px; }');
Sass.compile('@import "one"; @import "some-dir/two";',
function(result) {
  console.log(result.text);1
});
```

See also

▶ You can read more about sass.js at `https://github.com/medialize/sass.js`.

▶ Sass.js had been compiled with Emscripten. Emscripten is an LLVM-based project that compiles C and C++ into highly optimizable JavaScript in the asm.js format. You can read more about **Emscripten** at `http://kripken.github.io/emscripten-site/docs/introducing_emscripten/about_emscripten.html`.

Writing Sass or SCSS

Attentive readers have possibly already noticed that the SCSS code has been used to write Sass code. SCSS is the newer and more CSS-like syntax for Sass. This book uses SCSS code in lieu of the older indented Sass syntax. In this recipe, you will learn the differences between the Sass and SCSS syntaxes and why this book prefers SCSS.

Getting ready

For this recipe, you will need only a text editor and the Ruby Sass gem installed. In the *Installing Sass for command line usage* recipe of this chapter, you can read about how to install the Ruby Sass gem.

How to do it...

Use the following steps to learn how to convert SCSS code into the indented Sass syntax and find out that both syntaxes compile in exactly the same CSS code:

1. Use your text editor to create a simple SCSS file called `test.scss`. This file should contain the following SCSS code:

    ```scss
    $color: orange;

    p {
      color: $color;
    }
    ```

2. Then, run the following command in your console:

    ```
    sass-convert test.scss test.sass
    ```

3. The command from the previous step will create a new file named `test.sass`. Now, open the `test.sass` file with your text editor and you will find that its content looks as follows:

    ```sass
    $color: orange

    p
        color: $color
    ```

4. Now, you can run both the `sass test.sass` and the `sass test.scss` commands in your console. Both will give the following output:

    ```css
    p {
        color: orange; }
    ```

How it works...

Currently, two syntaxes are available to write Sass: the original indented syntax, mostly called Sass, and also the newer **Sassy CSS** (**SCSS**) syntax, which is an extension of **CSS3**.

When running the `sass test.sass` and the `sass test.scss` commands, the compiler uses the file extension to decide which syntax should be used. In your project, you can import partials in either syntax without any problem. Again, the compiler knows what to compile based on the file's extension. In the *Working with partials* recipe of this chapter, partials are discussed in more detail.

The `sass-convert` command-line tool used in this recipe ships with the Ruby Sass gem. After installing the gem, you can directly run the `sass-convert` command. This command looks at the file extensions too; `.sass` is converted into `.scss` or vice versa.

There's more...

As you already know, Sass has been written in Ruby. Ruby is the programming language. You can also use Ruby with Ruby on Rails. Ruby on rails is the Ruby framework for creating web apps. Ruby uses both Sass and **HAML**. HAML is a markup language used to clearly and simply describe the HTML of any web document without the use of inline code. HAML is a template system for HTML that tries to avoid repetition of code and unnecessary characters by relying on indentation and not the text to determine where the elements and blocks of code begin and end.

The original Sass syntax used the same method of declaration and coding that Ruby does and relies on indentation, as HAML does. This syntax is an excellent fit in Ruby (on rails) and feels already familiar for Ruby developers.

The newer SCSS focuses on the proposal of Sass in being an extension of CSS. Not only does SCSS look like CSS, but any valid CSS code is valid SCSS code too. Because this book is not only intended for Ruby developers, but for anyone who wants to learn Sass, this book uses the newer SCSS syntax for Sass.

See also

▶   In the *Playing on SassMeister* recipe of *Chapter 2, Debugging your code*, you can read about online test environments for Sass. Also, **SassMeister** has an option of switching easily between the SCSS and Sass syntaxes.

▶   You can read more about HAML at `http://haml.info/`.

▶   In *Chapter 2, Debugging your code*, you can read about how to use Sass with Ruby on rails.

▶   Visit `http://sass-lang.com/documentation/file.INDENTED_SYNTAX.html` if you want to learn more about the indented syntax.

Choosing your output style

When compiling Sass code into CSS code, you can choose between four different output styles: **expanded**, **nested**, **compacted**, and **compressed**. The nested style is the default style. In this recipe, you will learn the differences between these output styles and how to choose one for your projects.

Getting ready

You should have the Ruby Sass command line ready, as described in the _Installing Sass for command line usage_ recipe of this chapter. You will also need a text editor.

How to do it...

Perform the following step to see the differences between the Sass output styles:

1. Create an `output.scss` file and type the following Sass code into it:

    ```scss
    $base-color: blue;
    $link-color: orange;
    $hover-color: red;

    p {
      color: $base-color;

      a {
        color: $link-color;

        &:hover {
          color: $hover-color;
        }

      }
    }
    ```

    After creating the file mentioned earlier, you should compile this file into CSS with the four different output style options.

2. Firstly, compile the `output.scss` file with the option by running the following command in your console:

    sass --style expanded output.scss

    The preceding command outputs the CSS code as follows:

    ```css
    p {
      color: blue;
    }
    p a {
      color: orange;
    }
    p a:hover {
      color: red;
    }
    ```

3. Then, run the following command:

    sass --style nested output.scss

    The preceding command outputs as follows:

    ```
    p {
      color: blue; }
      p a {
        color: orange; }
        p a:hover {
          color: red; }
    ```

4. The third command you run will be:

    sass --style compacted output.scss

    The third command outputs the following CSS code:

    ```
    p {

      color: blue; }


    p a {

      color: orange; }


    p a:hover {

      color: red; }
    ```

5. Finally, run the following command:

    sass --style compressed output.scss

    The last command outputs the following line of CSS code:

    ```
    p{color:blue}p a{color:orange}p a:hover{color:red}
    ```

How it works...

Sass enables you to choose your output style by setting the --style command-line flag. In this recipe, you have seen the different output styles of Sass. The first expanded style produces CSS code formatted in a manner that would allow you to write it yourself when directly coding your CSS code. In fact, the output has not got any special syntax or format.

The second and default style you have tried is the `nested` style. In the *Using nested selectors* recipe of *Chapter 4, Nested Selectors and Modular CSS*, you can read about the ability of nesting selectors in Sass. The `nested` style makes the nesting of selectors in your Sass code visible in the compiled CSS code by adding additional indents before the selectors that are nested. Notice that the real nesting of selectors is not possible in a valid CSS code, so the selectors are not nested in the compiled CSS. Because the indent helps reflect the structure of the CSS styles and the HTML document, it will make your code more readable and easier to debug. In *Chapter 2, Debugging Your Code*, of this book, you can read more about testing and debugging your Sass and compiled CSS code.

Finally, the `compact` and `compressed` output styles reduce the file size of the compiled CSS code. The fewer the number of bytes of the CSS code to download, the faster your website or app will load, which improves user experience too. The `compact` output style reduces the number of white space by not having nesting and each selector on a single line, while the `compressed` output style only has minimal white spaces required to meet the CSS specification. When using the `compressed` output style, the compiled CSS code has no whitespace except that necessary to separate selectors and a newline at the end of the file.

The `compact` output style and especially the `compressed` output styles are not intended to be read by humans. In most situations, you will use the default `nested` output style for the development stage of your project. When taking your project into production, you should compile your CSS code with the compressed output style. When you are using CSS source maps to debug your code, as described in the *Using CSS* source maps to *debug your code* recipe of *Chapter 2, Debugging Your Code*, your output style for the development stage does not matter.

The `compressed` output styles also remove all your comments. You can read how to comment your code and which comments are preserved in the *Commenting your code in SCSS syntax* recipe of *Chapter 2, Debugging Your Code*.

There's more...

When using Compass, as described in *Chapter 6, Using Compass*, of this book, to compile your Sass code, you can choose the same output styles as described in the previous section. Output styles are set in the `config.rb` file of your Compass project. When not explicitly setting the environment option to production, Compass uses the `expanded` output style. In the production environment the `compressed` output style had been used.

You have already read that the `compressed` output style removes all the extra white space. Also, colors are converted to their shortest notation. Further optimization of your CSS code is possible, but it is not a task for Sass. Postprocessors, such as clean-css, also perform a more advanced optimization of your CSS code like selector, property, and media query merging. In the *Automatically prefixing your code with Grunt* recipe of *Chapter 16, Setting up a Build Chain with Grunt*, you can read about how to integrate the `clean-css` plugin and other postprocessors into your build chain.

See also

You can find the clean-css CSS minifier for node.js at `https://github.com/jakubpawlowicz/clean-css`.

Working with partials

When your project grows, you should not put all your SCSS code in the same file. You will have to find some logic to organize your Sass files. Splitting up your code over multiple files and applying the modularization of your code will help you create maintainable and reusable code. In this recipe, you can read about **partials**. Partials are special Sass files that can be imported in your project, but the partials themselves are not compiled into CSS.

Getting ready

This recipe requires the Compass installed as described in the *Installing Compass* recipe of this chapter. You can edit the Sass code in your favorite text editor.

How to do it

The steps beneath will show you that partial file are not compiled into the CSS code:

1. Create a file structure like the one shown in the following image:

   ```
   └── sass
        ├── layouts
        │    └── _grid.scss
        └── main.scss
   ```

2. The `main.scss` file should contain the following Sass code:

   ```scss
   @import 'layouts/grid';

   // scss-lint:disable PlaceholderInExtend
   section.custom {
       @extend .row;
   }
   ```

3. Write the following code beneath in the `layouts/_grid.scss` file:

   ```scss
   .row {
       width: 100%;
   }
   ```

4. Now run the following command in your working directory:

```
compass compile --force
```

5. After running the compile command, a new `stylesheets/main.css` file will be generated. This file should contain the compiled CSS code, as shown here:

```
/* line 1, ../sass/layouts/_grid.scss */
.row, section.custom {
  width: 100%;
}
```

6. Finally notice that `layouts/_grids.scss` does not compiles into a CSS file, because of it is a partial file and only its code is use to generate output in them main file.

How it works...

Sass files beginning with an underscore are called partials and won't be compiled to CSS, but they can be imported into other Sass stylesheets. Partials are useful for modularizing your code. When you split up your code into different files based on the type of function, you can easily reuse your code. When you modularize your code and use a file's structure with partials that reflects the modularization strategy, it will also be a lot of easier to find the needed code when you have to maintain your applications.

In this recipe, the partial has been imported with the `@import` directive; you can read more about this directive in the *Importing and organizing your files* recipe of *Chapter 9, Building Layouts with Sass*. Compass compiles all the files in the Sass folder, but ignores partial files starting with an underscore (_). When compiling your code with `node-sass`, as described in the *Using the sass-gulp plugin with Gulp* recipe of this chapter, files starting with an underscore are also ignored by default.

When you compile your project on the command line, you mostly automatically compile only the main file, as the command line compiler only accepts a single input file.

Also, the `@extend` directive possibly requires some more detailed explanation. You can learn more about the `@extend` directive in the *Utilizing the @extend directive* recipe of *Chapter 4, Nested Selectors and Modular CSS*. Finally, you should also notice that although the `layouts/_grid.scss` partial does not generate a compiled `layouts/grid.css` file, the `.row` selector declared in this partial outputs in the compiled `stylesheets/main.scss` CSS file. In the *Using placeholder selectors with the @extend directive* recipe of *Chapter 4, Nested Selectors and Modular CSS*, you will learn how to use the `@extend` directive, which prevents output in the compiled CSS. Also, mixins, as described in the *Leveraging mixins* recipe of *Chapter 3, Variables, Mixins, and Functions*, are not outputted in the final CSS code.

There's more...

Choosing a strategy to split up or modularize your code is not that easy. In the *Applying the OOCSS, SMACSS, and BEM methodologies* recipe of *Chapter 4, Nested Selectors and Modular CSS*, you can read about **OOCSS**, **SMACSS**, and **BEM**; these methodologies help you create modular, reusable, and maintainable CSS code. Applications and web pages are split up into modules and responsibilities, and each of them gets its own partial. Directory structures with partials can reflect your architectural strategy.

Hugo Giraudel, who maintains the Sass Guidelines project, introduced the **7-1 pattern**: 7 folders, 1 file. The 7-1 pattern based on SMACSS starts with the following file structure:

```
── base
── components
── layout
── main.scss
── pages
── themes
── utils
── vendors
```

Many projects will fit in the preceding structure, but you should realize that architecture is mostly very specific to the project. Depending on your project, you possibly should adapt the 7-1 pattern or even choose a quite different solution.

See also

▸   Giraudel's Sass Guidelines project can be found at `http://sass-guidelin.es/`.

▸   Vinay Raghu compared different Sass architectures and wrote an excellent blog post about it. You can find his blog post at `http://www.sitepoint.com/look-different-sass-architectures/`.

Writing your code in a text editor

You can write your Sass code in any text editor. Those who are familiar with the command line will even prefer an editor like **VIM**. VIM is an improved version of the vi editor distributed with most UNIX systems. This recipe will show you that you do not only have to choose your editor, but also have to find some SCSS style guidelines that fit your needs.

Many text editors have syntaxes highlighting for Sass and SCSS code. People who prefer a GUI should check out the *See also* section of this recipe.

Getting ready

You will only need your favorite text editor for this recipe.

How to do it...

Use the following steps to set up a new project according the style guidelines:

1. Read the **SCSS style guidelines** from the **See also** section and write down the style guidelines you are going to use when writing Sass code.

2. Set up your text editor to use a default indent according to the style guidelines from the previous step.

3. Open a new project and create a file structure. See the *Working with partials* recipe of this chapter to read more about file structures and Sass application architectures.

4. When you intend to use Compass, you can also run the `compass init` command, which automatically sets up an initial file structure for your project.

How it works...

Style guidelines will tell you how to write your code and guarantee that all the team members can work together on the same code base without spending too much time understanding the other's code. The guidelines should describe the indent in your code and how to nest your selectors. Also, naming conventions are part of the style guidelines. The names of your variables should not only be meaningful and descriptive, but they should also follow the guidelines. Sass variables are explained in *Chapter 3, Variables, Mixins, and Functions,* of this book.

Which style guidelines you chose does not matter so much, but when you have chosen, you should apply them correctly and consistently. Style guidelines keep your code readable, scalable, reusable, and maintainable.

Alternatively, you can use the `scss-lint` tool. This tool helps keep your SCSS files clean and readable. You can run it manually from the command line. You can find and read more about the `scss-lint` tool at `http://davidtheclark.com/scss-lint-styleguide/`.

The code examples in this book have all been linted with the `scss-lint` tool. When linting the code, the `ColorKeyword` linter will be excluded:

```
scss-lint --exclude-linter ColorKeyword
```

The `ColorKeyword` linter checks for usages of the HTML color keywords. The guidelines of the `scss-lint` tool tell you to use the (short) hexadecimal color notation instead of color keywords. In the examples in this book color names are used because of they are more easy to read.

In some situations, guidelines are ignored when the examples have to show a Sass feature that does not meet the guidelines. So, the `PlaceholderInExtend` linter does look for usages of the @extend directive without a placeholder, while the *Working with partials* recipe of this chapter explicitly shows you how the `@extend` directive can output without using a placeholder.

Also, plugins for the `scss-lint` tool are available for the **VIM, IntelliJ, Sublime Text, Atom,** and **Emacs** editors.

There's more...

In the *Editing and debugging your Sass code in a browser* recipe of *Chapter 2, Debugging Your Code*, you can read how to write and debug your Sass code in a browser. Editing in a browser does not require a text editor at all. When editing your code in a browser, you should not ignore the style guidelines.

See also

Style guidelines

Next, you will find an overview of different style guidelines for SCSS. Read them and choose the one that best fits your needs. Feel free to combine more than one source to create your own unique guidelines:

▸ The Sass Guidelines project can be found at `http://sass-guidelin.es/`.

▸ A Sass style guide published by Chris Coyier can be found at `https://css-tricks.com/sass-style-guide/`.

▸ edX is a massive open online course provider and online learning platform. For developers, it is an easy-to-understand and compact CSS/Sass style guide available at `https://github.com/edx/ux-pattern-library/wiki/Styleguide:-Sass-&-CSS`.

▸ Also, read *An Auto-Enforceable SCSS Styleguide Powered by SCSS-Lint* by David Clark at `http://davidtheclark.com/scss-lint-styleguide/`.

GUIs for Sass

Those who do not want to work with the command line can search for a suitable GUI or application. Many text editors can highlight that Sass and SCSS code have abilities to compile and preview your code. Some editors can also run post process tasks for the compiled CSS code. They are as follows:

- **Brackets** is a modern, open source text editor that makes it easy to design in the browser. Brackets focuses on visual tools and preprocessor support and is released under the MIT License. You can use Brackets free of charge, and it runs on OS X, Windows, and Linux. Download Brackets at `http://brackets.io/`.

- **Sublime Text** is a sophisticated text editor for code, markup, and prose according its website. Sublime Text may be downloaded and evaluated for free; however, a license must be purchased for continued use. A per-user license will cost $70. Read more about Sublime Text at `https://www.sublimetext.com/`.

- **Prepros** is a tool to compile LESS, Sass, Compass, Stylus, Jade, and much more with automatic CSS prefixing. It comes with a built-in server for cross-browser testing. It runs on Windows and Mac. Prepros has a free trial version, and you can buy a single user license for $29. More information on Prepros can be found at `https://prepros.io/`.

- Finally, there's **Compass.app** that is a menubar-only app for Sass and Compass. It helps designers compile stylesheets easily without resorting to a command-line interface. Compass.app is available for OS X, Windows, and Linux. You can buy Compass.app for only $10 at `http://compass.kkbox.com/`.

2
Debugging Your Code

In this chapter, we will cover the following topics:

- ▸ Using CSS source maps to debug your code
- ▸ Editing and debugging your Sass code in a browser
- ▸ Commenting your code in the SCSS syntax
- ▸ Building style guides with tdcss.js
- ▸ Building style guides with the Kalei Styleguide
- ▸ Using the @debug, @warn, and @error directives
- ▸ Playing on SassMeister

Introduction

Sass helps you to write better, reusable, and more readable CSS. When writing, you should check any syntax and solve errors found when compiling your code. Although your CSS is valid, the compiled CSS code should be tested on different devices and browsers.

In this chapter, you will be introduced to CSS source maps that will help you find the source files of origin for the style rules of a certain HTML element in your page. You will also learn how to edit your Sass code in a browser.

Good code also contains constructive comments that make your code clearer for others. Adding comments to your code is the topic of the third recipe of this chapter.

Automated testing, as required for **Test-driven Development** (**TDD**), can be done with tools, such as **Wraith** (`https://github.com/BBC-News/wraith`) and **Huxley** (`https://github.com/facebook/huxley`). As well as these tools, you can also use style guides. **Style guides** show you the visual effect of your CSS code. In the fourth and fifth recipes, you can read about how to generate your style guides.

The sixth recipe describes how to use @debug, @warn, and @error directives to debug your code and force the correct usage of more complex code structures.

In the last recipe of this chapter, you will get to work with **SassMeister**, a playground for Sass, Compass, and LibSass.

Using CSS source maps to debug your code

Most Sass projects merge and compile code from multiple source files into a single CSS file. This CSS file has also been minified in most cases. When you are inspecting the source of CSS files with the developer tools of your browser, you cannot relate the style effects to your original Sass code. CSS source maps solve this problem by mapping the combined/minified file back to its unbuilt state.

Getting ready

This recipe requires only the Ruby Sass compiler to be installed. Read the *Installing Sass for command line usage* recipe of *Chapter 1, Getting Started with Sass*, to find out how to install the Ruby Sass compiler. Use a command-line editor, such as **VIM**, to edit your Sass files. Refer to the *Writing our code in a text editor* recipe of *Chapter 1, Getting Started with Sass*, to read more about editing your Sass files. Finally, you will need a modern browser with support for the source map protocol. Both Google Chrome and Firefox support source maps debugging for a while. Also, MS Internet Explorer version 11 and up support version 3 of the source map protocol.

How to do it...

Use the step beneath to find out how to use CSS source maps to debug your Sass code:

1. Create a file structure, as shown in the following image:

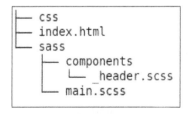

The main.scss file should only contain the following lines of code:

```
@import 'components/header';
```

2. In the `components/_headers.scss` file, type the SCSS code, as follows:

```scss
// CSS RESET
body, html {
  margin: 0;
  padding: 0;
}

@mixin header-styles($background-color) {
  background-color: $background-color;
  border: 3px solid darken($background-color, 20%);
  color: $header-default-font-color;
}

$header-margin: 10px !default;
$header-childs-padding: 10px !default;
$header-default-color: lightyellow !default;
$header-default-font-color: tomato !default;

.header {
  margin: $header-margin;
  * {
    padding: $header-childs-padding;
  }
}

.header-default {
  @include header-styles($header-default-color);
}
```

3. Now run the following command in your console:

```
sass sass/main.scss css/main.css
```

4. Finally, create an `index.html` file and use the `link` attribute in the `head` section of this file to link the compiled `css/main.css` file. You can use the following code to link the style sheet:

```html
<link rel="stylesheet" type="text/css" href="css/main.css" />
```

The complete HTML code of `index.html` should look as follows:

```html
<!doctype html>
<html lang="en">
<head>
  <meta charset="utf-8">
  <title>Sass with CSS source maps</title>
```

```
<meta name="description" content="Sass with CSS source maps">
<meta name="author" content="Bass Jobsen">
 <link rel="stylesheet" type="text/css" href="css/main.css" />
</head>
<body>
<header class="header header-default">
<h1>Write and debug Sass in brower</h1>
</header>
</body>
</html>
```

5. Open `index.html` from the previous step in your browser and open Developer Tools by right-clicking on the page and choosing the **Inspect element** option. You don't have to run a local web server, you can also open the file by using the `file://` protocol.

6. Then, select `<header class="header header-default">` in the **Elements** tabs and you will find that the style rules for the header element are indeed associated with your `_headers.scss` file instead of the `main.css` file. The following figure will show you that the `.header-default` style rules are defined in the `_headers.scss` file in line 25:

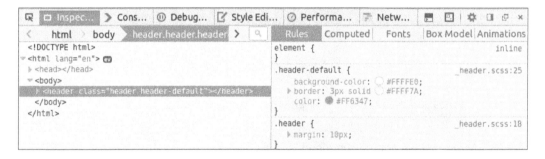

How it works...

The `sass   sass/main.scss css/main.css` command not only creates `css/main.css`, but also a `css/main.css.map` file. The `main.css.map` source map file contains the mapping for each selector and the style rule in the `main.css` file. The map itself is stored in a **base64** encoded-string and the source map file is in the JSON format.

In the beginning, source maps were introduced to map minify JavaScript to its origin source. Since version 3 of the source map protocol, support for CSS has been added. Sass generates the CSS source maps, as described previously, by default and adds a reference into the compiled CSS file, as follows:

```
/*# sourceMappingURL=main.css.map */
```

The web browser's developers tools use the preceding comment to read the source map and connect the style rules to their origin.

The `components/_header-styleseaders.scss` file in this recipe is a so-called partial file. You can read more about partials in the *Working with partials* recipe of *Chapter 1, Getting Started with Sass*. This partial file contains some Sass code for this demo that you might not be familiar with. The code uses variables and mixins, which are both discussed in *Chapter 3, Variables, Mixins, and Functions*, of this book. Variables in SCSS start with a `$` sign, and mixins are defined with the `@mixin` directive and called with the `@include` directive.

There's more...

In the last figure of the recipe, you found that the Sass source files are hyperlinked. Clicking on these links will take you to the source in the style editor, provided that the source files are reachable for the browser. In the *Editing and debugging your Sass code in a browser* recipe of this chapter, you can read how to use these features to edit and debug your Sass code.

The default `--sourcemap=auto` setting sets relative paths where possible and file URIs elsewhere. Alternatively, you can use the `--sourcemap=file` setting that forces the use of absolute file URIs always. The other settings are `--sourcemap=none` which completely disables sources maps, and the `--sourcemap=inline` setting which includes the source text in the source map.

In the past, people used the **FireSass** Firebug plugin together with the `--debug` option to find the Sass code source for a certain style rule. Because Sass, Compass, and all the major browsers support source maps now, you should not use the `--debug` option any more.

Both Sass and Compass also support the `--line-comments` option; this option emits comments in the generated CSS, indicating the corresponding source line. These comments will look like that shown in the example CSS code here:

```
/* line 18, components/_header.scss */
.header {
  margin: 10px; }
  /* line 20, components/_header.scss */
  .header * {
    padding: 10px; }
```

You can use these line comments when compiling your code on the command line or debugging your code without a browser. In the *Commenting your code in SCSS syntax* recipe of this chapter, you can read how comments in Sass compile into your final CSS code.

See also

The Source Map Revision 3 proposal can be found at `https://docs.google.com/a/` `google.com/document/d/1U1RGAehQwRypUTovF1KRlpiOFze0b-_2gc6fAH0KY0k/`. This proposal has been implemented by the Sass compiler, other preprocessors, and all the major browsers.

Editing and debugging your Sass code in a browser

When you directly edit your Sass code in a browser, you will immediately see the effects of your changes. To save your change, the browser should have access to your local file system. Browsers cannot access your file system by default. In this recipe, you will read about the steps required to edit in a browser and save your files.

Getting ready

In this recipe, the Google Chrome browser has been used. Browser editing is also possible with the Mozilla Firefox web browser.

Browser editing and debugging requires CSS source maps. CSS source maps are discussed in the next recipe of this chapter. You can repeat the steps in this recipe with any web page that uses CSS code built with Sass.

For this recipe, the Sass and HTML files from the *Using CSS source maps to debug your code* recipe are used again. These files are included in the download source code of this book. For a better understanding of the code used, it is recommended that you read the *Using CSS source maps to debug your code* recipe first before starting with the current recipe. Of course, you will also need Ruby Sass; refer to the *Installing Sass for command line usage* recipe of *Chapter 1*, *Getting Started with Sass*, to find out how to install Ruby Sass.

How to do it...

Copy the source files from the *Using CSS Source maps to debug your code* recipe. Follow these steps:

1. Use the following command to compile your Sass code:

   ```
   sass sass/main.scss css/main.css
   ```

2. Then, start watching the Sass and CSS files by running the following command:

   ```
   sass --watch sass:css
   ```

3. Open your `index.html` file in Google Chrome with the `file://` protocol.

4. Right-click with your mouse and choose the Inspect Element option to open Chrome's Developer Tools.

5. Click on the **Settings** icon in the upper-right corner; the setting panel should open now. In the **Settings** panel, you can add a folder to your workspace. Add the folder that contains both the `sass` and `css` folders of your project. The following screenshot will show you how the workspace's settings should look:

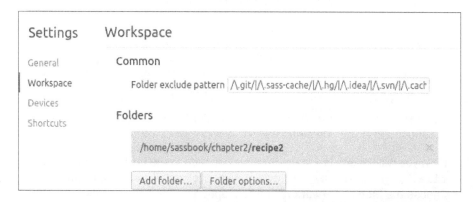

6. Make sure that both the **Enable CSS source maps** and **Auto-reload generated CSS** options in the **Settings** panel are enabled, as is shown in the following screenshot:

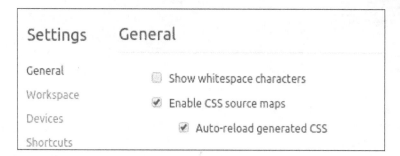

7. Then, in the **Element** tab of the developer tools, select an element of your HTML page and click on the hyperlink to the `.scss` file on the right-hand side. This should open your `.scss` file in the file editor.

8. Now, you will see your file and folder structure twice under the **Sources** tab, as seen in the next screenshot:

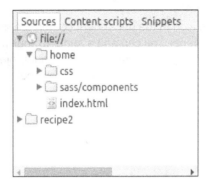

The first folder group represents the files under the `file://` protocol, while the second group is your file system.

9. Now, you will have to link your `filesystem` files to the files served under the `file://` protocol by the browser. Right-click on a `.scss` file of your filesystem. Choose the **Map to network resource...** option and connect the file with the same file under the `file://` protocol. You can see how this step should look in the following screenshot:

10. Restart the developer tools when the browser asks you to do so. Now, both file structures should be merged under the **Sources** tab, as seen in the following screenshot:

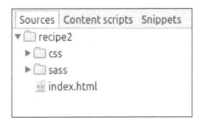

11. Now you can edit the .scss files in the file editor. Use *Ctrl + s* or right click on the mouse menu to save your files.

12. After saving your changes, the browser will reload the newly compiled CSS code, and you can immediately see how your new style rules will look.

How it works...

When you save your file in the browser, the changes are saved to your local filesystem due to the mapping done in the tenth step of this recipe with the network resources.

The Sass compiler, which runs with the --watch option, watches for file changes and recompiles the CSS code when a file change is detected. The browser in turn automatically reloads the linked CSS files when changes are detected.

As you have already read in the *Using CSS source maps to debug your code* recipe of this chapter, you do not have to explicitly set the required source map option. Sass creates source maps by default.

There's more...

In this recipe, you have linked the resource using the file:// protocol with your local filesystem; you can also run a local web server and connect your resource via the http:// protocol with your local filesystem. You can even use an external web server. When using an external web server, you should realize that changes are only saved on your local filesystem.

When using a browser other than Google Chrome, the first step is to compile and check whether your files of this recipe will not differ. Further steps may differ depending on your browser.

In the *Getting grunt watch for Sass, and LiveReload to work* recipe of *Chapter 16, Setting up a Build Chain with Grunt*, you can read how to watch your files with the gulp-watch plugin. With the gulp-watch plugin and live reload, you can use an external text editor to change your files and see the effects in your browser without having to reload your page. Instead of the Gulp build chain, you can also use the compilation process described in this recipe together with live reload.

In the *Installing Compass* recipe of *Chapter 1, Getting Started with Sass*, you can read about how you can install Compass. After installing Compass, you can use the Compass mixins in your code by using the --compass option. When running Sass to watch your files, you should specify both the options, as follows:

```
sass --watch sass:css --compass
```

In the same way, you can load other libraries by using the --require option.

See also

▶ You can read more about live reload at `http://livereload.com/`.

▶ Instructions for in-browser editing for the Mozilla Firefox browser can be found at `https://hacks.mozilla.org/2014/02/live-editing-sass-and-less-in-the-firefox-developer-tools/`.

Commenting your code in the SCSS syntax

Commenting your code will help you and others to better understand the code. Comments can also be used by other tools. If you or someone else has to change your code, maybe after a long period since the code has been written, comments should make clear what a block of code does and why it has been added in the first place.

Getting ready

For this recipe, you will only have to install Ruby Sass. The *Installing Sass for command line usage* recipe of *Chapter 1, Getting Started with Sass*, explains how you can install Ruby Sass.

How to do it...

Perform the following step to find out the differences between the three types of comments supported by Sass:

1. Create a Sass template called `comments.scss`. In this file, write down the SCSS code as follows:

```scss
// start comments

$author: 'Bass Jobsen';

// scss-lint:disable Comment
/*!
 * Copyright 2015 #{$author}
 */

// scss-lint:disable PropertySpelling
//compilles into invalid CSS
.code {
  author: $author;
}

// scss-lint:disable Comment
/*
```

```
* this comment does compile into the CSS code unless a compressed
output style is used.
*/
```

2. Now run the following command in your console:

```
sass comments.scss
```

3. The preceding commands output the CSS code, as follows:

```
/*!
* Copyright 2015 Bass Jobsen
*/
.code {
  author: "Bass Jobsen"; }

/*
* this comment does compile into the CSS code unless a compressed
output style is used.
*/
```

4. Then, run the preceding command with the --style compressed option in your console, as follows:

```
sass --style compressed comments.scss
```

5. Finally, you will find that the compiled CSS code looks as follows:

```
/*!
* Copyright 2015 Bass Jobsen
*/.code{author:"Bass Jobsen"}
```

How it works...

Sass supports three types of comments: single line, multiline, and special. In this recipe, all three types of allowed comments are used and demonstrated. Multiline comments written between /* */ are part of the official CSS syntax. Multiline comments are compiled in the CSS code unless the output's style is set to compressed. You can read more about these output styles in the *Choosing your output style* recipe of *Chapter 1, Getting Started with Sass*.

Single line comments starting with // can be used for developers to help them understand the code. Single line comments are not compiled into the CSS code.

Special comments are written between /*! */. They will always be rendered into a CSS output even in the compressed output modes. You can, for instance, use special comments to add a copyright notice at the beginning of your style sheet. The special comment syntax is also supported by most **postprocess minifiers**, such as clean-css. You can read more about these minifiers in the *Automatically prefixing your code with Grunt* recipe of *Chapter 16, Setting up a Build Chain with Grunt*.

There's more...

Comments are not always only intended for developers; you can also use comments to instruct the compiler or other computer programs. Some examples are mentioned in the following text.

In the *Using CSS source maps to debug your code* recipe of this chapter, you have already seen that the source map reference used by the browser is added to the compiled CSS code by using a comment. A source map comment will look like the following:

```
/*# sourceMappingURL=main.css.map */
```

In the *Writing your code in a text editor* recipe of *Chapter 1, Getting Started with Sass*, you can read about the `scss-lint` tool. Special comments help the `scss-lint` tool to ignore some checks for some parts of your code. In this recipe, single line comments, such as the `// scss-lint:disable PropertySpelling` comment, are used by the `scss-lint` tool.

The last example can be found in the *Building styleguides with tdcss.js* recipe of this chapter. The *tdcss.js* tool uses comments in your code to automatically build a style guide.

In the *Interpolation of variables* recipe of *Chapter 3, Variables, Mixins, and Functions*, you can read about variable interpolation. You can apply variable interpolation to your comments too, which can be used in the recipe to set the author's name.

The following code is from the recipe:

```
$author: 'Bass Jobsen';

// scss-lint:disable Comment
/*!
 * Copyright 2015 #{$author}
 */
```

This Sass code will compile into the CSS code, as follows:

```
/*!
 * Copyright 2015 Bass Jobsen
 */
```

As you can see, the `#{$author}` code has been replaced by the author's name assigned to the `$author` variable. Get a grip on variables by reading *Chapter 3, Variables, Mixins, and functions*, of this book.

See also

Some thoughts on whether to comment or not to comment your code by Neil McAllister can be referred to at `http://www.javaworld.com/article/2078485/core-java/how-to-get-developers-to-document-their-code.html`.

Building style guides with tdcss.js

In **TDD**, tests are written to test functional blocks of code and match the specification. After this, you write the code that makes `test pass`.

When applying test-driven CSS, the style guide is your test. After making changes in your Sass code, all the user interface elements in your style guide should still look as required.

Jakob Løkke Madsen (@jakobloekke) promotes test-driven development for CSS code. Madsen wrote the tdcss.js framework, which is a super simple style guide tool. The `tdcss.js` framework only depends on jQuery, and it is especially well-suited for adopting a test-driven approach to CSS styling. You can also use the tdcss.js framework to build a regular online style guide.

Getting ready

Download the `tdcss.js` file at `https://github.com/jakobloekke/tdcss.js/archive/master.zip`. Unzip this file in your working directory, which will create a folder called `tdcss.js-master`. Rename the `tdcss.js-master` folder to match the directory structure used in this recipe. You can use Ruby Sass on the command line to compile your Sass templates into CSS code. The *Installing Sass for command line usage* recipe of *Chapter 1, Getting Started with Sass*, explains how to install Ruby Sass.

How to do it...

Perform the following steps to build a styleguide with `tdcss.js`:

1. Create the following folder and file structure after downloading and unzipping the `tdcss.js` files:

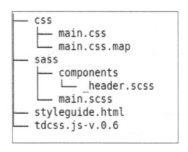

```
├── css
│   ├── main.css
│   └── main.css.map
├── sass
│   ├── components
│   │   └── _header.scss
│   └── main.scss
├── styleguide.html
├── tdcss.js-v.0.6
```

2. Edit your `sass/components/_header.scss` file to style some headers:

```scss
// CSS RESET
body, html {
  margin: 0;
  padding: 0;
}

@mixin header-styles($background-color) {
  background-color: $background-color;
  border: 3px solid darken($background-color, 20%);
  color: $header-default-font-color;
}

$header-margin: 10px !default;
$header-childs-padding: 10px !default;
$header-default-color: lightyellow !default;
$header-default-font-color: black !default;

$warning-color: red;

.header {
  margin: $header-margin;
  * {
    padding: $header-childs-padding;
  }
}

.header-default {
  @include header-styles($header-default-color);
}

.header-warning {
  @include header-styles($warning-color);
}
```

3. The `sass/main.scss` file should contain only the following line of code:

```scss
@import 'components/header';
```

4. Use the following command to compile your Sass code:

```
sass sass/main.scss css/main.css
```

5. Edit the HTML5 file called `styleguide.html` and make it look as follows:

```html
<!doctype html>
<html lang="en">
<head>
  <meta charset="utf-8">

  <title>Building styleguides with tdcss.js</title>
  <meta name="description" content="Building styleguides with
tdcss.js">
  <meta name="author" content="Bass Jobsen">

  <link rel="stylesheet" type="text/css" href="css/main.css" />
  <!-- TDCSS -->
  <link rel="stylesheet" href="tdcss.js-v.0.6/src/tdcss.css"
type="text/css" media="screen">
  <script type="text/javascript" src="http://code.jquery.com/
jquery-2.1.4.min.js"></script>
  <script type="text/javascript" src="tdcss.js-v.0.6/src/tdcss.
js"></script>
  <script type="text/javascript">
    $(function(){
        $("#tdcss").tdcss();
})
  </script>
</head>

<body>

<div id="tdcss">

<!-- # Header styles -->
<!-- & Collection of headers. -->

<!-- : Default header -->
<header class="header header-default">
    <h1>Write and debug Sass in brower</h1>
</header>

<!-- : Warning header -->
<header class="header header-warning">
    <h1>Write and debug Sass in brower</h1>
</header>
</div>

</body>
</html>
```

6.   Now, you can load the `styleguide.html` file in your browser.

7.   Finally, you will find a style guide similar to the one shown in the following screenshot:

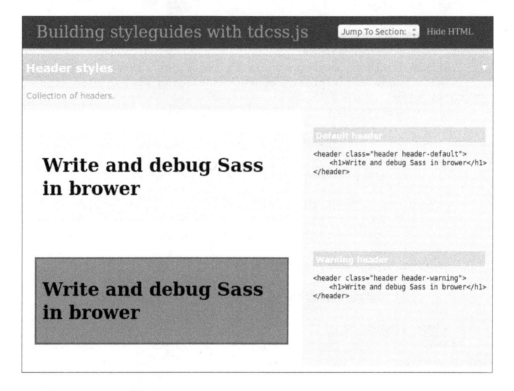

How it works...

Style guides built with the `tdcss.js` framework are not generated automatically without some special comments in the HTML code of the `styleguide.html` file.

The `styleguide.html` file contains styled user interface elements. You can group and describe these elements with HTML comments. All the user interface elements should be wrapped inside the `<div id="tdcss"></div>` tags.

The following HTML comments can then be used to build your style guide:

▸   To create a section, use the following comment style:

```
<!-- # Section name -->
```

▸   Descriptive texts can be added everywhere in your document with the following style:

```
<!-- & Descriptive text -->
```

▸ Finally, the HTML code of your elements should be preceded by the following:

<!– : Element title –>

The `tdcss.js` framework builds the style guide using these HTML comments.

There's more...

Some other tools to generate style guides use special comments inside the Sass and compiled SCSS code. In the *Building style guides with Kalei Styleguide* recipe of this chapter, you can read how to generate a style guide by adding special comments formatted in **Markdown** inside your Sass code. The recipe uses the same Sass code as the one used here, except for the additional comments required for the Kalei Styleguide tool.

StyleDocco is another tool used to generate style guides. Also, the StyleDocco tool requires some special comments inside your Sass templates.

See also

▸ You can visit `http://jakobloekke.github.io/tdcss.js/` to learn more about the `tdcss.js` framework and the test-driven CSS. This website also contains an introductory video and presentation about the `tdcss.js` framework.

▸ An introduction to test-driven development by Chris Maiden can be read at `https://www.codeenigma.com/community/blog/introduction-test-driven-development`.

▸ Read more about StyleDocco at `https://jacobrask.github.io/styledocco/`.

Building style guides with the Kalei Styleguide

Style guide shows you the visual effect of your CSS code. When integrating a style guide into your Sass workflow, you can easily check whether your changes have had the desired effect or, on the other hand, do not break your design. In this recipe, you will be introduced to the **Kalei Styleguide** tool.

Getting ready

Install Ruby Sass, as described in the *Installing Sass for command line usage* recipe of *Chapter 1, Getting started with Sass*, to compile your SCSS code into CSS code. The Kalei Styleguide tool used in this recipe can be downloaded at `https://github.com/thomasdavis/kaleistyleguide/archive/gh-pages.zip`. You should download and unzip this file into your current working directory.

The Kalei Styleguide tool requires an up and running web server, so you should serve the code for this recipe on an HTTP server. Setting up a web server for your projects is out of the scope of this book. In this recipe, **WEBrick** has been used to server the files. WEBrick is a Ruby library that provides simple HTTP web server services and is part of the Ruby standard library for Ruby 1.9.3. How to install Ruby can be read in the *Installing Sass for command line usage* recipe of *Chapter 1, Getting Started with Sass*, too.

In the *There's more...* section of this recipe, you can read a short description on how to use the Kalei Styleguide tool with Ruby on Rails. Ruby on rails also uses WEBrick to test applications.

How to do it...

The following steps will show you how to build a style guide by using the Kalei Styleguide tool:

1. Create the following folder and file structure after downloading the Kalei Styleguide and unzipping the files:

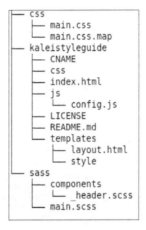

```
── css
│   ├── main.css
│   └── main.css.map
── kaleistyleguide
│   ├── CNAME
│   ├── css
│   ├── index.html
│   ├── js
│   │   └── config.js
│   ├── LICENSE
│   ├── README.md
│   └── templates
│       ├── layout.html
│       └── style
── sass
    ├── components
    │   └── _header.scss
    └── main.scss
```

2. Edit your `sass/components/_header.scss` file to style some headers and add your comment for the Kalei formatted in Markdown:

```
// CSS RESET
body, html {
  margin: 0;
  padding: 0;
}

@mixin header-styles($background-color) {
  background-color: $background-color;
  border: 3px solid darken($background-color, 20%);
  color: $header-default-font-color;
}
```

```
$header-margin: 10px !default;
$header-childs-padding: 10px !default;
$header-default-color: lightyellow !default;
$header-default-font-color: black !default;

$warning-color: red;

.header {
  margin: $header-margin;
  * {
    padding: $header-childs-padding;
  }
}

/*
## Header default
```

<header class="header header-default">
    <h1>Write and debug Sass in browser</h1>
</header>
```

*/

.header-default {
  @include header-styles($header-default-color);
}

/*
## Header warning
special header to show a warning
```

<header class="header header-warning">
    <h1>Write and debug Sass in browser</h1>
</header>
```

*/

.header-warning {
  @include header-styles($warning-color);
}
```

3. The `sass/main.scss` file should contain only the following line of code:

```
@import 'components/header';
```

4. Compile your code by running the following command in your console:

   ```
   sass sass/main.scss css/main.css
   ```

5. Edit the `kaleistyleguide/css/js/config.js` file to point the tool to the compiled `css/main.css` file. The `css_path` variable should be set as follows:

   ```
   css_path: '/css/main.css'
   ```

6. Now, server the file from your current working directory over HTTP on port 8080 with WEBrick by running the following command in your console:

   ```
   ruby -run -e httpd . -p 8080
   ```

7. Open `http://localhost:8080/kaleistyleguide/` in your browser. You will find that your style guide looks as follows:

How it works...

The Kalei Styleguide tool uses the comments formatted in Markdown in your style sheets to build a style guide. Markdown is a plain text formatting syntax, which can be easily converted into HTML. Stackoverflow (`http://stackoverflow.com/`), the popular developer forum, uses Markdown for comments and asking questions. Markdown is readable and easy to learn, and it does not require any special software.

To use the Kalei Styleguide tool, you should add Markdown comments in your Sass code. You should use multiline comments before each selector or class that you want to display in your style guide. You can add a title with a line starting with the chars. Normal text will be displayed as paragraphs. The HTML code on which the style should be applied should be written down between ``` ` ``` and ``` ` ``` backticks.

Because multiline comments are used, these comments are not compiled in the final CSS, provided that the `--style compressed` option is used. The *Commenting your code in SCSS syntax* recipe of this chapter will give you more information about the usage of comments in your Sass templates, and the *Choosing your output style* recipe of *Chapter 1, Getting Started with Sass*, explains the differences between the available output styles for the compilation process.

Modularization of your code will help you create better and more useful style guides too. In the *Applying the OOCSS, SMACSS, and BEM methodologies* recipe of *Chapter 4, Nested Selectors and Modular CSS*, you can read about OOCSS, SMACSS, and BEM; these methodologies help you to create modular, reusable, and maintainable CSS code.

There's more...

The Sass code used for this recipe is similar to that used for the *Building style guides with tdcss.js* recipe of this chapter. The tdcss.js tool requires HTML templates for your styles and leaves the Sass and CSS code untouched. **Styledocco** is another style guide that uses comments formatted in Markdown to build the style guide.

In *Chapter 14, Ruby on Rails and Sass*, you can read about how to build a Ruby on Rails application. A gem that provides an easy way to add the Kalei Styleguide to your existing Ruby application can be found at `https://github.com/andrewhavens/kalei-ruby-gem`.

See also

▶ The official website for the Kalei Styleguide tool can be found at `http://kaleistyleguide.com/`. This website itself demonstrates the tool and also contains an instruction video.

▶ If you are not familiar with Markdown, you can learn it in about 10 minutes at `http://markdowntutorial.com/`.

- ▶ **Nadarei KSS Styleguides** lets you create pretty style guides for your Rails 3.2 projects. KSS is a standard for documenting stylesheets. You can find it at `https://github.com/nadarei/nkss-rails`.

- ▶ Read more about StyleDocco at `https://jacobrask.github.io/styledocco/`.

Using the @debug, @warn, and @error directives

In this recipe, you will learn how to use the `@debug`, `@warn`, and `@error` directives to debug your code or validate the input for mixins and functions.

Getting ready

This recipe requires the command-line Ruby Sass compiler installed. In the *Installing Sass for command-line usage* recipe of *Chapter 1, Getting Started with Sass*, you can read about how to install Ruby and Ruby Sass. You can edit the Sass templates with your favorite text editor.

How to do it...

Use the following steps to learn how to use the `@debug`, `@warn`, and `@error` directives to debug your Sass code:

1. Create a Sass file `test.scss` that contains the following SCSS code:

```scss
@mixin set-width($width) {

  @if $width < 50 {
    @error "width should be >= 50";
    $width: 1px * $width;
  }

  @if unit($width) not 'px' {
    @warn "width (#{$width}) converted to pixels";
    $width: 1px * $width;
  }

  $width: $width * 10;
  @debug "width: #{$width}";
  width: $width;
}

div {
  @include set-width(50);
}
```

2. Then, run the following command in your console:

   ```
   sass test.scss test.css
   ```

3. You will find that the preceding command creates both a `test.css` and a `test.css.map` file. In your console, you should find the following output:

   ```
   WARNING: width (50) converted to pixels
            on line 9 of test.scss, in `set-width'
            from line 19 of test.scss


   test.scss:14 DEBUG: width: 500px
   ```

4. Finally, change `@include set-width(50);` into `@include set-width(49);` in the `test.scss` file and run the command from the second step again.

5. Now, the output to the console will look as follows:

   ```
   Error: width should be >= 50
          on line 4 of test.scss, in `set-width'
          from line 19 of test.scss
      Use --trace for backtrace.
   ```

How it works...

SassScript is a small set of extensions used by Sass in addition to the plain CSS property syntax. SassScript enables you to use variables, arithmetic, and extra functions to set the values of your CSS properties. You can also use SassScript to set property and selector names via interpolation (refer to *Chapter 3, Variables, Mixins, and Functions*). In the *Using Sass interactive mode and SassScript* recipe of *Chapter 1, Getting Started with Sass*, you can read how to test SassScript by running Sass in the interactive mode.

The `@debug`, `@warn`, and `@error` directives enable you to write SassScript expressions to the standard error output stream. You can use this information to debug your code or verify the correct usage of reusable and complex code, such as mixins and functions. You can read more about mixins and the `@function` directive in *Chapter 3, Variables, Mixins and Functions* of this book, and Sass the `@if` directive is described in the *Using @if* recipe of *Chapter 8, Advanced Sass Coding*.

The `@debug` and `@warn` directives only write a message to the output stream. The `@error` directive generates an error, just like a normal Sass error and stops the compilation process.

There's more...

The output of the @debug and @warn directives can be suppressed by using the -quiet option. You can repeat the command from the second step of this recipe with the -quiet option by writing the following command in your console:

```
sass --quiet test.scss test.css
```

The preceding command compiles your Sass code without generating any output to the standard error output stream. The @error directive cannot be suppressed or ignored. Although the @error directive stops the compilation process, Sass does generate the test.css file. After an error is thrown by the @error directive, the test.css file does not contain valid CSS code; instead, the error trace is saved to it. A test.css.map source map file will not be generated.

Playing on SassMeister

SassMeister is a project of Jed Foster and Dale Sande. SassMeister is a playground for Sass, Compass, and LibSass. You can easily test and share your Sass code on SassMeister. In this recipe, you will be introduced to SassMeister.

Getting ready

For this recipe, you will only need a web browser to visit SassMeister at http://sassmeister.com.

How to do it...

The steps below demonstrate you how to test your code on the SassMeister playground for Sass:

1. In your browser, navigate to http://sassmeister.com.

2. You can directly start using SassMeister or you can log in with your GitHub account.

3. Write down the following SCSS code in the upper-left SCSS input area of SassMeister:

```scss
@mixin set-width($width) {
  @if $width < 50 {
    @error "width should be >= 50";
    $width: 1px * $width;
  }
  @if unit($width) not "px" {
    @warn "width (#{$width}) converted to pixels";
    $width: 1px * $width;
  }
```

```
    $width: $width * 10;
    @debug "width: #{$width}";
    width: $width;
}

div {
    @include set-width(50);
    background-color: red;
    color: white;
    padding: 20px;
}
```

4. In the upper-right HTML area, you should write down the following line of HTML code:

    ```
    <div>Playing on SassMeister</div>
    ```

5. Now you will find the compiled CSS code in the middle area. The HTML will be rendered in the bottom area.

Your **SassMeister** page should look like the following screenshot:

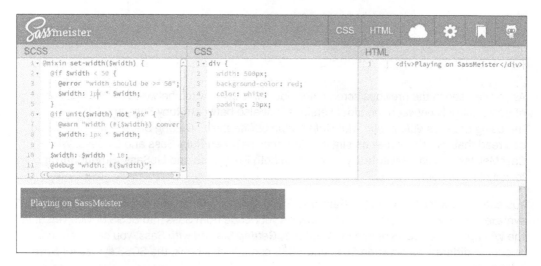

How it works...

SassMeister compiles your SCSS online and applies the compiled CSS directly to your HTML code. The code used in this recipe is the same code as the one used for the *Using the @debug, @warn and @error directives* recipe of this chapter. Read this recipe to learn more about the directives and find references for the SCSS code used.

SassMeiser does not output the @debug and @warn messages. The @error messages are outputted and stop the compilation process.

There's more...

Via the **Settings** button in the right corner of the UI of SassMeister, you can configure the compilation process. The **Settings** panel looks like the following screenshot:

As you can see in the previous screenshot, you can easily switch between different versions of Sass, not only between the older versions, but also between Ruby Sass and LibSass. In the *Using the sass-gulp plugin with Gulp* recipe of *Chapter 1, Getting Started with Sass*, you can read that that there may be slight differences between Ruby Sass and LibSass. With SassMeister, you can easily test your code on both Ruby Sass and LibSass without having to install them both.

You can also switch between the Sass and SCSS syntaxes. When you switch between the syntaxes, SassMeister automatically converts your code from Sass into SCSS or vice versa. In the *Writing Sass or SCSS* recipe of *Chapter 1, Getting Started with Sass*, you can read more about the differences between Sass and SCSS code. In this book, the SCSS syntax for Sass will be used.

Another interesting feature is the ability to add and integrate Sass extensions in your code. The list of extensions includes, among others, Compass, as discussed in *Chapter 6, Using Compass*; Bourbon and Neat, as discussed in *Chapter 13, Meeting the Bourbon Family*; Foundation, as discussed in *Chapter 11, Foundation and Sass*; and Susy, as discussed in *Chapter 10, Building Grid-based Layouts with Susy and Sass*. So, you can easily test these extensions without having to install them first.

Finally, you can choose the output style for your compiled code, as described in the *Choosing your output style* recipe of *Chapter 1, Getting Started with Sass*.

See also

▸ **GitHub** is a code host and a place to share code with friends, co-workers, classmates, and complete strangers. You can find GitHub at `https://github.com/`. GitHub is free to use for public projects.

▸ **CodePen** is an HTML, CSS, and JavaScript code editor in your browser with instant previews. Also, CodePen can compile SCSS and indented Sass code, and it enables you to easily include Sass add-ons, such as Compass, Bourbon, and Breakpoint. You can find CodePen at `http://codepen.io/`.

3
Variables, Mixins, and Functions

In this chapter, we will cover the following topics:

- ▸ Using variables
- ▸ Applying operations in Sass
- ▸ Declaring variables with !default
- ▸ Interpolation of variables
- ▸ Leveraging mixins
- ▸ Writing mixins with arguments
- ▸ Duplicating mixins and name collisions
- ▸ Creating pure Sass functions

Introduction

In the *Using Sass interactive mode and SassScript* recipe of *Chapter 1, Getting started with Sass*, and the *Using the @debug, @warn and @error directives* recipe of *Chapter 2, Debugging your code*, you have already read about SassScript. In this chapter, you will get a better grip on SassScript. SassScript is small set of extensions of the plain CSS property syntax. You can use SassScript to set property values or generate property or selector names.

Variables enable you to define common use values at a single place. In the first recipe of this chapter, you will get a grip on variables. The second recipe talks about using operations in SassScript to set your property values. It is followed by two recipes, which will explain in detail why and how to use variables.

The next three recipes talk about **mixins**. Mixins can be used to create CSS code for your output. You can use mixins to set properties, and you can also dynamically create selectors and property names. You can use SassScript inside your mixins. The parameters for your mixins should be values defined by SassScript too.

The seventh recipe discusses the @function directive. You can use this directive to define a Sass function. Sass functions do not generate any output, but return a single value.

Using variables

When writing CSS code, you will have to repeat identical values and colors all around the place. Variables enable you to define commonly used values at a single place and solve the problem of repeating identical values in your code.

Getting ready

For this recipe, you will use the command-line Sass compiler and Compass. Read the *Installing Sass for command line usage* recipe of *Chapter 1, Getting Started with Sass*, to find out how to install it. In the *Installing Compass* recipe of *Chapter 1, Getting Started with Sass*, you can read about how to install Compass. You can edit the SCSS code in your favorite text editor. Finally, you will need a modern web browser to inspect the results.

How to do it...

The following steps help you to understand how to use variables in Sass:

1. Create a file called `variables.scss`. This file should contain the following Sass code:

```
@import 'compass/utilities/color/contrast';

// scss-lint:disable ColorKeyword
$warning-color: orange;
$warning-font-color: contrast-color($warning-color);

.button-warning {
  background-color: $warning-color;
  border-color: darken($warning-color, 20%);
  border-radius: 20px;
  color: $warning-font-color;
  padding: 20px;

  &:hover {
    background-color: darken($warning-color, 30%);
  }
}
```

2. Compile the `variables.scss` Sass template from the previous step by running the following command in your console:

```
sass --compass variables.scss variables.css
```

3. Then, create a `index.html` HTML file that will link the compiled `variables.css` file and contain the HTML elements, as follows:

```
<h1>Using variables in Sass</h1>
<h1 class="warning">Using variables in Sass</h1>
<button class="button-warning">Warning!</button>
```

4. Open `index.html` in your web browser and find that it will look like that shown in the following image:

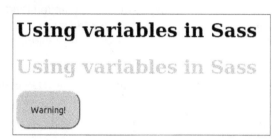

5. Now, you can change the value of the `@waring-color` variable in the `variables.scss` file from `orange` to `red` and repeat the preceding steps.

How it works...

When you are creating the CSS code for you website or app, you may repeat some values more than once. You may possibly use a color pallet for your styling. When these commonly used values change, you should find and replace every usage in your CSS code. Variables enable you to define these values only once at a single place. Variables will make your code DRY (don't repeat yourself) and your projects more easy to maintain.

Variables begin with dollar signs, and are declared like CSS properties, using a colon between the name and the values and ending with a semicolon:

```
$variable: value;
```

Variable names can use hyphens and underscores interchangeably. Besides the data types supported by SassScript, any other valid CSS value can be assigned to a variable. SassScript supports seven **data types**: `numbers`, `quoted` and `unquoted` `strings`, `colors`, `booleans`, `nulls`, `lists`, and `maps`.

In *Chapter 5, Built-in Functions*, you can read about Sass built-in functions, which can be used to use and manipulate the data types as described earlier.

In this recipe, the built-in `darken()` color function has been used. The `darken()` function makes, as its name tells you already, a color darker. You can read more about functions to manipulate colors in the *Color functions* recipe of *Chapter 5, Built-in Functions*.

The `contrast-color()` function used to set the value of the `$warning-font-color` variable is a part of Compass. Compass is a style library for Sass. You can read more about Compass in *Chapter 6, Using Compass*, of this book. The `contrast-color()` function will be described in a detailed way in the *Creating color contrasts automatically* recipe of *Chapter 8, Advanced Sass Coding*.

There's more...

When you start working with Sass variables, you will have to understand that these variables are scoped. Variables defined in the main scope, not nested inside a selector, mixin, or function, are available everywhere in your code. These kinds of variables are called global variables.

This can easily be seen when inspecting the following example SCSS code:

```scss
$color: red;

.link {
  color: $color;
}
```

The preceding code will compile into CSS as follows:

```css
.link {
  color: red; }
```

On the other hand, variables defined inside a selector are called local variables. Local variables are only available inside their nesting (local scope). Consider the following SCSS code:

```scss
$primary: red;

.link {
  $primary green;
  color: $primary;

  &:hover {
    color: $primary;
  }
}
p {
  color: $primary;
}
```

The preceding Sass code will compile into CSS as follows:

```
.link {
  color: green; }
  .link:hover {
    color: green; }


p {
  color: red;
}
```

Inside the `.link` selector, the locally defined `$primary` variable will be used.

In the *Referencing parent selectors with & sign* recipe of *Chapter 4, Nested Selectors and Modular CSS*, you can learn about the `&` reference used to create the `.link:hover` CSS selector. Now, you can see that the nested `&:hover` used the `$primary` variable defined in its parents' scope and not the globally defined `$primary` color variable. The compiled CSS code of the `p` selector shows that the global `$primary` variable is still `red`.

You can override variables in the same scope by defining a variable with the same name again. The new assigned value will only be used in the code after the overriding definition, which can be seen when inspecting the following example Sass code:

```
$primary: red;

.link {
  color: $primary;
}

$primary: green;

.other-link {
  color: $primary;
}
```

The preceding SCSS code compiles into CSS code as follows:

```
.link {
  color: red; }

.other-link {
  color: green; }
```

Finally, you can use the `!global` keyword to override a globally defined variable in a local scope.

The following example demonstrates the effect of the `!global` keyword in your code:

```
$color: red;

.link {
  $primary: green !global;
}

.other-link {
  color: $primary;
}
```

This compiles into the CSS code as follows:

```
.other-link {
  color: green; }
```

Here, the `!global` keyword sets the value of the `$primary` variable in the global scope to green.

When you use a variable before declaring it, the compiler will throw an `Undefined variable` error and stop the compilation process. In the *Declaring variables with !default* recipe of this chapter, you can read how to prevent these errors by using the `!default` keyword.

See also

When you study other CSS precompilers, such as **Less** or **Stylus**, you will find that the scope of definitions with the `!global` keyword are a unique feature of Sass. You can compare different CSS precompilers and their features at `http://csspre.com/compare/`.

Applying operations in Sass

You can use SassScript to assign a value to a property or variable. SassScript enables you to apply standard **arithmetic operations** (adding, subtracting, multiplying, dividing, and modulo) when assigning values. Other operations are available per data type. In this recipe, you will learn how to use operations in SassScript to assign values.

Getting ready

For this recipe, you will use the command-line Sass compiler. Read the *Installing Sass for command line usage* recipe of *Chapter 1, Getting Started with Sass*, to find out how to install it. Operations with SassScript can easily be tested in the interactive mode of Ruby Sass. In the *Using Sass interactive mode and SassScript* recipe of *Chapter 1, Getting Started with Sass*, you can read how to use this interactive mode.

How to do it...

Perform the following steps to find out how to apply operation on assigned values:

1. Create a Sass template called `operations.scss`. This file should contain the SCSS code as follows:

   ```
   // scss-lint:disable ColorKeyword, PropertySortOrder,
   PropertySpelling
   $color1: blue;
   $color2: red;
   $distance: 10px;

   .operations {
     color: $color1 + $color2;
     width: $distance * 100;
     height: ($distance + 10) * 5;
     height-2: $distance + 10 * 5;
     font-family: sans- + 'serif';
   }
   ```

2. Compile the file into the CSS code by running the following command in your console:

   ```
   sass --watch operations.scss
   ```

3. Now you will find that the compiled CSS looks as follows:

   ```
   .operations {
     color: magenta;
     width: 1000px;
     height: 100px;
     height-2: 60px;
     font-family: sans-serif; }
   ```

How it works...

If you use arithmetic operations to assign values with SassScript, all the common mathematical rules will be applied. Mathematical rules are also applied to the units, as described in detail in the *There's more...* section of the *Creating pure Sass functions* recipe of this chapter. Parentheses can be used for precedence rules.

As you can see, operations can not only be applied to numbers, but also to other data types supported by SassScript. SassScript supports seven data types: `numbers`, `quoted` and `unquoted` `strings`, `colors`, `booleans`, `nulls`, `lists`, and `maps`. The `color: $color1 + $color2;` declaration shows you that you can sum up two colors. For the summation, you can add the color values of each color of the **RGB** triplet; `#ff0000` (red) + `#0000ff` (blue) = `#ff00ff` (magenta). For colors, `ff` is the highest hexadecimal value; color calculations are not circular, so `ff + 01 = ff`.

Operations on colors defined with the `rgba()` and `hsla()` **CSS color values** can only be applied when the colors have the same alpha channel. Notice that Sass supports its own `rgba()` and `hsla()` functions too. In Sass, the `rgba(blue,0.5)` call compiles into the `rgba(0,0,255,0.5)` CSS code. When working with colors, you should possibly prefer the color functions, as described in the *Color functions* recipe of *Chapter 5, Built-in Functions*, rather than just applying operations.

The `font-family: sans- + 'serif';` declaration shows you how to concatenate string by using the + operator.

You cannot apply operations on `lists` and `maps`. Also, for these data types, you can use the built-in functions, as described in the *List functions* recipe and *Map functions* recipe of *Chapter 5, Built-in Functions*.

Finally, the `height: ($distance + 10) * 5;` declaration also shows you that precedence rules are correctly applied.

Sass math functions preserve units during arithmetic operations. Units must be the same or compatible to preserve them. For example, you cannot mix `px` with the `em` values. You can read more about unit and arithmetic operations in the *There's more...* section of the *Creating pure Sass functions* recipe of this chapter.

There's more...

With the `calc()` CSS function, you can perform calculations to determine CSS property values. Nowadays, most of the major web browsers support the `calc()` function. The following CSS code will show you a use case for the `calc()` function:

```
div {
  width: calc(100% - 20px); }
```

When your Sass code to compile the preceding CSS code contains one or more variables, the compiler tries to apply the operation and solve `100% - 20px`. The preceding operation generates an `Incompatible units` error in the first place. Secondly, it should compile into unwanted CSS code. You can solve this issue by using variable or string interpolation. Consider a SCSS code like that shown here:

```
$border-margin: 20px;
div {
  width: calc(100% - #{$border-margin});
}
```

The preceding SCSS code will compile into CSS code, as described in the use case at the beginning of this section. You can read more about variable interpolation in the *Interpolation of variables* recipe of this chapter.

When developing and maintaining style sheets for your website or app, colors are often subjects of change. It seems to be a good practice to use global variables for colors everywhere in your code; this makes it easy to update the color, as you only need to change it at one place. In the *Writing your code in a text editor* recipe of *Chapter 1, Getting Started with Sass*, you can read about the `scss-lint` tool. This tool checks your Sass code for hard coded color values and throws an error when found.

See also

▶   The CSS Color Module Level 3, which includes the `rgba()` and `hsla()` CSS color values, can be found at `http://www.w3.org/TR/css3-color/`.

▶   Read more about the `calc()` CSS function at `https://developer.mozilla.org/en-US/docs/Web/CSS/calc`.

▶   You can counsel the Can I Use database to find out which browsers support a CSS feature or not. You can find this database at `http://caniuse.com/`.

Declaring variables with !default

When you start using frameworks, such as **Bootstrap** and **Foundation**, as discussed further on in this book, you will also start using variables for customization. The usage of the `!default` keyword when declaring the framework's variables makes it possible to customize the code without changing the original code. Keeping the original code untouched enables you to update the framework source code without destroying your modifications.

Getting ready

Install Ruby Sass as described in the *Installing Sass for command line usage* recipe of *Chapter 1, Getting Started with Sass*. You can edit the SCSS code of this recipe with a text editor.

How to do it...

The following steps will show you how to use the !default operator when declaring variables:

1. Create a Sass template called `default.scss` and write down the following SCSS code into this file:

```scss
// scss-lint:disable ColorKeyword

$color: red;
$color: green !default;

.green {
  color: $color;
}
```

2. Now run the following command in your console:

`sass default.scss`

3. You will find that the command from the previous step outputs the CSS code like that shown here into the command line:

```css
.green {
  color: red; }
```

4. When you remove the first `$color: red;` declaration in the `default.scss` file, the default `green` value of the `$color` variable is used by the compiler. And the compiled CSS code will look as follows:

```css
.green {
  color: green; }
```

How it works...

If you are writing reusable code for your project, it will make sense to define your variable in a single place. When you use a variable before declaring it, the compiler will throw an `Undefined variable` error and stop the compilation process. So, your code should have default values for the variables used for customization. In Sass, you can create default variable values with ease by putting the `!default` keyword after the variable's value. Your variable's declaration with a default value should look as follows:

```scss
$variable: value !default;
```

To override a default value, you should declare a variable with the same name and a different value. Because the default values are used elsewhere in your code, you should override them before or directly after their declaration. If you override your default value after using it, any usage before the override will get the original default value. In case your default variables are declared in a partial file, you should declare your overriding variable before the declaration of the @import directive. You can learn more about the @import directive in the *Importing and organizing your files* recipe of *Chapter 9, Building Layouts with Sass*.

The example code in this recipe defines all the Sass code in a single file. In practice, your default variables will be declared in one or more partials. You can read more about partials in the *Working with partials* recipe of *Chapter 1, Getting Started with Sass*.

Consider the situation that you got a partial called _default-variables.scss that contains, for instance, the following code:

```
$color: red !default;
```

Now, you can create a main.scss file for your project, which will contain the following code:

```
// customization
$color: green;
// default variables
@import "default-variables"
// import other code that uses the variables defined above here
```

The compiler will use green now for every $color usage in your code. You can easily change the $color variable without having to change the _default-variables.scss file. If the _default-variables.scss file contains many variables, you will have to override only the variables you want to change.

There's more...

In the *There's more...* section of the *Using variables* recipe of this chapter, you can read about the variable's scope in Sass. You can also use the !default keyword in a local scope so that the global scope can override the default value. In the following example, you can see that the local scope inside the .link selector used the color value assigned to the $color variable in the global scope:

```
$color: red;
.link {
 $color: green !default;
 color: $color;
}
```

The preceding SCSS code compiles into CSS code as follows:

```
.link {
  color: red; }
```

In *Chapter 12, Bootstrap and Sass*, of this book, you can read about Bootstrap. All Bootstrap's variables are defined with the `!default` keyword in a single partial file called `_variables.scss`. Foundation, as described in *Chapter 11, Foundation and Sass*, also uses a special `_settings.scss` partial file with default variables.

Interpolation of variables

Variable interpolation means the ability to build a string by using the values assigned to variables. In Sass, you can use variable interpolation to dynamically create property and selectors' names. In this recipe, you will learn how to apply variable interpolation in your code.

Getting ready

You can test variable interpolation in Sass with the Ruby Sass compiler. The *Installing Sass for command line usage* recipe of *Chapter 1, Getting Started with Sass*, describes how to install Ruby Sass on your system.

How to do it...

Perform the steps beneath to learn how to use variable interpolation in Sass to dynamically create property and selector names:

1. Write down the Sass code as follows in a Sass template called `interpolation.scss`:

    ```
    $name: class;
    $direction: left;
    $units: px;

    .#{$name} {
      margin-#{$direction}: 20#{$units};
    }
    ```

2. Compile the Sass template from the previous step with Ruby Sass by running the following command in your console:

    `sass interpolation.scss`

3. The compiled CSS code from the first three steps should look like that shown here:

    ```
    .class {
      margin-left: 20px;
    ```

How it works...

In Sass, you can use string interpolation by using the #{ } interpolation syntax. The syntax enables you to use SassScript variables in selectors' and property names and values.

SassScript supports quoted and unquoted strings. In SassScript, quoted strings are compiled into quoted strings. But when you're using quoted strings for interpolation, the value is unquoted first. Consider the following SCSS code:

```
// scss-lint:disable PropertySortOrder, PropertySpelling
$value1: unquoted;
$value2: 'quoted';

test {
    p1: $value1;
    p2: $value2;
    p3: $value1 #{$value2};
    p4: $value1#{$value2};
    p5: $value1 + #{$value2};
    p6: $value1 + $value2;
    p7: $value1 $value2;
}
```

The preceding Sass code compiles into CSS code as follows:

```
test {
    p1: unquoted;
    p2: "quoted";
    p3: unquoted quoted;
    p4: unquotedquoted;
    p5: unquoted + quoted;
    p6: unquotedquoted;
    p7: unquoted "quoted"; }
```

In the preceding CSS code, you can see that the quotes are removed from the $value2 variable for the p3, p4, and p5 properties when applying string interpolation with the #{ } interpolation syntax. For the p5 property, the + operator has not been applied, while the p6 and p7 properties will show how the strings are concatenated, as described in the *Applying operations in Sass* recipe of this chapter.

There's more...

Other use cases of variable interpolation can be found elsewhere in this book too. In the *Commenting your code in the SCSS syntax* recipe of *Chapter 2, Debugging Your Code*, you can read how to use variable interpolation to generate copyright notices in your CSS code. The *Applying operations in Sass* recipe of this chapter describes why you should use variable interpolation when using the `calc()` CSS function in your code.

Variable interpolation can also be used inside mixins and functions to dynamically compile a list of selectors or values. You can read more about mixins in the *Leveraging mixins* and *Writing mixins with arguments* recipes of this chapter.

Leveraging mixins

Mixins play an important role in Sass and help you write reusable code and use **semantic HTML** code.

Mixins are like macros and allow you to reuse properties and selectors. People used to functions programming will tend to see mixins like functions. Mixins do not return a value at runtime, but generate an output at compile time. For functions in Sass, read the *Creating pure Sass functions* recipe of this chapter.

Getting ready

You can test the mixins in this recipe with the Ruby Sass compiler. The *Installing Sass for command line usage* recipe of *Chapter 1, Getting Started with Sass*, describes how to install Ruby Sass on your system.

How to do it...

The steps beneath will help you to understand how to use mixins in your Sass code:

1. Create a Sass project file, which contains the following code:

```scss
@import 'components/responsive-utilities';

// scss-lint:disable ColorKeyword
$side-bar-background-color: orange !default;

.side-bar {
  @include hidden-mobile;

  background-color: $side-bar-background-color;
```

```
  li {
    list-style: square;
  }
}

.banner {
  @include hidden-mobile;

  img {
    float: right;
  }
}
```

2. The project file from the first step imports the `components/_responsive-utilities`.scss file. This file should contain the following Sass code:

```
@mixin hidden-mobile {
    @media (max-width: 767px) {
        // scss-lint:disable ImportantRule
        display: none !important;
    }
}
```

3. Now, compile your project by running the following command in your console:

   sass sass/main.scss

4. Finally, the compiled CSS code should look as follows:

```
.side-bar {
  background-color: orange; }
  @media (max-width: 767px) {
    .side-bar {
      display: none !important; } }
  .side-bar li {
    list-style: square; }

@media (max-width: 767px) {
  .banner {
    display: none !important; } }
  .banner img {
    float: right; }
```

How it works...

Mixins enable you to define styles, which can be reused everywhere in your code. You can define a mixin with the `@mixin` directive. Mixins do not only contain properties, but also selectors and other valid CSS code. You can use SassScript inside your mixins too, which will enable you to dynamically create selectors' and property names. Mixins can also have arguments; you can read more about this in the *Writing mixins with arguments* recipe of this chapter.

After defining your mixins, you can import them by using the `@import` directive. You can read more about the `@import` directive in the *Importing and organizing your files* recipe of *Chapter 9, Building Layouts with Sass*.

The `hidden-mobile` mixin used in this recipe contains a media query. You can read more about the `@media` rules and Sass in the *Creating responsive grids* recipe of *Chapter 9, Building Layouts with Sass*. By using the `hidden-mobile` mixin, you can directly hide your elements on small screens without the need of having an additional `.hidden-mobile` class for hiding. You can also apply the mixins to semantic HTML5 elements, such as the `header`, `footer`, `section`, and `aside` elements.

When your mixin generates a selector, you can import it in the global scope without the need to nest the `@include` directive in a selector. The following example code shows how a mixin can be imported in the document's root:

```
@mixin half {
  footer {
    width: 50%;
  }
}

@include half;
```

This code will compile into CSS as follows:

```
footer {
  width: 50%; }
```

There's more...

CSS' clear fixes are frequently used in layouts with floated elements. The clear fix clears the float of an element's child element without any additional markup.

Bootstrap, as discussed in *Chapter 12, Bootstrap and Sass*, used the clear fix mixin shown here. The clear fix itself is adopted from `http://nicolasgallagher.com/micro-clearfix-hack/`:

```
@mixin clearfix() {
  &:before,
```

```
&:after {
  content: " "; // 1
  display: table; // 2
}
&:after {
  clear: both;
}
```

You can include this mixin everywhere in your project's code to clear the floats. Notice that mixins are not only reusable in your project, but are portable too. You can easily import the clear fix mixins from Bootstrap in your project by using the @import directive, as described in the *Importing and organizing your files* recipe of *Chapter 9, Building Layouts with Sass*.

Every time that you use the clear fix mixin, the same properties will be copied in your compiled CSS code. Repeating the same properties again and again will make the compiled CSS code larger than strictly necessary. While you are writing modular CSS code, refer to *Chapter 4, Nested Selectors and Modular CSS*; maybe, you don't care about these additional bytes of code. You possibly prefer the grouping of connected codes together in favor of some duplicate code. If you do not care about the order of the compiled CSS code, you can consider using the @extend directive instead of a mixin. You can read more about the @extend directive in the *Utilizing the @extend directive* recipe of *Chapter 4, Nested Selectors and Modular CSS*.

See also

To learn more about semantic HTML code, you should read the *Let's Talk about Semantics* article by Mike Robinson. You can find Robinson's article at `http://html5doctor.com/lets-talk-about-semantics/`.

Writing mixins with arguments

As already mentioned in the *Leveraging mixins* recipe of the chapter, mixins enable you to define styles, which can be reused everywhere in your code. Mixins can also have arguments. Mixins with arguments enable you to create different types of the same pattern based on the parameters set by your mixins' call. In this recipe, you will create cross-browser **background gradients** with Sass.

Getting ready

You can test the mixins in this recipe with the Ruby Sass compiler. The *Installing Sass for command line usage* recipe of *Chapter 1, Getting Started with Sass*, describes how to install Ruby Sass on your system. You also will need a text editor and a browser to inspect the compiled CSS code.

How to do it...

Perform the following step to get grips on using mixins with arguments:

1. Create your main project file called `main.scss`. This file should import the gradient partial file. So, the `main.scss` file should contain the SCSS code like that shown here:

```
// scss-lint:disable ColorKeyword, ColorVariable

@import 'components/gradients';

header {
  @include gradient-horizontal(yellow, green);

  color: white;
  padding: 20px;
}
```

2. The gradient partial, the `components/_gradients.scss` file, should contain the mixin that creates your background gradient. The SCSS code in this file will look as follows:

```
// scss-lint:disable ColorKeyword, ColorVariable

@mixin gradient-horizontal($start-color: #555, $end-color: #333,
$start-percent: 0%, $end-percent: 100%) {
  background: $start-color; // Old browsers
  background-image: linear-gradient(to right, $start-color $start-
percent, $end-color $end-percent); // Standard, IE10, Firefox 16+,
Opera 12.10+, Safari 7+, Chrome 26+
  background-repeat: repeat-x;
  filter: progid:DXImageTransform.Microsoft.
gradient(startColorstr='#{ie-hex-str($start-color)}',
endColorstr='#{ie-hex-str($end-color)}', GradientType=1); // IE9
and down
}
```

3. Now, compile your project by running the following command in your console:

```
sass sass/main.scss main.css
```

4. Create a `index.html` file that will link the compiled `main.css` file from the previous step and will contain the HTML markup code like that shown here:

```
<header>Background gradients with Sass</header>
```

5. Finally, open `index.html` in your browser and find that your background gradient will look as follows:

How it works...

In the *Leveraging mixins* recipe of this chapter, you can read about how to use mixins without parameters. The `gradient-horizontal()` mixin used in this recipe accepts four arguments. Mixin's arguments are set SassScript values, such as variables. Inside the mixin, you can use the parameters that are assigned to local variables with the name of the parameter.

Inspect the declaration of the mixin used in this recipe again for better understanding. This mixin's definition looks as follows:

```
@mixin gradient-horizontal($start-color: #555, $end-color: #333,
$start-percent: 0%, $end-percent: 100%) {}
```

The `gradient-horizontal()` mixin accepts four arguments. These arguments are separated by commas and written within parentheses after the mixin's name. The first `$start-color` argument has a default value of #555, followed by the `$end-color` argument with a default value of #333, the `$start-percentage` argument with a default value of 0%, and finally, the fourth `$end-percentage` argument with a default value of 100%. As you can see, default values are set with a semicolon between the name and the value.

You can include the mixin without any parameter. Without parameters, the default values are used by the mixin. Notice that parameters are only optional if the default values are set. Consider the following SCSS code that throws a `Mixin bar is missing argument $height` error because the `bar()` mixin is included without the required height parameter:

```
@mixin bar($height) {
  height: $height;
}
.bar {
  @include bar;
}
```

Now turn back to the example code of the recipe. You can include the `gradient-horizontal()` mixin with one, two, three, or four parameters, because all the parameters of this mixin have a default value. The following SCSS code will show you how to set a background gradient from red to blue:

```
@include gradient-horizontal(blue, red);
```

For a different start and end percentage, you will have to set the third and fourth parameters too, as it can be seen in the following SCSS code:

```
@include gradient-horizontal(blue, red, 50%, 75%);
```

Finally, you can also include mixins using explicit keyword arguments. For the example `gradient-horizontal()` mixin can look like that shown here:

```
@include gradient-horizontal($end-color: red);
```

Named arguments, as used here, can be passed in any order, and the arguments with default values can be omitted.

There's more...

Sass supports variable arguments also known as variadic arguments. Variable arguments are available as a list inside the mixin. Variable arguments can be useful to set CSS properties, which accept a list of values. For instance, the `background-image` CSS property accepts a list of images separated by commas.

A mixin can only accept a single variable argument; the variable argument should be at the end of the arguments' list. The variable arguments look just like normal arguments, but are followed by the . . ., syntax.

The following SCSS code shows you how a mixin that accepts an unknown number of arguments can look:

```
@mixin background($background-color: black, $background-images...) {
background-color: $background-color;
background-image: $background-images;
}
```

The preceding mixin can now be called with an unknown number of arguments, as follows:

```
$background-color: red;

.single-background-image {
  @include background($background-color, url('../image1.png'));
}
```

```scss
.multiple-background-image {
  @include background($background-color, url('../image1.png'),
url('../image2.png'), url('../image3.png'));
}
```

Notice that you can also include a mixin with a parameter being a list. Consider the following SCSS code:

```scss
// scss-lint:disable ColorKeyword

@mixin background($color, $image-list) {
  background-color: $color;
  background-image: $image-list;
}

$background-color: red;

.background {
  @include background($background-color, (url(2), url(3)));
}
```

This SCSS code compiles into CSS code like that shown here:

```css
.background {
  background-color: red;
  background-image: url(2), url(3); }
```

Because the variable argument becomes available as a list inside the mixins, you can also use the built-in list function to build more dynamic mixins. You can read more about built-in list functions in the *List functions* recipe of *Chapter 5, Built-in Functions*. Also, the @each directive, as described in the *Using the @each directive* recipe of *Chapter 8, Advanced Sass Coding*, can be used with lists.

A block of styles can be passed to a mixin. Inside the mixins, the @content directives hold the styles. An example of passing blocks of styles can be found here:

```scss
@mixin small-screens {
  @media (max-width: 767px) {
  @content;
  }
}

test {
  color: black;
  @include small-screens {
    color: red;
  }
```

```
  }
@include small-screens {
    h1 { font-size: 2em; }
}
```

The preceding SCSS code compiles into CSS code like that shown here:

```
test {
  color: black; }
  @media (max-width: 767px) {
    test {
      color: red; } }

@media (max-width: 767px) {
  h1 {
    font-size: 2em; } }
```

Finally, you should pay some attention to the background gradient CSS code itself. In the past, browsers have used different syntaxes with different browser prefixes to support gradient backgrounds. You can read more about browser prefixes in the *Using vendor prefixes* recipe of *Chapter 7*, *Cross-Browser CSS3 Mixins*. This recipe discusses gradient backgrounds too. If you have to support older browsers, the background gradient code will become more complex.

See also

More information about the CSS background-image property can be found at `https://developer.mozilla.org/en/docs/Web/CSS/background-image`.

Duplicating mixins and name collisions

When you define mixins with the same name, you may possibly get conflicting code. This recipe explains how to prevent name collisions in Sass.

Getting ready

Read the *Installing Sass for command line usage* recipe of *Chapter 1*, *Getting Started with Sass*, to install Ruby Sass on your system. This recipe uses Ruby Sass to compile your CSS code. The SCSS code can be edited in your favorite text editor.

How to do it...

The following steps will demonstrate you how duplicate mixin names may influence the compiled CSS code:

1. Create a Sass template called `mixins.scss`. This file should contain the SCSS code like that shown here:

   ```scss
   // scss-lint:disable PropertySpelling
   @mixin mixin {
     property: first;
   }

   s1 {
     @include mixin;
   }

   @mixin mixin {
     property: second;
   }

   s2 {
     @include mixin;
   }
   ```

2. Compile the SCSS code from the first step by running the following command in your console:

   sass mixins.scss

3. The command outputs the following CSS code in your console:

   ```css
   s1 {
     property: first; }

   s2 {
     property: second; }
   ```

How it works...

In this recipe, two mixins with the same name are defined. As you can see, the second mixin overrides the first one, but only for calls after the second's declaration.

Overriding of mixins can be complicated when using more than one mixin library.

Collision of class names in the compiled CSS code can be prevented by wrapping the `@import` directive inside a class selector, as shown next. You can read more about the `@import` directive in the *Importing and organizing your files* recipe of Chapter 5, *Building Layouts with Sass*:

```
.bootstrap {
@import 'bootstrap';
}
```

The preceding SCSS code wraps all the classes compiled by `@import 'bootstrap';` in the `.bootstrap` class, so you can use the compiled classes and selectors together with the `.bootstrap` class in your HTML. Bootstrap's mixins are not reusable and selectors cannot be extended with the `@extend` directive. Read more about Bootstrap in *Chapter 12, Bootstrap and Sass*.

The **Scut** mixin library prevents the earlier mentioned problem with conflicting names by adding a prefix to every class and mixin. Sass functions, as described in the *Creating pure Sass functions* recipe of this chapter, should also be prefixed to prevent name collisions.

There's more...

Sass also does not support the **overloading** of mixins. You can use default values as parameters to make a mixin callable with a different number of arguments. Read the *Writing mixins with arguments* recipe to learn more about parametric mixins. The following example shows you how to create a mixin with default values:

```
@mixin transparent-backgrounds($color, $opacity: 1) {
   background-color: $color;
   opacity: $opacity;
}
```

Now, you can include the preceding mixin with both the `@include transparent-backgrounds(blue)` and the `@include transparent-backgrounds(blue, 0.5)` declarations. The opacity level describes the transparency level of an element. The opacity level ranges from `1` (not transparent) to `0` (completely transparent). The default value for the `opacity` property is `1`. So, when using `1` as the default value for the mixin too, the effect will be the same as not setting the opacity.

Most CSS properties have a default value and the default value for many of them is `initial` (the specified value that is designated as the property's initial value; this value does not have to be the browser default) or `inherit` (inherit the value from the parent). Also, the `initial` and `inherit` values can be used as the default value for a mixin.

The recipe also makes clear that the compiler tests the SCSS/CSS syntax, but does not complain about the nonexisting or wrongly spelled properties. The `property` property used in this recipe is not defined in the CSS(3) specifications. The SCSS linter tool described in the *Writing your code in a text editor* recipe of *Chapter 1, Getting Started with Sass*, also checks for naming errors and gives a warning for the unknown properties. Neither the compiler nor the linter tool throws an error or warning when assigning an invalid value to a property. You will need a **CSS validator** to check for nonsyntax-related CSS errors.

See also

▶ **Scut** is a collection of Sass utilities to ease and improve our implementations of common style-code patterns. You can find the Scut library at `http://davidtheclark.github.io/scut/`.

▶ **PrettyCSS** is a CSS3-compliant parser, lint checker, and pretty printer. With this tool, you can check for CSS' format violations and then beautify the code to standardize it. You can find PrettyCSS at `https://www.npmjs.com/package/PrettyCSS`.

Creating pure Sass functions

Since Sass version 3.3.1., you can not only use the `@mixin` directive, but also the `@function` directive. Pure Sass functions created with the `@function` directive do not generate output in the compiled CSS code, but return a single value. In this recipe, you will create a Sass function that converts value in `px` (pixel) units to values in `em` units.

Getting ready

Read the *Installing Sass for command line usage* recipe of *Chapter 1, Getting Started with Sass*, and install Ruby Sass on your system. In the *Using Sass interactive mode and SassScript* recipe of *Chapter 1, Getting Started with Sass*, you can read how to use the interactive Sass mode. Operations with units, as used in this recipe, can easily be tested in the interactive Sass mode.

How to do it...

Perform the steps below to build a pure Sass function yourself:

1. Create a Sass template that contains an `em` function, which looks as follows:

   ```
   $browser-context: 16;

   @function px_to_em($pixels, $context: $browser-context) {
     @return ($pixels / $context) * 1em;
   }
   ```

2. Now you can compile the SCSS like that shown here:

```
h1 {
font-size: px_to_em(20);
}
```

3. The SCSS code from the previous step should compile into CSS code like that shown here:

```
h1 {
  font-size: 1.25em; }
```

How it works...

As already mentioned, Sass functions created with `@function` directive return a single value based on their input parameters. You must call the `@return` directive to set the return value of the function. You can use the `@function` directive instead of the `@mixin` directive if you have to assign the same kind of value to different properties. The `@function` directive will help you make your code more DRY. You can replace mixins, which set the same kind of value for different properties with a single `@function` directive to get the same output.

Functions can access any globally defined variables as well as accept arguments just like mixins. Also, keyword and variable arguments are supported for functions. Read more about using mixins with arguments in the *Writing mixins with arguments* recipe of this chapter.

You can calculate the em equivalent for any pixel value using this formula:

em = desired pixel value / font-size of the parent element in pixels

In this recipe, the px_to_em function has been used to calculate the corresponding em value of a pixel value. An em value is equal to the size of the font that applies to the parent of the element in question. Using em values for your designs will make your applications easier to scale and resize.

There's more...

In the *Applying operations in Sass* recipe of this chapter, the standard arithmetic operations (adding, subtracting, multiplying, dividing, and modulo) for the data types supported by SassScript, including the data types supported by vanilla CSS already, are discussed. When applying operations in Sass, the rules for units are the same as used for normal mathematical operations.

In the normal mathematical/physical context, you cannot add or subtract numbers with different units; `1 kilometer + 2 hours` makes no sense. The same will be true for SassScript values when compiling `1px + 1em` results in an `Incompatible units` **SyntaxError**.

For the same reason, the unit will get lost when dividing two values with the same unit. Multiplying a unitless value with 1 x unit will result in a value with the unit used for multiplying. In this recipe, the preceding had been used to get a value in em units. First divide two unitless values and then multiply the result with `1 x 1em`.

You can easily test the outcome of an operation by using the interactive mode of Sass, as described in the *Using Sass interactive mode and SassScript* recipe of *Chapter 1, Getting Started with Sass*.

When using the `@if` directive, as describe in the *Using the @if directive* recipe of *Chapter 8, Advanced Sass Coding*, you can also change your function so that it always uses two pixel values, even when you call it with some unitless values. A more robust function for the pixels to em conversion will look like that shown here:

```
@function px_to_em($pixels, $context: $browser-context) {

    @if (unitless($pixels)) {
        $pixels: $pixels * 1px;
    }

    @if (unitless($context)) {
        $context: $context * 1px;
    }

    @return ($pixels / $context) * 1em;
}
```

Besides the `@if` directive, the built-in `unitless` function is also used in the preceding SCSS code. You can read more about the built-in function in *Chapter 5, Built-in Functions*.

Instead of using math, you can also use string interpolation to get the correct em values. You can read more about string interpolation in the *Interpolation of variables* recipe of this chapter. The following Sass code compiles in the same CSS code as you have seen in the recipe before:

```
$browser-context: 16;
@function px_to_em($pixels, $context: $browser-context) {
    @return #{$pixels/$context}em;
}
```

In the preceding code, `#{$ pixels/$context}em` compiles into a single string value.

See also

▸ Some code used in this recipe has been adapted from `https://css-tricks.com/snippets/sass/px-to-em-functions/`. On this page, you can read more about these functions and their source of origin.

▸ Also read *Why ems?* by Chris Coyier at `https://css-tricks.com/why-ems/`.

▸ More information about the `font-size` CSS property can be found at `/developer.mozilla.org/en-US/docs/Web/CSS/font-size`.

4

Nested Selectors and Modular CSS

In this chapter, you will learn the following topics:

- ▶ Using nested selectors
- ▶ Creating more intuitive code and making inheritance clear
- ▶ Referencing parent selectors with the & sign
- ▶ Using multiple & signs to refer to the parent selector more than once
- ▶ Using the & operator to change the selector order
- ▶ Utilizing the @extend directive
- ▶ Using placeholder selectors with the @extend directive
- ▶ Using the @extend directive together with the @media at-rule
- ▶ Using the @extend directive with care
- ▶ Emitting rules at the root of the document
- ▶ Avoiding nested selectors too deeply for more modular CSS
- ▶ Applying the OOCSS, SMACSS, and BEM methodologies

Introduction

When coding Sass, you should realize that SCSS code compiles into valid CSS code. Sass does not guarantee that the CSS is modular, readable, or well-organized, and so easy to maintain. In this chapter, you will learn how to use nesting in your Sass code to reflect the visual hierarchy of your HTML and extend selectors to reduce the size of the compiled CSS code.

Also, the parent reference will be explained. You can use the & parent reference to use the parent selector in your code without having to explicitly use its name. The recipes in this chapter describe many useful use cases of the parent reference.

Sass does not generate bad code, but coders can. When you apply the Sass features described in this chapter, you should always keep the final result in your mind. For instance, nesting your code to follow the visual hierarchy of your HTML will make your code easier to read and maintain. On the other hand, nesting too deeply will produce overspecified CSS and will be considered to be a bad practice.

In the last recipe, you will learn about the **Object-Oriented CSS (OOCSS)**, **Scalable and Modular Architecture for CSS (SMACSS)**, and **Block Element Modifier (BEM)** methodologies. These methodologies can help you better organize your CSS code.

Using nested selectors

In contrast to vanilla CSS code, Sass allows you to nest selectors. Nesting of selectors may help create better organized and more readable CSS code.

Getting ready

You can use the Ruby Sass compiler to compile the Sass code in this recipe into CSS code. Read the *Installing Sass for command line usage* recipe of *Chapter 1, Getting Started with Sass*, to find out how to install Ruby Sass. Use a text editor, as described in the *Writing your code in a text editor* recipe of *Chapter 1, Getting Started with Sass*, to edit your SCSS code.

How to do it...

The following steps will show you how to use nested selectors in Sass:

1. Create a Sass template called `main.scss` that will contain the following SCSS code:

```scss
// scss-lint:disable ColorKeyword

$text-color: black;
$link-color: red;

p {
  color: $text-color;

  a {
    color: $link-color;
  }
}
```

2. Compile the `main.scss` file from the previous step into CSS code by running the following command in your console:

   `sass main.scss`

3. You will find that the CSS code outputted to your console will look as follows:

```
p {
  color: black; }
  p a {
    color: red; }
```

How it works...

Because nested selectors in Sass can follow the structure of your HTML code, your CSS code will become more easy to read and maintain. Another advantage of nesting your selectors is when you change the name of a selector/element; you only need to change it in one place (the outer selector) instead of in numerous places, like you would when writing CSS. The SCSS for a certain HTML element or structure becomes portable and can be reused in more than one project.

When inspecting the compiled CSS code from the last step of this recipe, you will find that the nested SCSS code compiles into unnested and valid CSS code. The a selector, which has been nested inside the p selector, compiles as expected into a p a selector.

There's more...

We call the compiled p a selector in the compiled CSS code of this recipe a descendant selector. The preceding descendant selector selects all the a selectors that are nested anywhere in a p selector of your HTML markup structure.

Other types of selectors supported by CSS are the child combinator, the adjacent sibling combinator, and the general sibling combinator. The following SCSS code shows how you can easily build these selectors with Sass using nesting too:

```
// scss-lint:disable ColorKeyword
$light-color: green;
$default-color: red;
$dark-color: darkred;

nav {
  ul {
    li { // descendant selector
      color: $light-color;
    }
    > li { // child combinator
```

```
        font-size: 1.2em;
      }
    }

  ~ p { // general sibling combinator
    color: $default-color;
  }

  + p { // adjacent sibling combinator
    color: $dark-color;
  }
}
```

The preceding code compiles into CSS code as follows:

```
nav ul li {
  color: green; }
nav ul > li {
  font-size: 1.2em; }
nav ~ p {
  color: red; }
nav + p {
  color: darkred; }
```

Also, pseudo classes can be nested in your SCSS. You can read more about nesting pseudo classes in the *Referencing parent selectors with the & sign* recipe of this chapter.

Using nesting to group-related selectors together makes your Sass code more readable. But when you nest too deep, your code becomes less portable. In the *Avoiding nested selectors too deeply for more modular CSS* recipe of this chapter, you can read more about the best practice for nesting.

See also

Read also the Child and Sibling Selectors by Chris Coyer at `https://css-tricks.com/child-and-sibling-selectors/` to learn more about the selectors discussed in this recipe.

Creating more intuitive code and making inheritance clear

While HTML code already has a nested structure of HTML elements, CSS code has no nesting. Sass extends CSS with nesting, which enables you to create selectors that follow the same nested structure as your HTML.

Getting ready

Read the *Installing Sass for command line usage* recipe of *Chapter 1*, *Getting Started with Sass*, to find out how to install Ruby Sass.

How to do it...

Learn how to make your code more intuitive by performing the steps shown beneath:

1. Create a Sass template called `main.scss` that will contain the following SCSS code:

```
// scss-lint:disable ColorKeyword

$link-color: black;

p {
  font-size: 1em;
  a {
    color: $link-color;
  }
}
```

2. Compile the `main.scss` file from the previous step into CSS code by running the following command in your console:

```
sass main.scss
```

3. You will find that the CSS code outputted to your console will look like that shown here:

```
p {
  font-size: 1em; }
  p a {
    color: black; }
```

How it works...

Web browsers use the hierarchy of your HTML structure to calculate CSS property values that have not been explicitly set. Consider an HTML structure like that shown here:

```
<div>
  <h2>blue</h2>
</div>
```

Here, the font color set by the `color` CSS property of the `h2` HTML element inherits its value from the div HTML element. Note that the color CSS property has a default value of inheritance.

Now, you can use an SCSS code like that shown here to visualize this inheritance:

```
div {
  color: blue;

  h2 {
    font-size: 1.3em;
  }
}
```

In the preceding SCSS code, it is directly clear that the nested `h2` selector got a calculated color value of blue inherited from the `div` element.

There's more...

Although nesting your selectors can make your code more intuitive, it can equally break other things. For instance, when considering OOCSS principles, this does not allow the nesting of headings (`h1` - `h6`). Headings are considered to be built-in objects in OOCSS, so their appearance should be consistent across an entire website. You can read more about OOCSS in the *Applying the OOCSS, SMACSS, and BEM methodologies* recipe of this chapter.

You should restrict the levels of nesting in your SCSS code. If you apply too much nesting to your selectors, your CSS will get broken for every change in your HTML structure. Read more about this topic in the *Avoiding nested selectors too deeply for more modular CSS* recipe of this chapter.

See also

▸ Read more about the inherited CSS values at `https://developer.mozilla.org/en-US/docs/Web/CSS/inherit`.

▸ To understand more about the CSS selector's performance, you can start reading the CSS performance revisited: selectors, bloat, and expensive styles article by Ben Frain. You can find this article at `http://benfrain.com/css-performance-revisited-selectors-bloat-expensive-styles/`.

Referencing parent selectors with the & sign

In Sass, you can use the **ampersand (&)** sign to reference the parent selector in the nested code. Referencing the parent can be useful to create constituted selectors from your nested code.

Getting ready...

In this recipe, you will have to compile your SCSS into CSS code. You can use the Ruby Sass compiler to do this. More information on the Ruby Sass compiler can be found in the *Installing Sass for command line usage* recipe of *Chapter 1, Getting Started with Sass*. Alternatively, you can also use SassMeister to compile your code. SassMeister is an online compiler for Sass, Compass, and LibSass. You can read more about SassMeister in the *Playing on SassMeister* recipe of *Chapter 2, Debugging Your Code*.

How to do it...

Learn how to use parent selectors in your Sass code to create maintainable code:

1. Create a Sass template called main.scss that will contain the following SCSS code:

```scss
// scss-lint:disable ColorKeyword

$link-color: black;
$hover-color: red;

.link {
  color: $link-color;

  &:hover {
    color: $hover-color;
  }
```

2. Compile the `main.scss` file from the previous step into CSS code by running the following command in your console:

   sass main.scss

3. You will find that the CSS code outputted to your console will look as follows:

   ```
   .link {
     color: black; }
     .link:hover {
       color: red; }
   ```

How it works...

A CSS pseudo-class is a keyword added to selectors that specifies a special state of the element to be selected. The most well-known pseudo-class is the `:hover` pseudo-class that describes the mouse hover state of an element. In contrast to pseudo-classes, CSS pseudo-elements do not describe the states of an element; they select certain parts of your document. The most well-known pseudo-elements are the `::before` and `::after` pseudo-elements.

In this recipe, you can see how to create a `.link` selector with `:hover` pseudo-class. In your code, the `&` reference will be replaced with the parent selector as it appears in the CSS.

Nested selectors are concatenated with a space between them by default. The & reference can be used to avoid the space between the selectors.

When your nesting is more than one level deep, the parent selector will be fully resolved before the & reference is replaced. The following SCSS code makes the meaning of this clear:

```scss
// scss-lint:disable ColorKeyword

$link-color: black;
$hover-color: red;

p {
  .link {
    &:hover {
      color: $hover-color;
    }
  }
}
```

The preceding SCSS code compiles into CSS code as follows:

```css
p .link:hover {
  color: red; }
```

As you can see, the `p   .link` selector is the compiled concatenated selector.

The & reference is very useful for compiling `pseudo` classes and `pseudo` elements. The & reference helps you clarify the relation between the selector and the pseudo classes and elements. Nesting of pseudo classes and pseudo elements improves the readability of your code and makes it easier to maintain.

You can also use the & reference to merge two compound selectors. The following SCSS code will show you how to merge two compound selectors:

```
.test {
    &-link {
        display: none;
    }
}
```

The preceding SCSS code compiles into CSS code like that shown here:

```
.test-link {
    display: none; }
```

Also, in case you have to concatenate two selectors without a space, you can use the & reference. An SCSS code like that shown here concatenates two selectors into one:

```
.first {
    &.second {
        width: 90%;
    }
}
```

The preceding SCSS code compiles into CSS code as follows:

```
.first.second {
    width: 90%; }
```

Here, `.first.second` selects HTML elements having both the `.first` and `.second` classes.

Finally, the & reference can also be used with variable interpolation. Read more about variable interpolation in the *Interpolation of variables* recipe of *Chapter 3, Variables, Mixins, and Functions*. An example of variable interpolation and the & reference can be found when compiling the following SCSS:

```
$name: test;

.#{$name} {
    display: inline-block;
```

```scss
@at-root {
  .ie8-#{$name} {
  display: block;
  }
 }
}
```

The preceding SCSS compiles into CSS code like that shown here:

```css
.test {
  display: inline-block; }
  .ie8-test {
    display: block; }
```

You can read more about the `@at-root` directive used here in the *Emitting rules at the root of the document* recipe of this chapter.

There's more...

When you use the & reference in SassScript, it will also reference the parent selectors and will be set to null if there is no parent selector. Consider the following example SCSS code:

```scss
// scss-lint:disable PropertySpelling

selector1,
selector2 {
  $var: &;
  value: $var;
}
```

The preceding SCSS code compiles into CSS code like that shown here:

```css
selector1, selector2 {
  value: selector1, selector2; }
```

Note that the & reference in SassScript always is a comma-separated list of space-separated lists, even if the parent selector does not contain a comma or space. You can read more about the built-in list functions of Sass in the *List functions* recipe of *Chapter 5, Built-in Functions*. The following SCSS code will show you that the & reference in SassScript is a list (or null) indeed:

```scss
// scss-lint:disable PropertySpelling

@mixin parent-selector() {
  length: length(&);
}
```

```
p {
  @include parent-selector;
}

a,
b {
  @include parent-selector;
}
```
The SCSS code above compiles into CSS code as follows:
```
p {
  length: 1; }

a,
b {
  length: 2; }
```

As you can see, the & reference is a list, which indeed can be used as an argument for the Sass length() built-in function, in the preceding code.

See also

▶ Read more about pseudo-classes at https://developer.mozilla.org/en-US/docs/Web/CSS/pseudo-classes

▶ Read more about pseudo-elements at https://developer.mozilla.org/en-US/docs/Web/CSS/Pseudo-elements

Using multiple & signs to refer to the parent selector more than once

In the *Referencing parent selectors with the & sign* recipe of this chapter, you can read about how to use the & parent reference for selectors in SassScript. This recipe will show you how to use multiple & parent references.

Getting ready

Read the *Installing Sass for command line usage* recipe of *Chapter 1, Getting Started with Sass*, to find out how to install Ruby Sass. You can use the Ruby Sass compiler to compile the Sass code in this recipe into CSS code.

How to do it...

The following steps will show you that you can use the same parent selector more than once:

1. Create a Sass template called `main.scss` and write down the SCSS code like that shown here into it:

```
.link {
  &, .&-small {
  color: blue;
  }
}
```

2. Compile the main.scss file from the first step into CSS code by running the following command in your console:

```
sass main.scss
```

3. Now, you will find the following CSS code outputted to your console:

```
.link, .link-small {
   color: blue; }
```

How it works...

The & parent reference may appear more than once within a selector. For each appearance, the & reference is replaced by the parent selector. This enables you to repeatedly refer to a parent selector without repeating its name.

There's more...

If the parent selector is a list of selectors, you can use the & parent reference to create a list of all the possible permutations of these selectors. The following example SCSS code will show you how this works:

```
a, b {
  & + & {
    color: black;
  }
}
```

The preceding SCSS code compiles into CSS code as follows:

```
a + a, b + a, a + b, b + b {
  color: black; }
```

Using the & operator to change the selector order

The & operator, described as the & parent reference in the *Referencing parent selectors with the & sign* and *Using multiple & signs to refer to the parent selector more than once* recipes of this chapter, can be used to change the selector order. Changing the selector order may help you compile different style rules for special pages or situations.

Getting ready

Read the *Installing Sass for command line usage* recipe of *Chapter 1, Getting Started with Sass*, to find out how to install Ruby Sass. You can use the Ruby Sass compiler to compile the Sass code in this recipe into CSS code.

How to do it...

Learn how to change the selector order with the & operator by performing the following steps:

1. Create a Sass template called `main.scss`, which will contain an SCSS code like that shown here:

    ```scss
    // scss-lint:disable ColorKeyword
    $normal-color: red;
    $home-color: orange;

    .normal {
      color: $normal-color;

      .home & {
        color: $home-color;
      }
    }
    ```

2. Now, run the following command in your console to compile the Sass template from the first step into a static CSS files called main.css:

    ```
    sass main.scss main.css
    ```

3. The main.css file should contain a CSS code like that shown here:

    ```css
    .normal {
      color: red; }
      .home .normal {
        color: orange; }
    ```

4. Now, you can create an HTML that will link the compiled main.css file from the second step. The HTML file can contain a body element with a special home class. The body element should look like that shown here:

```
<body class="home">
```

How it works...

As you can see, the text color set by the color CSS property only gets the value assigned to the `$home-color` variable if the normal class in your HTML has been nested inside a home class. By assigning the home class to the body element in your HTML document, each appearance of the normal class will be selected by the .home .normal descendant selector in your compiled CSS code.

Repeating the technique of changing the selector order enables you to create some special style rules for your homepage or other special pages.

All your CSS files will compile into a single file, which can be used on every page of your project. Because of the nesting of different styles inside the default style, your code is well-organized and easy to maintain.

In this recipe, you will compile all your CSS code into a single CSS file. This file also contains CSS code only used on the homepage (pages with the home class added to the body tag). Although unused CSS code plays an important role in the performance of your CSS code, you can ignore this when the number of differences is limited.

Compiling the different styles into the same CSS file will also result in a larger file size. When the number of differences is limited, the larger number of bytes will load faster than a smaller amount of code with an additional http request. Also, notice that your browser can cache the CSS file, because this file is static and used on every page of your project.

There's more...

Modernizr is a JavaScript library that detects HTML5 and CSS3 features in the user's browser. For each feature detected by Modernizr, a special class will automatically be added to the HTML element in your HTML document.

The beginning of your HTML document can look like that shown here:

```
<html lang="en" dir="ltr" id="modernizrcom" class="no-js">
```

When Modernizr runs, it removes the `no-js` class and replaces it with JS. This is a way to know, in your CSS, whether or not JavaScript support is enabled. Now, you can again use the changing selector order technique to write some different style rules for the browsers not supporting JavaScript. An SCSS code, such as that shown here, will give you another example of changing the selector order with the parent references technique described in this recipe:

```scss
.notice {
  display: none;

  .no-js & {
    display: block;
  }
}
```

In 2008, Paul Irish described HTML's conditional classes in a blog post. These conditional classes were used to detect different versions of the Microsoft Internet Explorer browser and did not require JavaScript.

When using this technique introduced by Irish, the beginning of your HTML document could look like that shown here:

```html
<!--[if lt IE 7]>      <html class="ie6"> <![endif]-->
<!--[if IE 7]>         <html class="ie7"> <![endif]-->
<!--[if IE 8]>         <html class="ie8"> <![endif]-->
<!--[if gt IE 8]><!--> <html>             <!--<![endif]-->
```

See also

▸ The CSS performance revisited: selectors, bloat, and expensive styles article by Ben Frain can be found at `http://benfrain.com/css-performance-revisited-selectors-bloat-expensive-styles/`. This article describes how unused styles influence the performance of your CSS code.

▸ You can read more about Modernizr at `http://modernizr.com/`.

▸ Irish's blog post about HTML's conditional classes can be found at `http://www.paulirish.com/2008/conditional-stylesheets-vs-css-hacks-answer-neither/`.

Utilizing the @extend directive

If the styling of an HTML element requires more than one class, you can use the `@extend` directive to merge these classes into a single class. In this recipe, you will learn how to use the `@extend` directive for your projects.

Getting ready

Read the *Installing Sass for command line usage* recipe of *Chapter 1, Getting Started with Sass*, to find out how to install Ruby Sass. You can use the Ruby Sass compiler to compile the Sass code in this recipe into CSS code.

How to do it...

Learn how to use the @extend directive to create a list of selectors that share the same properties:

1. Create an HTML file that will contain the following HTML code used to style two buttons:

   ```
   <button class="button button-default">Default</button>
     <button class="button button-alert">Alert</button>
   ```

2. Then, create your SCSS code to style the buttons from the first step. This SCSS code will look as follows:

   ```scss
   // scss-lint:disable ColorKeyword

   $default-color: red;
   $warning-color: orange;

   .button {
     display: inline-block;
     margin-bottom: 0;
     font-weight: bold;
     text-align: center;
   }

   .button-default {
     background-color: $default-color;
   }

   .button-alert {
     background-color: $warning-color;
   }
   ```

3. Now, you can rewrite the SCSS code from the previous step by using the `@extend` directive as follows:

```scss
// scss-lint:disable ColorKeyword

$default-color: red;
$warning-color: orange;

.button {
  display: inline-block;
  font-weight: bold;
  margin-bottom: 0;
  text-align: center;
}

.button-default {
  @extend .button;
  background-color: $default-color;
}

.button-alert {
  @extend .button;
  background-color: $warning-color;
}
```

4. The SCSS from the third step compiles into CSS code as follows:

```css
.button, .button-default, .button-alert {
  display: inline-block;
  font-weight: bold;
  margin-bottom: 0;
  text-align: center; }

.button-default {
  background-color: red; }

.button-alert {
  background-color: orange; }
```

How it works...

The `@extend` directive creates a list of selectors that share the same properties. The grouping of selectors avoids repetition of the same properties more than once in the compiled CSS code.

In this recipe, the button, button-default, and button-alert are grouped together and share the same properties. This means that you do not have to use the `.button` class in your HTML any more.

The final compiled CSS code of this recipe also contains also an unused `.button` class. In the *Using placeholder selectors with the @extend directive* recipe of this chapter, you can read how to avoid classes that are only intended for extensions in your compiled CSS code. When using the `scss-lint` tool, as described in the *Writing your code in a text editor* recipe of *Chapter 1, Getting Started with Sass*, you will also get a `PlaceholderInExtend` warning (prefer using placeholder selectors (for example, `%some-placeholder`) with `@extend`) when linking your code.

There's more...

Instead of the `@extend` directive, you could also use an attribute selector to avoid the `button` class in your HTML. In the SCSS of the second step of this recipe, you can replace the `.button` selector with the `[class^="button-"], [class*=" button-"]` attribute selector.

Some people avoid attribute selectors because of some older browsers have performance issues around attribute selectors.

See also

You can read more about attribute selectors in CSS at `https://developer.mozilla.org/en-US/docs/Web/CSS/Attribute_selectors`.

Using placeholder selectors with the @extend directive

Placeholder selectors in Sass enable you to create selectors that can be extended but never outputted into the compiled CSS code.

Getting ready

This recipe reuses the code from the fourth step of the *Utilizing the @extend directive* recipe of this chapter. You can use the Ruby Sass compiler, as described in the *Installing Sass for command line usage* recipe of *Chapter 1, Getting Started with Sass*, to compile the Sass code in this recipe into CSS code.

How to do it...

After performing the following steps you have learn how to use placeholder selectors in your Sass code to avoid unused selectors in the compiled CSS code:

1. Copy the SCSS code from the fourth step of the *Utilizing the @extend directive* recipe of this chapter. In this SCSS, replace the `.button` selector three times with the `%button` placeholder selector. Now, your code should like that shown here:

   ```scss
   // scss-lint:disable ColorKeyword

   $default-color: red;
   $warning-color: orange;

   %button {
     display: inline-block;
     font-weight: bold;
     margin-bottom: 0;
     text-align: center;
   }

   .button-default {
     @extend %button;
     background-color: $default-color;
   }

   .button-alert {
     @extend %button;
     background-color: $default-color;
   }
   ```

2. Then, save the SCSS code from the previous step into a Sass template called `buttons.scss`.

3. Run the following command in your console:

   `sass buttons.scss`

4. Finally, a compiled CSS code like that shown here should be outputted to your console:

   ```css
   .button-default, .button-alert {
   display: inline-block;
   font-weight: bold;
   margin-bottom: 0;
   text-align: center; }
   ```

```
.button-default {
  background-color: red; }

.button-alert {
  background-color: orange; }
```

How it works...

The `.button` selector in this recipe should not be directly used in HTML. The `@extend` directive has been used to avoid this base class.

Placeholder selectors work just like normal classes or ID selectors, except that the leading # or . signs are replaced by the % sign.

There's more...

Mixins, as discussed in the *Leveraging mixins* recipe of *Chapter 3, Variables, Mixins, and Functions*, will generate an output every time you use it. In case the generated output is not depending on contextual variables, you should prefer extending it with placeholder selectors to avoid duplicate code and large style sheets.

Using the @extend directive together with the @media at-rule

In this recipe, you will see that the `@extend` directive can only be used to extend selectors in the same `@media` block. In the *Media Queries with Breakpoint* recipe of *Chapter 8, Advanced Sass Coding*, and in the *Creating responsive grids* recipe of *Chapter 9, Building Layouts with Sass*, the `@media` at-rule will be discussed in more detail.

Getting ready

In this recipe, you will create style rules with the `@media` print media query blocks; styles within these blocks will only be applied while generating printed output. If you want to test your compiled print style sheets, your system should be able to print web pages. You can print the output to both paper and files (PDF).

You can edit Sass templates with your favorite text editor. The *Writing your code in a text editor* recipe of *Chapter 1, Getting Started with Sass*, describes how to edit these templates with a text editor. Then, compile your templates with the Ruby Sass compiler. Read the *Installing Sass for command line usage* recipe of *Chapter 1, Getting Started with Sass*, to find out how to install Ruby Sass.

How to do it...

The following steps will help you to get grips on using the @extend directive together with the @media at-rule:

1. Create a Sass template called media.scss. Write down the following SCSS code into this file:

    ```scss
    @media print {
      .text {
        color: $print-color;
      }
    }

    h1 {
      @extend .text;
    }

    @media print {
      h2 {
        @extend h1;
      }
    }
    ```

2. Now run the following command in your console:

    sass media.scss

3. Finally, you will find that the CSS code, like that shown here, has been outputted to your console:

    ```css
    @media print {
      .text, h1, h2 {
        color: black; } }
    ```

How it works...

As you can see in the preceding compiled CSS code, all the selectors are extended inside the same @media block.

Notice that if the h1 selector, defined outside the @media print block, also has its own properties, these properties will not compile into the @media block.

Sass does not even allow you to @extend an outer selector from within @media, and throws an error.

The following example SCSS code shows what happens if the h1 selector looks like that shown here:

```
h1 {
    @extend .text;
    property: value;
}
```

After adding the property: value; property declaration inside the h1 selector, the output to your console will look like that shown here:

```
Error: You may not @extend an outer selector from within @media.
        You may only @extend selectors within the same directive.
        From "@extend h1" on line 16 of media.scss.
```

There's more...

Earlier, you saw that you cannot extend from a selector within a @media block. For the same reason, a selector within a @media block cannot extend from a selector without a @media block or inside a different @media block. Also, the following SCSS code will throw an error:

```
$print-color: black;

h1 {
    color: $print-color;
}

@media print {
    h2 {
        @extend h1;
    }
}
```

Using the @extend directive with care

When extending a selector, it will extend all the occurrences of the selector. This recipe shows why you should use the @extend directive with care to prevent your CSS code from containing unwanted or unexpected selectors.

Getting ready

You can use either the Ruby Sass compiler or the online SassMeister compiler to compile the SCSS of this recipe into static CSS code. More information about the Ruby Sass compiler and SassMeister can be found in the *Installing Sass for command line usage* recipe of *Chapter 1, Getting Started with Sass*, and the *Playing on SassMeister* recipe of *Chapter 2, Debugging Your Code*.

How to do it...

Perform the following steps to understand why you should use the @extend directive with care:

1. Create a Sass template called example.scss. Write down the following SCSS code into this file:

   ```scss
   .example {
     color: $base-color;

     &:hover {
       color: lighten($base-color,20%);
     }
   }

   .parent .example {
     width: 500px;
   }

   .test {
     @extend .example;
   }
   ```

2. Compile the SCSS code from the previous code into CSS code by running the following command in your console:

   ```
   sass example.scss
   ```

3. After running the command from the second step, you will find in your console a CSS like that shown here:

   ```css
   .example, .test {
     color: red; }
     .example:hover, .test:hover {
       color: #ff6666; }

   .parent .example, .parent .test {
     width: 500px; }
   ```

How it works...

As you can see, when inspecting the compiled CSS code of this recipe, not only the `.example` selector, but also the `.parent .example` selector is extended. As already mentioned, a selector will extend all the occurrences of the selector.

In many situations, the extending of the `.parent .example` selector is not desired. The not desired extending of selectors may cause your compiled CSS code to contain many unwanted or unexpected selectors.

Notice that the extending of the `.example` selector also includes the nested `:hover` pseudo classes. Extending the hover effect too can be useful in some situations. When your hover color depends on the normal style color, you should possibly prefer using mixins in favor of extends. You can read more about mixins in *Chapter 3, Variables, Mixins, and Functions* of this book.

Sass also allows you to extend complex selectors, such as the `.example:hover` selector, in the recipe's code.

There's more...

When using third-party mixin libraries for your project, these libraries may define selectors with the same name as the one already used in your project. When extending these selectors with the same name, all the occurrences of the selector are extended, which may give you unexpected results.

On the other hand, extending a selector that does not exist may result in an error. You can use the `!optional` flag to prevent these errors.

Finally, notice that `@extend` works by inserting the extending selector anywhere in the style sheet such that the extended selector appears. The following SCSS example code will show you that this means that `@extend` may possibly unexpectedly influence the source order of your CSS code.

Consider the following example SCSS code:

```
// scss-lint:disable ColorKeyword

$first-color: red;
$second-color: blue;

.first {
color: $first-color;
}
```

```
.second {
color: $second-color;
@extend .first;
}
```

The preceding SCSS code compiles into CSS code as follows:

```
.first, .second {
  color: red; }

.second {
  color: blue; }
```

Here, using `@extend` after the declaration in your SCSS code does not set the text color for the `.second` selector. In your browser, the calculated value of the color property for the `.second` selector will be equal to blue.

Both the declarations for the color property have the same CSS specificity value, so the last declaration in the compiled CSS code wins.

Also, read the *Using placeholder selectors with the @extend directive* recipe of this chapter. Using placeholders prevents you from having unused selectors in your compiled CSS in many situations.

See also

▶ The calculation of the CSS specificity value is explained at `https://css-tricks.com/specifics-on-css-specificity/` by Chris Coyer

▶ You can find the CSS Cascading and Inheritance Level 3 recommendation at `http://www.w3.org/TR/css-cascade-3/`

Emitting rules at the root of the document

This recipe will explain how to use the `@at-root` directive to move nested styles out from within a parent selector. This enables you to write SCSS code that follows the visual nesting of your HTML code, as described in the *Creating more intuitive code and making inheritance clear* recipe of this chapter, but on the other hand, emits the rules at the root of the document in your compiled CSS code.

Getting ready

Use the Ruby Sass compiler to compile the SCSS code of this recipe into static CSS code. Read the *Installing Sass for command line usage* recipe of *Chapter 1, Getting Started with Sass*, to find out how to install Ruby Sass.

How to do it...

Learn how to move nested styles out from within a parent selector by using the `@at-root` directive:

1. Create a Sass stylesheet called `atroot.scss`. This file should contain an SCSS code like that shown here:

    ```scss
    // scss-lint:disable ColorKeyword

    $form-text-color: black;
    $form-header-color: orange;

    form {
      color: $form-text-color;

      @at-root .form-header {
        color: $form-header-color;
      }
    }
    ```

2. Compile the SCSS code from the previous step into CSS code by running the following command in your console:

    ```
    sass atroot.scss
    ```

3. After running the command from the second step, you will find, in your console, a CSS code like that shown here:

    ```css
    form {
     color: black; }
      .form-header {
        color: orange; }
    ```

How it works...

As you can see, when inspecting the compiled CSS code of this recipe, the selector that has been nested in Sass is at the root of the style sheet after compiling the code. So, we have the `@at-root` directive to move nested styles out from within a parent selector. As explained further on in this recipe, finding use cases for the `@at-root` directive is not that easy.

The Sass code in this recipe can possibly be used with an HTML code like that shown here:

```html
<header class="form-header">form header</header>
<form>
 <!-- form fields here -->
</form>
```

In the preceding HTML code, the `form-header` class is related to the form HTML elements, but the `form-header` class is not nested inside the form in the hierarchical HTML structure. Now, you can use the `@at-root` directive to make the relation between the `.form-header` class and the form element clear by nesting.

In the *Applying the OOCSS, SMACSS, and BEM methodologies* recipe of this chapter, you can read more about organizing your CSS to make relations between elements more clear.

There's more...

Finding use cases for the `@at-root` directive is not easy. Some people suggest to use the `@at-root` directive to nest the keyframe declarations inside the selector that uses it. An example of using the `@at-root` directive with nested keyframe declarations can look like the following SCSS code:

```
.box {
  animation: blink 5s infinite;

  @at-root { @keyframes blink {
      0% { opacity: 0; }
      100% { opacity: 1; }
    }
  }
}
```

The preceding SCSS compiles into CSS code as follows:

```
.box {
  animation: blink 5s infinite; }
@keyframes blink {
  0% {
    opacity: 0; }
  100% {
    opacity: 1; } }
```

In the preceding example, only the official W3C syntax for the keyframe animations is used. Animations in CSS3 require vendor-prefixes to support older browsers. You can read more about these vendor-prefixes in the *Chapter 7, Cross-Browser CSS3 mixins* of this book.

Another use case of the `@at-root` directive can be found in the *Referencing parent selectors with the & sign* recipe of this chapter. In this recipe, the `@at-root` directive has been used together with variable interpolation (refer to the *Interpolation of variables* recipe of *Chapter 3, Variables, Mixins, and Functions*) to create a compound selector at the root of the document.

By default, the `@at-root` directive just excludes selectors, but when using it with the `@at-root (without: …)` syntax, you can use it to move out of nested directives. The preceding syntax moves your selector out of all directives. You can also specify the directives to move out by using the following syntax: `@at-root (without: media, supports)`.

On the other hand, the `@at-root(with: rule)` syntax moves your selectors out all directives, but will preserve any CSS rules.

For better understanding, consider an SCSS like that shown here:

```scss
@media print {
  .page {
    width: 8in;
    @at-root (without: media) {
      .t {color: red;}
    }
  }
}
```

The previous SCSS code compiles into CSS as follows:

```css
@media print {
  .page {
    width: 8in; } }
  .page .t {
    color: red; }
```

This shows you that the `.page .t descendant` selector is now at the root of the style sheet and not nested inside the `@media` directive.

See also

- ▸ Read the Using Sass 3.3s @at-root for the piece of mind blog post by Stuart Robson at `http://www.alwaystwisted.com/articles/2014-03-08-using-sass-33s-at-root-for-piece-of-mind`, which describes the usage of the `@at-root` directive to nest keyframe declarations

- ▸ Read more about keyframes and animations in CSS3 at `http://www.smashingmagazine.com/2011/05/17/an-introduction-to-css3-keyframe-animations/`

Avoiding nested selectors too deeply for more modular CSS

As discussed in the *Creating more intuitive code and making inheritance clear* recipe of this chapter too, you should avoid nesting selectors too deeply. The risk of nesting too deep is creating an overspecified CSS, which is not easy to maintain. In this recipe, you will learn how to prevent nesting your selectors to deep.

Getting ready

You can use the Ruby Sass compiler to compile the Sass code in this recipe into CSS code. Read the *Installing Sass for command line usage* recipe of *Chapter 1, Getting Started with Sass*, to find out how to install Ruby Sass. The `scss-lint` tool, as described in the *Writing your code in a text editor* recipe of *Chapter 1, Getting Started with Sass*, will be used to check your SCSS code for nesting problems.

How to do it...

To keep your CSS code maintainable and reusable you should set up it modular. In the following steps you will create some deep nested SCSS code which demonstrates that deep nesting will make your CSS code less reusable:

1. Create a Sass template called `deepnesting.scss`. This file should contain an SCSS code like that shown here:

```scss
// scss-lint:disable ColorKeyword, IdSelector

$light-color: blue;
$dark-color: darkblue;
$sidebar-background-color: yellow;
$sidebar-padding: 20px;
$nav-background-color: white;

#main {
  aside {
    background-color: $sidebar-background-color;
    padding: $sidebar-padding;

    nav {
      background-color: $nav-background-color;

      ul {
        li { // descendant selector
          color: $light-color;
```

```
            &:hover {
              color: $dark-color;
            }
          }
        }
      }
    }
  }
}
```

2. Now, compile the SCSS from the previous step into CSS code by running the following command in your console:

   sass deepnesting.scss

3. The command from the second step will output the following CSS code to your console:

   ```
   #main aside {
     background-color: yellow;
     padding: 20px; }
     #main aside nav {
       background-color: white; }
       #main aside nav ul li {
         color: blue; }
         #main aside nav ul li:hover {
           color: darkblue; }
   ```

4. Then, run the scss-lint tool by running the following command in your console:

   scss-lint deepnesting.scss

5. The scss-lint command from the fourth step will now give you warnings, such as that shown here:

   deepnesting.scss:17 [W] SelectorDepth: Selector should have depth of applicability no greater than 3, but was 4

   deepnesting.scss:17 [W] NestingDepth: Nesting should be no greater than 3, but was 4

How it works...

You should restrict the levels of nesting in your SCSS code. If you apply too much nesting to your selectors, your CSS will break with every global change of your HTML structure.

In this recipe, the nav selector has been nested inside the #main aside selector. When you want to reuse the navigation styled with the nested nav selector, you will have a problem if the other project does not have an element with #main id selector or it needs the navigation outside the aside element. The preceding code shows you why nesting too much makes your CSS code not easy to reuse.

Also, notice that, in the recipe, the nested selectors of the navigation compile into the `#main aside nav ul li` selector in your CSS code. The `#main aside nav ul li` selector has a high specificity value. When you have to change a property inside this selector by overriding it, you will need to create a selector with the same or higher specificity. Long descendant selectors are difficult to maintain and reuse.

There's more...

When linting the SCSS code with the `scss-lint` tool in the fifth step of this recipe, you found two different warnings regarding the nesting of the selectors in your code. The first warning says: `selectorDepth:`. Selectors should have a depth of applicability no greater than 3, but it was 4. As it is mentioned already, a large depth of applicability leads to your CSS code being tightly coupled to your HTML structure. When your CSS code is coupled too tight to your HTML structure, each change of yours requires the change of both your CSS code and HTML code, which will make it more difficult to maintain or change your code. Also, reusing your Sass code is not possible, unless all your projects have exactly the same HTML structure.

The documentation of the `scss-lint` tool also mentions that deep selectors may affect rendering times, especially on mobile devices.

Notice that the `selectorDepth` warning checks the compiled CSS for deep selectors, because Sass enables you to create deep selectors without nesting too. On the other hand, the `selectorDepth` linter checks your Sass code for nesting too deep. Because nesting too deep will result in overqualified CSS that could prove hard to maintain and output unnecessary selectors, you should check the nesting depth apart from the `selectorDepth`.

Finally, notice that the `idSelector` linter was ignored in this recipe. Styles bound to an `idSelector` cannot be reused in your HTML code because an HTML document cannot have more than one element with the same ID.

See also

▶ The calculation of the CSS specificity value will be explained at `https://css-tricks.com/specifics-on-css-specificity/` by Chris Coyer.

▶ The complete documentation of the linter supported by the `css-lint` tool can be found at `https://github.com/brigade/https://smacss.com/book/selectorsscss-lint/blob/master/lib/scss_lint/linter/README.md`.

▶ Read more about selector performance in the *Selector Performance* article by Jonathan Snook. Snook is the creator of SMACSS, as discussed in the *Applying the OOCSS, SMACSS, and BEM methodologies* recipe of this chapter. You will find Snook's article at `https://smacss.com/book/selectors`.

- Also, interesting to read is the *CSS performance revisited: selectors, bloat, and expensive styles* article by Ben Frain. You can find this article at `http://benfrain.com/css-performance-revisited-selectors-bloat-expensive-styles/`.

- Finally, Dave Gregory explains very well why you should not use ID selectors in his *Don't use ID selectors in CSS* blog post that can be found at `http://screwlewse.com/2010/07/dont-use-id-selectors-in-css/`.

Applying the OOCSS, SMACSS, and BEM methodologies

When reading the *Creating more intuitive code and making inheritance clear* and the *Avoiding nested selectors too deeply for more modular CSS* recipes of this chapter, you should have realized that creating maintainable and reusable CSS code with Sass, which performs well, means to find a compromise between using class selectors for everything and using deep selector rules that create tight coupling between HTML and CSS. Creating modular CSS code can be such a compromise.

The methodologies described in this recipe will help you better organize your CSS code. These methodologies build your CSS code as round reusable objects, modules, or blocks. Reusable components can be reused in all your projects without the need to write the same CSS again and again for every new project.

For teams using the same methodology for writing CSS (and Sass), the methodology not only helps to write reusable CSS code, but also guarantees that each team member can more easily understand the meaning of the code written by other team members. The methodologies described in this recipe do not only affect the CSS code, but also the HTML code.

Getting ready

Read the *Installing Sass for command line usage* recipe of *Chapter 1, Getting Started with Sass*, to find out how to install Ruby Sass. You can use the Ruby Sass compiler to compile the Sass code in this recipe into CSS code. You should also get introduced to the BEM methodology. You can learn more about BEM by reading the *An Introduction to the BEM Methodology* article by John Medeski. You can find Medeski's article at `http://webdesign.tutsplus.com/articles/an-introduction-to-the-bem-methodology--cms-19403 nesting.scss`.

How to do it...

Learn how to apply the BEM methodology for your compiled CSS code and HTML code:

1. Consider an HTML like that shown here:

```
<nav class="nav" role="navigation">
    <ul class="nav__list">
        <li class="nav__list__item"><a href="#" class="nav__list__
link--active">First link</a></li>
        <li class="nav__list__item"><a href="nav__list__link"></
a>Second link</li>
        <li class="nav__list__item"><a href="#" class="nav__list__
link"></a>Third link</li>
    </ul>
</nav>
```

2. Now, create a Sass template called bem.scss, which will contain the following SCSS code:

```
// scss-lint:disable ColorKeyword

$list-background-color: green;
$link-color: navy;
$link-color-active: red;

.nav {
  width: 100%;

  &__list {
    background-color: $list-background-color;

    &__item {
      float: left;
    }

    &__link {
      color: $link-color;

      &--active {
        color: $link-color-active;
      }

    }
  }
}
```

3. Now, compile the SCSS code from the previous step by running the following code in your console:

sass bem.scss

4. The compiled CSS code from the third step will look like that shown here and can be used to style the HTML code from the first step:

```
.nav {
  width: 100%; }
  .nav__list {
    background-color: green; }
    .nav__list__item {
      float: left; }
    .nav__list__link {
      color: navy; }
      .nav__list__link--active {
        color: red; }
```

How it works...

In this recipe, the BEM methodology has been used to create the CSS and HTML code. The BEM methodology splits your HTML code into reusable blocks (modules). After this, these blocks are split up again into elements. Each block and element has its own CSS class. The class name of the elements is created by concatenating the block and element names with two underscores (__). In this recipe, the .nav selector is the block, while the .nav__list selector is an element of the .nav block.

The .nav__list__link--active is a modifier of the .nav__list__link element. As you can see, modifier classes are created by concatenating the element or block class and the modifier name with a double hyphen (--). You should use modifiers when you need to modify the style of a specific element.

When you lint the SCSS code of this recipe with the scss-lint tool, as described in *Writing your code in a text editor* recipe of *Chapter 1, Getting Started with Sass*, you will get a nestingDepth warning. See also the *Avoiding nested selectors too deeply for more modular CSS* recipe of this chapter to learn about nesting depth. This warning will be due to the nest active modifier of the navigation links. Of course, you can ignore this warning, but on the other hand, you should consider whether nesting all the selectors of a block is the best way to implement the BEM methodology.

In many situations, the element or block and the modifier will share the same properties. Only one or a few of these properties will be changed by the modifier. The modifier cannot inherit the properties of the element when it is nested to build the concatenated class name. The following SCSS code will show you how to create a default class to style a button and its modifier, which styles a warning button:

```
// scss-lint:disable ColorKeyword
$button-font-color: white;
$button-default: blue;
$button-warning: red;
```

```scss
.button {
  background-color: $button-default;
  border-radius: 10px;
  color: button-font-color;
  font-size: 2em;
}

.button--warning {
  @extend .button;
  background-color: $button-warning;
}
```

In the preceding SCSS code, you will have to repeat the `.button` class name to make the extending of the `.button` class possible. You can organize your code into partials, as describe in the *Working with partials* recipe of *Chapter 1, Getting Started with Sass*, to separate your code for each block. When each block is in its own partial, you do not have to nest your selector to make their relation clear.

There's more...

Instead of the BEM methodology, as described previously, you can also use the OOCSS or SMACCS methodologies.

The OOCSS methodology uses two principles. The first principle is the separation of structure and skin. Consider the button styling example used in the previous section. When you separate the structure and skin according to OOCSS, you can rewrite these styles as follows:

```scss
// scss-lint:disable ColorKeyword
$button-font-color: white;
$button-default: blue;
$button-warning: red;

.button {
  border-radius: 10px;
  font-size: 2em;
}

.button-default {
  background-color: $button-default;
  color: button-font-color;
}
.button-warning {
  background-color: $button-warning;
  color: button-font-color;
}
```

Here, the `.button` selector holds the structure for your buttons, while the `.button-defualt` and `.button-warning` selectors hold the skins of your different button types. In your HTML, a button should have both the `.button` (style) and `.button-warning` (skin) classes. In the *Using placeholder selectors with the @extend directive* recipe of this chapter, you can read about how to merge these classes in your compiled CSS code.

The second principle of OOCSS is the separation of containers from their content. For the button example, the principle mean, you should use a `.button` class selector instead of a `button` element selector. Using element selectors disables the use of button styles for other elements. Maybe, you want to style an anchor element, such as a button. Now, you can simply add the `.button` class to it in your HTML.

SMACSS is an approach to web development written by Jonathan Snook. SMACCS splits your CSS code up into base, layout, module, state, and theme rules. Modules are an interesting part when writing SMACSS with Sass.

The SCSS code for a module can look like that shown here:

```scss
.module {

  > h2 {
    padding: 5px;
  }

  span {
    padding: 5px;
  }
}
```

The SMACSS state rules can be compared to the skin selectors used with OOCSS. For instance, all the active elements in your HTML have the same `.is-active` class. The SCSS code `.is-active` can look like that shown here:

```scss
$active-color: darkred;

.is-active {
  color: $active-color;
}
```

See also

- BEM was developed by the team at Yandex. You can find their website at `https://en.bem.info/`.
- Learn how to use OOCSS at `http://oocss.org/`.
- The official SMACSS website can be found at `https://smacss.com/`.

5
Built-in Functions

In this chapter, you will learn the following topics:

- ▶ Color functions
- ▶ String functions
- ▶ Number functions
- ▶ List functions
- ▶ Map functions
- ▶ Selector functions
- ▶ Introspection functions
- ▶ Conditional assignments
- ▶ Adding Custom functions to Sass

Introduction

Sass offers you many useful built-in functions, also called instance methods, for manipulating colors and other values. In this chapter, you will learn how to use these built-in functions to set property values or assign variables in SassScript. Each recipe in this chapter describes a different type of function. Finally, the last recipe will introduce you to creating your own custom Sass functions.

Color functions

Sass comes with some built-in color functions. You can use these functions to create and manipulate CSS color values. You can also use these functions in your designs to generate color schemes dynamically based on a single input color.

Getting ready

The example code of this recipe will be compiled into CSS code using Ruby Sass. You can learn how to install Ruby Sass in the *Installing Sass for command line usage* recipe of *Chapter 1, Getting Started with Sass*. You can also easily test the color functions in the Sass interactive mode. Read the *Using Sass interactive mode and SassScript* recipe of *Chapter 1, Getting Started with Sass*, to learn more about using the interactive mode of Sass. For those who are not familiar with the different color models supported by CSS, it's highly recommended to study the CSS Color Module Level 3 first.

How to do it...

The following are the steps to implement color functions:

1. Create a Sass template called `main.scss`, which will contain the SCSS code like the one shown here:

```scss
$startcolor: rgb(255,0,0); // red

.link {
    &:link {
      color: rgba($startcolor, 0.5);
    }
    &:hover {
      @if red($startcolor) > 200 {
        color: $startcolor;
      }
      @else {
        color: darken($startcolor, 10%);
      }
    }
}
```

2. Compile the SCSS file from the previous step by running the following command in your console:

```
sass main.scss
```

3. Finally, you will find a CSS code like the one shown here outputted in your console:

```
.link:link {

  color: rgba(255, 0, 0, 0.5); }

.link:hover {

  color: red; }
```

How it works....

In CSS and Sass, colors are either a keyword or a numerical specification. The **RGB color model**, which has three channels: red (R), green (G), and blue (B), can be used to specify a color. The rgb() and rgba() notations are RGB color values in CSS and built-in functions in Sass. An example of these RGB color values can be found in the *Using Sass in browser* recipe of *Chapter 1, Getting Started with Sass*. The rgba() call in Sass is not a color declaration but a color function; this function can be overloaded, which will enable you to call it with two parameters too. By default, you will have to set all four parameters when calling rgba(). The first three parameters are the red, green, and blue channel values of the color; these values can be set with a list of three numerical values. The integer value 255 corresponds to 100%, and to F or FF in the **hexadecimal notation**: rgb(255,255,255) = rgb(100%,100%,100%) = #FFF. Instead of numerical values, percent values can also be used to set the colors' values. The last parameter of the rgba() function call is called the alpha value. The alpha parameter allows you to specify the opacity of a color, where the alpha value is a number from the range 0.0 (fully transparent) to 1.0 (fully opaque).

The red(), green(), and blue() functions will give you the value of the corresponding color channels of a color.

There's more...

Another color model is the **HSL color model**. HSL colors are encoded as a triplet (hue, saturation, and lightness). For transparent HSL colors, the **HSLA model** is available. Just like RGBA colors, in the HSLA model, the last alpha is a number from the range 0.0 (fully transparent) to 1.0 (fully opaque).

In the HSL model, the hue(), saturation(), and lightness() functions can be used to get the value of the corresponding color channel of a color value. Other color functions like the darken() function are related to the HSL model too. The darken() function, as described in the *Using variables* recipe of *Chapter 3, Variables, Mixins, and Functions*, is an example of such an HSL-related color function. You can use these HSL color functions to manipulate color values and dynamically generate color schemes.

You should note that both hsl() and hsla() with alpha=1 return a color value in the hexadecimal notation (#rrggbb) or a **color keyword**. See the *String functions* recipe of this chapter to compile your colors in the hsl() and hsla() formats.

Other special color functions are the adjust-color() and ie-hex-str() functions. The adjust-color() function can be use to increase or decrease one or more components of a color. This function can change the red, green, blue, hue, saturation, lightness, and alpha properties of a color. The properties are specified as keyword arguments and are added to or subtracted from the color's current value for that property. The following SCSS code shows some examples of the usages of the adjust-color() function:

```
adjust-color(#ff0000, $red: -50);
adjust-color(hsl(0, 100%, 50%), $red: -50);
```

Here, both the function calls will return the #cd0000 color value.

As it is also been discussed in the *Applying operations in Sass* recipe of *Chapter 3, Variables, Mixins, and Functions*, operations on colors defined with the rgba() and hsla() **CSS color values** can only be applied when the colors have the same alpha channel.

The ie-hex-str() function returns a color value in the #rrggbbaa notation used by the Internet Explorer filters. In the *Writing mixins with arguments* recipe of *Chapter 3, Variables, Mixins, and Functions*, the ie-hex-str() function was used to create cross-browser gradients.

See also

- ▶ The CSS Color Module Level 3 can be found at http://www.w3.org/TR/css3-color/.
- ▶ Color schemer is a robust color toolset for Sass. It expands on the existing Sass color functions and adds things, such as RYB manipulation, * set-hue, * set-lightness, tint, shade, and more. You can find Color Schemer at https://github.com/at-import/color-schemer.
- ▶ A complete list of the Sass built-in color functions can be found at http://sass-lang.com/documentation/Sass/Script/Functions.html.

String functions

Sass has some built-in functions to manipulate strings. In this recipe, you will learn about the quote() and unquote() functions. These functions add or remove surrounding quotes from a string value.

Getting ready

Read the *Installing Sass for command line usage* recipe of *Chapter 1, Getting Started with Sass*, to install Ruby Sass. After this, you can also use Sass interactive to evaluate the results of the string functions, as described in the *Using Sass interactive mode and SassScript* recipe of *Chapter 1, Getting Started with Sass*.

How to do it...

The following are the steps for implementing string function:

1. Create a Sass template called `main.scss`. This template should contain the SCSS code like the following:

   ```
   // scss-lint:disable DuplicateProperty

   .test {
     color: hsla(0, 100%, 50%, 1); //fall-back
     color: unquote('hsla(0, 100%, 50%, 1)');
   }
   ```

2. Compile the SCSS file from the previous step by running the following command in your console:

   ```
   sass main.scss
   ```

3. Finally, you will find a CSS code like that shown here outputted in your console:

   ```
   .test {
     color: red;
     color: hsla(0, 100%, 50%, 1); }
   ```

How it works...

The color functions, as described in the recipe of this chapter, return a color value in the hexadecimal notation (`#rrggbb`) or a color keyword. So, if you prefer having colors in the `hsl(a)` notation in your compiled CSS code, you cannot use the `hsl()` function. In this recipe, strings are used to write down colors in the `hsl(a)` notation; they are surrounded by quotes. The `unquote()` function removes the surrounding quotes from the string. Now, the compiled CSS code contains the `hsla(0, 100%, 50%, 1)` notation, which is a valid CSS color value representing the `red` color.

There's more...

Many developers are already used to using RGB values for colors in HTML and CSS. The `hsl(a)` color notation is considered to be more intuitive because the meaning of changing the saturation (second channel) of lightness (third channel) of a color is directly clear. The `hsl(a)` color notation also makes changing color values programmatically much easier.

The CSS code in the recipe contains a declaration for the color property twice. Older browsers do not support the HSLa color model. These browsers will use the first declaration to calculate the color value.

See also

- ▶ More about the HSLa color model in CSS can be read in the *Yay for HSLa* article by Chris Coyier. Coyier's article can be found at `https://css-tricks.com/yay-for-hsla/`.
- ▶ A complete list of the Sass built-in string functions can be found at `http://sass-lang.com/documentation/Sass/Script/Functions.html`.

Number functions

Sass also provides some functions that can be used to manipulate numbers in SassScript. In this recipe, you will learn how to use these functions. You will also learn how to apply other mathematical operations by using Compass.

Getting ready

Read the *Installing Sass for command line usage* recipe of *Chapter 1, Getting Started with Sass,* to find out how to install Ruby Sass. You will also need Compass, so read the *Installing Compass* recipe of *Chapter 1, Getting Started with Sass.* You can also read more about Compass in *Chapter 6, Using Compass.* You can edit the SCSS code in your favorite text editor.

How to do it...

Perform the steps beneath to calculate the circumference and the area of a circle, it will show you how to manipulate numbers in SassScript:

1. First, create some SCSS code that will calculate the circumference and the area of a circle in SassScript. You can write down this SCSS code in a Sass template called `circle.scss`. The contents of the `circle.scss` file should now look like the following:

   ```
   // scss-lint:disable PropertySpelling
   ```

```scss
@mixin circle($radius: 1) {
  r: $radius;
  C: round(2 * pi() * $radius); // Circumference of Circle
  A: round(pi() * pow($radius, 2)); // Area of Circle
}

.circle {
  @include circle;
}

.big-circle {
  @include circle(4);
}
```

2. Compile the SCSS from the first step by running Sass with Compass in the console. You should run the following command to do this:

   ```
   sass --compass circle.scss
   ```

3. The command from the previous step should output the following CSS code in your console:

   ```css
   .circle {
     r: 1;
     C: 6;
     A: 3; }

   .big-circle {
     r: 4;
     C: 25;
     A: 50; }
   ```

How it works...

In the *Applying operations in Sass* recipe of *Chapter 3, Variables, Mixins, and Functions,* you can read about how to apply basic on numerical values in SassScript. Sass extends the basics operation with some more complex functions. In the recipe, only the round () function is built-in in Sass, and the pi (), pow (), and trigonometric functions are only available when using Sass with Compass. Read the *Installing Compass* recipe of *Chapter 1, Getting Started with Sass,* to find out how to use Compass on the command line.

In the *Adding Custom Functions to Sass* recipe of this chapter, you will learn how to create your own custom functions for pi.

There's more...

Sass also has a random() function that returns a random number. So, you can use the Sass random() function to create dynamical stylesheets. You should realize that Sass compiles into static CSS code. The random number only changes when you recompile your Sass code and not when you reload the compiled CSS code in your browser. Only when running Sass in browser, as described in the *Using Sass in a browser* recipe of *Chapter 1, Getting Started with Sass*, does your CSS recompile for every page reload. For the same reason, you should not use Sass.js in a browser in your production environments.

For the same reasons as described earlier, unique-id(), which returns a unique CSS identifier, only generates unique identifiers for every call at compile time. The identifiers created do not change when reloading the compiled and static CSS code.

See also

▸ Learn how to calculate the circumference and the area of a circle at `http://www.math.com/tables/geometry/circles.htm`

▸ The complete list of the Sass built-in numerical functions can be found at `http://sass-lang.com/documentation/Sass/Script/Functions.html`

▸ An overview of the Compass Math Helper function can be found at `http://compass-style.org/reference/compass/helpers/math/`

List functions

A list in Sass can be any **comma- or space-separated list** of values. In this recipe, you will learn how to use lists in your code with the built-in list functions.

Getting ready

Read the *Writing mixins with arguments* recipe of *Chapter 3, Variables, Mixins, and Functions* first if you have not already done so. Install Ruby Sass to compile your SCSS code on the command line. Read the *Installing Sass for command line usage* recipe of *Chapter 1, Getting Started with Sass*, to find out how to install Ruby Sass.

How to do it...

Here are the steps showing implementation of list functions:

1. Create a Sass template called `listexample.scss`, which will contain the following CSS code:

    ```scss
    // scss-lint:disable PropertySpelling

    @mixin list($values...) {
      number: length($values);
      last: nth($values, length($values));
      values: $values;
    }

    .list1 {
      @include list(value1);
    }

    .list2 {
      @include list(value1, value2, value3);
    }
    ```

2. Then, run the following command in your console to compile the CSS code into static CSS code:

    ```
    sass listexample.scss
    ```

3. The command from the second step of this recipe will output the following CSS code into your console:

    ```css
    .list1 {
      number: 1;
      last: value1;
      values: value1; }

    .list2 {
      number: 3;
      last: value3;
      values: value1, value2, value3; }
    ```

How it works...

Lists in Sass are immutable; all the list's functions return a new list rather than updating the existing list in place.

In the *There's more...* section of the *Writing mixins with arguments* recipe of *Chapter 3, Variables, Mixins, and Functions*, it was made clear that the variable arguments of mixins are available as an list in SassScript inside the mixin. The SCSS code of this recipe shows that the variable argument (`$values...`) is indeed a list.

Because the `$values` variable inside the mixin is a list, you can apply the list function to it. The `length()` function returns the number of items in the list. The `nth()` function returns a specific item in a list; this function requires two parameters. The first parameter is the list and the second parameter is the position of the requested item in the list. Notice that the indexes of the lists start at 1, not 0.

There's more...

You can also nest lists in Sass, and there is no limit to the level of depth you can have with nested lists. Consider a SCSS code like that shown here, which will declare a comma-separated list with a depth of two levels:

```
// scss-lint:disable PropertySpelling

$nested-list: (
(a, b, c),
(d, e, f)
);

.test {
  property: nth(nth($nested-list, 2), 3);
}
```

The preceding SCSS code compiles into CSS code as follows:

```
.test {
  property: f; }
```

See also

- ▶ The `@each` directive, as discussed in the *Using the @each directive* recipe of *Chapter 8, Advanced Sass Coding*, works with both lists and maps. Sass treats maps, as discussed in the *Map functions* recipe of this chapter, as lists of pairs.

- ▶ The complete list of the Sass built-in list functions can be found at http://sass-lang.com/documentation/Sass/Script/Functions.html.

Map functions

Since version 3.3, Sass has not only supported lists, as discussed in the *List functions* recipe of this chapter, but also maps. Maps are a list of key value pairs, also called **associative arrays** or **hashes** in other languages.

Getting ready

Install Ruby Sass to compile your SCSS code on the command line. Read the *Installing Sass for command line usage* recipe of *Chapter 1, Getting Started with Sass*, to find out how to install Ruby Sass.

How to do it...

Here are the steps showing implementation of map functions:

1. Create a file called `main.scss`, which will contain the following SCSS code:

```scss
$configuration: ( //defaults
  width: 768px,
  colors: (
    default: #ff0,
    alert: #f00
  )
);

$configuration: map-merge($configuration, (width: 1024px)); // customization

element {
  background-color: map-get(map-get($configuration, colors), default);
  width: map-get($configuration, width);
}
```

2. Then, run the following command in your console:

   `sass main.scss`

3. The command from the previous step should output a CSS code like the one shown here in your console:

```css
element {
  background-color: #ff0;
  width: 1024px; }
```

How it works...

Each key on a Sass map points to a certain value. Sass map functions enable you to look up values based on their key and perform other operations on maps. Maps in Sass are immutable; all map functions return a new map rather than updating the existing map in place.

In this recipe, you built a simple configuration object with Sass maps. You can store the default configuration in a partial file; also read the *Working with partials* recipe of *Chapter 1, Getting Started with Sass*. The SCSS to store a configuration for your code in this recipe is only intended to demonstrate the Sass map functions; it is not a recommendation on how to store your configuration.

The `map-merge($map1, $map2)` function merges two maps because a map can only contain one key with the same name. Key value pairs with the same key will override each other. Keys in `$map2` will take precedence over keys in `$map1`. All the keys in the returned map that also appear in `$map1` will have the same order as in `$map1`. New keys from `$map2` will be placed at the end of the map.

You can also use the `map-merge()` function to add new values to your map. The following SCSS code shows how to add the `newkey` key and its associated `newvalue` value to a `$map` map:

```
$map: map_merge($map, (newkey: newvalue));
```

The features of the `map-merge()` function described earlier are used to override the value for the `width` key in the example's configuration of this recipe.

Sass maps can be nested. In fact, keys and values can be any valid Sass type, including lists and other maps. The `map-get($map, $key)` function returns the value associated with the `$key` key `$map` in the map. In the recipe's code, the `colors` key has been associated with another nested map, so you will have to call the `map-get()` function twice to get the required color for the `background-color` property.

There's more...

Just like Sass lists, the `@each` directive also works with Sass maps. Read more about lists in the *List functions* recipe of this chapter. Examples of the `@each` directive can be found in the *Using @each* recipe of *Chapter 8, Advanced Sass Coding*. Notice that Sass treats maps as lists of pairs.

See also

- Using Sass maps for configuration is described in more detail in the *Bringing configuration objects to Sass* article by Hugo Giraudel. You can find Giraudel's article at `http://hugogiraudel.com/2014/05/05/bringing-configuration-objects-to-sass/`.

- Sassy-Maps is a library of map helper functions for Sass 3.3 and up. You can find the Sassy-Maps library at `https://github.com/at-import/Sassy-Maps`.

- A complete list of the Sass built-in map functions can be found at `http://sass-lang.com/documentation/Sass/Script/Functions.html`.

Selector functions

Selector functions in Sass can help you build compound selectors in SassScript. In this recipe, you will learn how to use these functions.

Getting ready

Read the *Installing Sass for command line usage* recipe of *Chapter 1, Getting Started with Sass*, to find out how to install Ruby Sass and compile your Sass templates into CSS code.

How to do it....

Here are the steps showing implementation of selector functions:

1. Create a Sass template called `selectors.scss`. Write the following SCSS into this file:

```scss
@mixin selector($selector) {

  .#{$selector} {
    #{selector-append('.child-', $selector)} {
      width: 100%;
    }
  }

}

@include selector(test);
```

2. Compile the Sass template from the previous step into CSS by running the following command in your console:

```
sass selectors.scss
```

3. After running the command from the second step, you will find the following CSS code in your console:

```
.test .child-test {
  width: 100%; }
```

How it works...

In this recipe, as described in *Chapter 3, Variables, Mixins, and Functions*, of this book, a mixin has been used to create the compound selector. The `selector-append()` selector function has to be called with two arguments; the function concatenates both the arguments and returns the new selector.

Notice that string interpolation is applied to `selector-append()` by wrapping it inside the `#{}` interpolation syntax. You can read about string interpolation in Sass in the *Interpolation of variables* recipe of *Chapter 3, Variables, Mixins, and Functions*.

There's more...

Other selectors are the `selector-parse()` and the `is-superselector()` functions, among others.

The `selector-parse()` function parses a selector into the format returned by the `&` parent reference. The `&` parent reference in SassScript returns a list of selectors that reflect the nesting.

The `is-superselector($selector1,$selector2)` call returns whether the `$selector1` selector is a superselector of the `$selector2` selector. Being a superselector means matching all the elements that match the other selector. So, the `is-superselector('.a','.a.b')` call returns true, while `is-superselector('.a.b','.a')` does not.

See also

The complete list of the Sass built-in selector functions can be found at `http://sass-lang.com/documentation/Sass/Script/Functions.html`.

Introspection functions

Some of the introspection functions of Sass can be used to test whether a certain condition is true or not. Other introspection functions call a Sass function or return the type of a variable.

Getting ready

Read the *Installing Sass for command line usage* recipe of *Chapter 1, Getting Started with Sass*, to find out how to install Ruby Sass. You will also need Compass, so read the *Installing Compass* recipe of *Chapter 1, Getting Started with Sass*. You can edit the SCSS code in your favorite text editor. This recipe uses the same SCSS code as the one used for the *Adding Custom Functions to Sass* recipe of this chapter.

How to do it...

Here are the steps showing implementation of introspection functions:

1. Create a Sass template called cos.scss. The `cos.scss` file should contain the following lines of SCSS code:

    ```scss
    // scss-lint:disable PropertySpelling

    @function cosine($x) {

      @if function-exists(cos) {
        @return cos($x);
      } @else {
        @warn 'cos() function not found!';
        @return null;
      }

    }

    .test {
      cosine: cosine(1);
    }
    ```

2. Then, try to compile your code without Compass by running the following command in your console:

    ```
    sass cos.scss
    ```

3. You will find that the command from the previous step outputs a warning to your console. The warning in your console should look like the following:

```
WARNING: cos() function not found!
        on line 8 of cos.scss
```

4. Now, repeat the second step using the Compass library by running a command like the following:

```
sass --compass cos.scss
```

5. Finally, the last command from the fourth step should output the following CSS code in your console:

```
.test {
  cosine: 0.5403; }
```

How it works...

In this recipe, the `function-exists()` introspection function was used to find out whether the `cos()` trigonometric function does exist or not. In the *Number functions* recipe of this chapter, you will read that Sass does not support trigonometric functions. Compass extends Sass with more complex mathematical functions, including trigonometric functions. So, the example code throws a warning when compiling it without Compass.

In the *Adding Custom Functions to Sass* recipe of this chapter, you will learn how to create your own custom `cos()` trigonometric function.

There's more...

Some of the introspection functions can be used together with the conditional `@if` statement; an example of using the function together with the `@if` statement can be found in the *Creating pure Sass functions* recipe of *Chapter 3, Variables, Mixins, and Functions*. You can read more about the `@if` directive in the *Using @if* recipe of *Chapter 8, Advanced Sass Coding*. For conditional assignments of values, you can also use the `if()` function, as described in the *Conditional assignments* recipe of this chapter.

See also

▶ The complete list of the Sass built-in introspection functions can be found at http://sass-lang.com/documentation/Sass/Script/Functions.html.

▶ An overview of the Compass Math Helper function can be found at http://compass-style.org/reference/compass/helpers/math/.

▶ The complete list of the Sass built-in introspection functions can be found at http://sass-lang.com/documentation/Sass/Script/Functions.html.

Conditional assignments

In this recipe, you will learn how to perform a conditional assignment of a variable or a property with SassScript.

Getting ready

Read the *Installing Sass for command line usage* recipe of *Chapter 1, Getting Started with Sass*, to find out how to compile your SCSS code into CSS code.

How to do it...

Perform the following step to learn more about conditional assignments in Sass:

1. Use your text editor to create a Ruby file called `if.rb`. Write down the following SCSS code into this file:

   ```scss
   // scss-lint:disable ColorKeyword

   $dark: true;
   $dark-color: black;
   $light-color: white;

   .element {
     color: if($dark, $dark-color, $light-color);
   }
   ```

2. Then, run the following command in your console to compile the Sass template from the first step into CSS code:

   ```
   sass if.scss
   ```

3. Finally, a CSS code like the one shown here should be outputted in your console:

   ```css
   .element {
     color: black; }
   ```

How it works

The condition `if()` function should be called with three parameters. The first parameter sets the condition, followed by two values. When the expression, which sets the condition, returns anything other than `false` or `null`, the first value (second parameter) will be assigned, otherwise the last parameter will be assigned.

There is more...

As you can see, the `if()` function can only be used for a simple conditional assignment. For more complex **if-then-else logic** in SassScript, you will have to use the `@if` directive. Read more about the `@if` directive in the *Using @if* recipe of *Chapter 8, Advanced Sass Coding*.

The conditional assignment used in this recipe can easily be rewritten with the `@if` directive. When using `@if` directive instead of the condition `if()` function, your SCSS code will look like the following:

```
.element2 {
  @if(dark) {
    color: $dark-color;
  } @else {
    color: $light-color;
  }
}
```

The preceding SCSS code will also compile into CSS code, as shown here:

```
.element2 {
  color: black; }
```

Adding custom functions to Sass

The other recipes in the chapter describe functions already built into Sass. In this recipe, you will learn how to extend Sass with your own custom functions.

Getting ready

This recipe requires some basic knowledge of Ruby programming. To learn more about Ruby, you can read the *Ruby and MongoDB Web Development Beginner's Guide* book by Gautam Rege. You can find more about Rege's book at `https://www.packtpub.com/web-development/ruby-and-mongodb-web-development-beginners-guide`. Also, read the *Installing Sass for command line usage* recipe of *Chapter 1, Getting Started with Sass*, to find out how to compile your SCSS code into CSS code. This recipe uses the same SCSS code as the one used for the *Introspection Functions* recipe of this chapter.

How to do it...

Here are the steps showing the implementation of adding custom functions:

1. Use your text editor to create a Ruby file called `cos.rb`. Write down the following Ruby code into this file:

```ruby
module Sass::Script::Functions
  def cos(number)
    number(Math.cos(number.value))
  end
  declare :cos, [:number]
end
```

2. Create a Sass template called `cos.scss`. The `cos.scss` file should contain the following lines of SCSS code:

```scss
// scss-lint:disable PropertySpelling

@function cosine($x) {

  @if function-exists(cos) {
    @return cos($x);
  } @else {
    @warn 'cos() function not found!';
    @return null;
  }

}

.test {
  cosine: cosine(1);
}
```

3. Now run the following command in your console:

```
sass --require ./cos.rb cos.scss
```

4. Finally, you will find a CSS like the one shown here in your console:

```css
.test {
  cosine: 0.5403; }
```

How it works...

The Ruby code in the first step of this recipe extends the `Sass::Script::Functions` module and adds a `cos()` trigonometric function. When writing your own custom functions for Sass, you should keep in mind that first of all, the arguments passed are value objects. Value objects are also expected to be returned. Also, see `http://sass-lang.com/documentation/Sass/Script/Value.html` to learn more about the value object.

In the third step, the Ruby Sass compiler has been called with the `--require` option. This option can be used to load any Ruby library before Sass runs.

There's more...

In this recipe, you have created your own custom function to calculate the cosine of a numerical value. The Compass library, as discussed in the *Installing Compass* recipe of *Chapter 1*, *Getting Started with Sass*, and *Chapter 6*, *Using Compass*, already extends Sass with more complex mathematical functions, including the `cos()` trigonometric function to calculate the cosine of a value. The *Introspection Functions* recipe of this chapter will demonstrate how to use this trigonometric function in your SCSS code with Compass.

In the *Creating pure Sass functions* recipe of *Chapter 3*, *Variables, Mixins, and Functions*, you can read about how to create functions with the `@function` directive. Functions defined with the `@function` directive are written in SassScript, while the built-in functions are written in Ruby. In most situations, you can use both the methods to create a function to assign a property value. Custom functions written with the `@function` directive can ship with your code or library; you can use partials, as described in the *Working with partials* recipe of *Chapter 1*, *Getting Started with Sass*, to distribute your customs functions. Those who have grown familiar with SassScript after reading this book do not have to learn Ruby to create custom functions with the `@function` directive.

The cosine trigonometric function created in this recipe is only a wrapper for the `Math.cos()` function already built in Ruby. Sass does not have built-in trigonometric functions. You can use the Taylor series to create your own trigonometric functions in SassScript. To do so, you will have to create your own power and factorial functions first.

Also, note that you should not use these custom functions to create dynamical code, since Sass files are by default only compiled once.

See also

> ▶ Those who want to try to create their own trigonometry functions in SassScript should read the *Trigonometry in Sass* article by Daniel Perez Alvarez. This article can be found at `https://unindented.org/articles/trigonometry-in-sass/`.

> ▶ A simple explanation about using the Taylor series to approximate cosine can be found at `http://www.mathsisfun.com/algebra/taylor-series.html`.

6
Using Compass

In this chapter, you will learn the following topics:

- ► Extending Sass with Compass helper functions
- ► Truncating Text with ellipses
- ► Tuning vendor prefixes from Compass stylesheets
- ► Adding Compass to an existing Sass project
- ► Maintaining your applications with Compass
- ► Using Bootstrap with Compass

Introduction

According to their website, **Compass** is an open source **CSS Authoring Framework**. It extends Sass with useful and reusable functions, and it helps you write cross-browser CSS code with ease. In this chapter, you will learn how to use and integrate Compass in your projects.

Read the *Installing Compass* recipe of *Chapter 1, Getting Started with Sass*, to find out how to install Compass.

You will finally notice that the Compass Framework is a charityware. This means that it is free to download and use; but if you use it, you are asked to donate to the **United Mitochondrial Disease Foundation** (**UMDF**).

Extending Sass with Compass helper functions

In *Chapter 5*, *Built-in functions*, you can read about useful functions already built in Sass. After installing Compass, you can also use helper functions provided by Compass in your code. This recipe demonstrates how to use some of these helper functions.

Getting ready

In this recipe, you will compile your SCSS code with Compass. First, read the *Installing Compass* recipe of *Chapter 1*, *Getting Started with Sass*, to find out how to install Compass. Also, read the *Adding Compass to an existing Sass project* and *Maintaining your applications with Compass* recipes of this chapter to learn more about using Compass for your project.

How to do it...

After installing Compass you can use it to compile your Sass code. Perform the following step to see Compass in action:

1. Create a new Compass project by running the following command in your console:

   ```
   compass create
   ```

2. Then, create a new sass/main.scss file that will contain the SCSS code like that shown here:

   ```
   div {
     background-image: inline-image('SassnotSASS.jpg');
   }
   ```

3. Finally, compile your new project by running the following command in your console:

   ```
   compass compile
   ```

4. The command from the previous step creates a new stylesheets/main.css CSS file. Write down the compiled CSS code as follows into it:

   ```
   /* line 1, ../sass/main.scss */
   div {
     background-image: url('data:image/jpeg;base64,/9j/4QAYRXhpZgAASU
   kqAAgAAAAAAAAAAAAAP/sABFEdWNreQABAAQAAAA3AAD/4QMtaHR0cDovL25zLmFk
   b2JlLmNv...');
   }
   ```

How it works...

First, note that the base 64 encoded string in the last step of this recipe has been truncated. The location of the `SassnotSASS.jpg` image does not require a path. You should save your images in the folder set by the `images_dir` setting in your `config.rb` Compass configuration file.

The `background-image` CSS property should be set to an URI. The function's notation for an URI is `url()`. Note that URIs may not only contain URLs, but also data URIs. Data URIs inline the content of the file into the CSS code. You can use the `inline-image()` function to create inline images in your CSS code. The `inline-image()` function can be called with the URL of the file to inline. It generates a string that holds the base 64 encoded content of the image file.

Notice that the `base64` part of this string also sets the encoding type of the inlined content of the file. Setting the encoding type is not required; inline code that is not base 64 encoded should be URL encoded.

 Some older browsers don't support data URIs. Internet Explorer supports data URIs since version 8. In version 8 of the Internet explorer data, a URI may not contain more than 32768 bytes.

The second argument for the `inline-image()` function, which sets the MIME type, is optional. The `inline-image()` function does not validate the MIME type string; neither does it check whether the URL content matches the MIME type set by the second parameter. But if the URL does not exist, it throws a `File not found or cannot be read` error. If no MIME type string is set, the file extension of the URL will be used to determine the MIME type.

There's more...

For small images, using data URIs seems to be a good or better alternative for image sprites, as described in the *Using image sprites with Compass* recipe in *Chapter 8, Advanced Sass Coding*. Data URIs should be used sparingly, as testing has revealed that, on some mobile views, a data URI is on an average six times slower than using a binary source. Other situations can be solved using an icon font, such as Font Awesome. Font Awesome can be found at `http://fontawesome.github.io/Font-Awesome/`.

Background images with data URI should only be used for images that are a part of your layout. Technically, there is no reason to not define all the images of your website as an inline image with a data URI. Because of screen reader, printer and also other devices running in a high contrast mode will ignore background images, you should always provide functional and semantically important images with the `img` tag in the document markup for accessibility proposals. For this reason, you should also set an alternative background color for situations when the image is unavailable.

You may have noticed that the number of bytes of the base 64 encoded URI is usually larger than the number of bytes of the original image. Base 64 encoded data can be compressed very well. So, when using http compression for your website, the side effect of larger number of bytes can be eliminated.

The `inline-font-files()` helper function provided by Compass is very similar to the `font-files()` function. You can use this function to embed a font file within the generated CSS file.

Compass also extends Sass with trigonometric functions. In the *Introspection Functions* recipe of *Chapter 5, Built-in Functions*, you can read about how to use the `cos()` function.

Besides functions, Compass also provides many mixins. You can read about the differences between functions and mixins in *Chapter 3, Variables, Mixins, and Functions*, of this book. The *Truncating Text with ellipses* recipe of this chapter will show you how to use the `overflow()` mixin, and in the *Creating a vertical rhythm for your website* recipe of *Chapter 8, Advanced Sass Coding*, you will learn how to create typographical patterns by using both: the Compass' functions and mixins.

See also

- More information on the usage of URIs in CSS can be found at `http://www.w3.org/TR/CSS21/syndata.html#value-def-uri`.

- Some background information about the usage of http compression with gzip or deflate for your website can be found at `http://css-tricks.com/snippets/htaccess/active-gzip-compression/`. For Apache, you can enable the compression via `.htaccess`. IIS users should use the `web.config` file.

- More information about the load time of data URIs by Peter McLachlan can be found at `http://www.mobify.com/blog/data-uris-are-slow-on-mobile/`.

- A complete list of Compass' helper functions can be found at `http://compass-style.org/reference/compass/helpers/`.

Truncating Text with ellipses

In this recipe, you will learn how to truncate text with ellipses using Compass. The `text-overflow` CSS property determines how overflowed content that is not displayed is signaled to users. It can be clipped; it can display an ellipsis or a custom string. The `overflow()` mixin of Compass helps you write cross-browser CSS code for truncating texts with ellipses.

Getting ready

For this recipe, you will need a modern web browser. Of course, you also have to install Compass. The *Installing Compass* recipe of *Chapter 1, Getting Started with Sass*, describes how to install Compass on your system.

How to do it...

The following steps will show you how to truncate text with the Compass helper functions:

1. Create a new Compass project by running the following command in your console:

   ```
   compass create
   ```

2. Then, create a new `sass/main.scss` file that will contain SCSS code like that shown here:

   ```scss
   @import "compass/typography/text/ellipsis";

   .truncated {
     @include ellipsis();
     width: 250px;
   }

   .truncated-wrap {
     @include ellipsis(false);
     width: 250px;
   }
   ```

3. Compile your project by running the following command in your console:

   ```
   compass compile
   ```

4. The preceding command creates a new `stylesheets/main.css` CSS file. Now, create an `index.html` file that includes this CSS file. The `index.html` file should look as follows:

   ```html
   <!doctype html>
   <html lang="en">
   <head>
     <meta charset="utf-8">

     <title>Truncating Text with Ellipses</title>
     <meta name="description" content="Truncating Text with
   Ellipses">
     <meta name="author" content="Bass Jobsen">

     <link rel="stylesheet" type="text/css" href="stylesheets/main.
   css" />

   </head>
   ```

```
<body>
<p class="truncated">Show how to truncate long text with
ellipses.</p>
<p class="truncated-wrap">Show how to truncate long text with
ellipses.</p>
<p class="truncated-wrap">Showhowtotruncatelongwordswith
ellipses.</p>
</body>
</html>
```

5. Now load the `index.html` file from the fourth step in your browser. You will find that the result will look like the following image:

> Show how to truncate long t...
>
> Show how to truncate long
> text with ellipses.
>
> Showhowtotruncatelongwor...
> ellipses.

How it works...

In *Chapter 7, Cross-Browser CSS3 Mixins*, of this book, you can learn more about vendor-prefixes in CSS3. The `text-overflow` CSS property requires vendor-prefixes for some browsers. The `overflow()` mixin of Compass helps you write this code with a single declaration.

When inspecting the source of the compiled `stylesheets/main.css` CSS file, you will find that the `@include ellipsis();` mixin call compiles into the CSS code as follows:

```
white-space: nowrap;
overflow: hidden;
-ms-text-overflow: ellipsis;
-o-text-overflow: ellipsis;
text-overflow: ellipsis;
```

The `ellipsis()` mixin accepts a single argument (`$no-wrap`). The `$no-wrap` parameter got a default value of `false`, which means that the ellipsis text is no-wrap. If you do not explicitly set this parameter to `true`, the mixins will compile the `white-space: nowrap;` declaration into your final CSS, which will limit the text to a single line.

Also, notice that the earlier only works when your HTML elements are declared with the `display` property set to the `block` or `inline-block` value.

There's more...

The *Tuning vendor prefixes from Compass stylesheets* recipe of this chapter discusses cross-browser support for CSS3 properties. The `ellipsis()` mixin does not give the desired result for older browsers. Especially, older versions of the Firefox web browser do not support ellipses. You can use the technique described here to fix this. Notice that you also can consider applying **progressive enhancement** or even **graceful degradation**, as described in the *Applying Progressive enhancement* recipe of *Chapter 7, Cross-Browser CSS3 Mixins*, because Mozilla added support for CSS ellipsis since version 7.0.

To add support for older versions of the Firefox web browser, you should run the following command in your console:

```
compass install compass/ellipsis
```

The preceding command installs a special XML file in the `stylesheets` folder of your project. The command also installs an example `sass/ellipis.scss` Sass file. The example file shows you how to use the ellipsis mixin. To use the ellipses fall-back for older browsers, you should set the `$use-mozilla-ellipsis-binding` variable to `true`. You should declare this variable before importing the mixin, as follows:

```
$use-mozilla-ellipsis-binding: true;
@import "compass/typography/text/ellipsis";
```

With the preceding SCSS settings, the SCSS code used in this recipe compiles into CSS code as follows:

```
.ellipsis {
  white-space: nowrap;
  overflow: hidden;
  -ms-text-overflow: ellipsis;
  -o-text-overflow: ellipsis;
  text-overflow: ellipsis;
  -moz-binding: url('/stylesheets/xml/ellipsis.xml#ellipsis'); }
```

The `ellipsis()` mixin is a part of the Text functions and a mixin of the Compass Typography module. The Compass Typography module provides some basic mixins for common text styling patterns. Besides patterns for truncating texts, this module also contains helpers for styling links and lists. In the *Creating a vertical rhythm for your website* recipe of *Chapter 8, Advanced Sass Coding*, you will learn how to create typographical patterns by using Compass' functions and mixins.

See also

▶ The official documentation for the `ellipsis()` mixin can be found at `http://compass-style.org/reference/compass/typography/text/ellipsis/`.

▶ More information about CSS String Truncation with Ellipsis by Justin Maxwell can be found at `http://mattsnider.com/css-string-truncation-with-ellipsis/`.

▶ Finally, read more about the `text-overflow` CSS property at `https://developer.mozilla.org/en-US/docs/Web/CSS/text-overflow`.

Tuning vendor prefixes from Compass stylesheets

Vendor-specific rules provide us with early implementations of standard properties and alternative syntaxes. These rules allow browsers to implement proprietary **CSS properties** that would otherwise have no working standards (and may never actually become standardized). Which vendor prefixes you will have to add depends on the browsers you have to support. In this recipe, you will learn how to configure Compass cross-browser support.

Since CSS3, you can give any block level element rounded corners without using images by using the `border-radius` property. The `border-radius` property should be prefixed for the best possible browser support. Compass can automatically add the right prefixes for you.

Getting ready

Of course, you will have to install Compass for this recipe. So, read the *Installing Compass* recipe of *Chapter 1, Getting Started with Sass*, to find out how to install Compass. Also, read *Chapter 7, Cross-Browser CSS3 Mixins*, of this book to learn more about cross-browser CSS3 code.

How to do it...

The following demonstrate you how to tuning vendor prefixes when working with Compass.

1. Create a new Compass project by running the following command in your console:

   ```
   compass create
   ```

2. Then, create a new `sass/main.scss` file that will contain SCSS code as follows:

   ```
   $graceful-usage-threshold: 0.1;
   $debug-browser-support: true;

   @import "compass";
   ```

```
.rounded-corners {

  @include border-radius(5px);

}
```

3. Compile your project into CSS code by running the following command:

```
compass import
```

4. The preceding command writes down the CSS as follows into the `stylesheets/main.css` file:

```
/* line 7, ../sass/main.scss */
```

```
.rounded-corners {
```

```
/* Capability border-radius is prefixed with -moz because
0.25036% of users need it which is more than the threshold of
0.1%. */
```

```
/* Creating new -moz context. */
```

```
  -moz-border-radius: 5px;
```

```
/* Capability border-radius is not prefixed with -ms because 0%
of users are affected which is less than the threshold of 0.1. */
```

```
/* Capability border-radius is not prefixed with -o because 0% of
users are affected which is less than the threshold of 0.1. */
```

```
/* Capability border-radius is prefixed with -webkit because
0.1583% of users need it which is more than the threshold of 0.1%.
*/
```

```
/* Creating new -webkit context. */
```

```
  -webkit-border-radius: 5px;
```

```
  border-radius: 5px;
```

```
}
```

How it works...

Cross-browser support is already built in the `border-radius()` mixin, but Compass enables you to fine-tune which browsers to support. Underneath the covers of Compass's vendor prefixing and legacy browser support is the very same data that drives the website `http://caniuse.com`. *Can I use* provides up-to-date browser support tables for the support of frontend web technologies on desktop and mobile web browsers. This data allows Compass to correlate browser support with browser usage statistics and browser versions for you.

In this recipe, the `$graceful-usage-threshold` variable was used and set to `0.1`. The preceding declaration means that less than `0.1%` of the users, according to the data provided by the *Can I use* website, will be affected if the required prefix is not added any more. Because `$debug-browser-support` was set to `true`, the comments in the code show you how graceful degrading works for the `border-radius` property.

Reconsider the part of CSS code from the recipe as shown here:

```
/* Capability border-radius is prefixed with -moz because 0.25036%
of users need it which is more than the threshold of 0.1%. */
/* Creating new -moz context. */
-moz-border-radius: 5px;
```

As you can see, the `-moz` prefix was added because `0.25036%` of the users need it, which is more than the `0.1%` set by the `$graceful-usage-threshold` variable. You can read more about graceful degradation in the *Applying progressive enhancement* recipe of *Chapter 7, Cross-Browser CSS3 Mixins*. For our example in the recipe with rounded corners, graceful degradation means that less than `0.1%` of the users see the web page without rounded corners. Rounded corners do not influence the basic functionalities of the page.

You can use the `$critical-usage-threshold` variable to set a threshold for properties that cannot be degraded gracefully. The CSS3 multicolumn layout module does not degrade gracefully because the layout meshes up when the columns don't work. The threshold for the Compass column mixins can be set by the `$multicolumn-support-threshold` variable too. The `$multicolumn-support-threshold` variable equals to the `$critical-usage-threshold` variable's default.

There's more...

In some situations, you will have to support some older browsers regardless of the thresholds described in the previous version. You can set the `$supported-browsers` variable to define which browsers your website should support. The `$browser-minimum-versions` variable enables you to set the oldest version of a browser to be supported.

Try to compile the SCSS code used in this recipe with the following variables:

```
$browser-minimum-versions: (firefox: '3.6');
$graceful-usage-threshold: 0.1;
$debug-browser-support: true;
```

Using these settings will result in the following piece of CSS code:

```
/* Capability border-radius is prefixed with -moz because firefox
3.6 is required. */
/* Creating new -moz context. */
-moz-border-radius: 5px;
```

Finally, notice that the Compass `border-radius()` mixin only adds vendor-prefixes to your properties for cross-browser support. Even when you explicitly set the $browser-minimum-versions variable to support some decent browsers, the mixin does not add any nonstandard code, polyfill, or other alternative solution to support older browsers.

Older versions of Compass also had mixins for the so-called CSS3 **Progressive Internet Explorer** (**PIE**). CSS3 PIE is a JavaScript library that enhances Internet Explorer older than version 10 to render many modern CSS3 capabilities wherever possible.

See also

▶ The complete documentation for tuning vendor prefixes can be found at `http://compass-style.org/help/documentation/tuning-vendor-prefixes/`

▶ Learn more about block-level and inline elements in HTML by reading *The Difference Between "Block and "Inline"* post by Louis Lazaris at `http://www.impressivewebs.com/difference-block-inline-css/`

▶ Read how to apply `border-radius` through CSS in more detail at `https://css-tricks.com/almanac/properties/b/border-radius/`

▶ Find the documentation for the Compass Column module at `http://compass-style.org/reference/compass/css3/columns/`

▶ Finally, the official website of the CSS3 PIE can be found at `http://css3pie.com`

Adding Compass to an existing Sass project

In the *Installing Compass* recipe of *Chapter 1, Getting Started with Sass*, you can read about how to create a new Compass project. In this recipe, you will learn how to add Compass to an existing Sass project.

Getting ready

Of course, you will have to install Compass before using it. Read the *Installing Compass* recipe of *Chapter 1, Getting Started with Sass*, to find out how to install Compass. This recipe uses the same SCSS code as was used in the *Introspection functions* recipe of *Chapter 5, Built-in Functions*, to demonstrate the cosine trigonometric function.

How to do it...

You can learn how to integrate Compass in a existing Sass project by performing the following steps:

1. Create a file structure like that shown here:

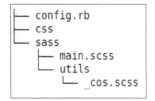

```
├── config.rb
├── css
└── sass
    ├── main.scss
    └── utils
        └── _cos.scss
```

2. Write down the following SCSS code into the `sass/main.scss` file:

```
// scss-lint:disable PropertySpelling

@import "utils/cos";

.test {
  cosine: cosine(1);
}
```

3. The `sass/utils/_cos.scss` file should contain the SCSS as follows:

```
@function cosine($x) {

  @if function-exists(cos) {
    @return cos($x);
  } @else {
    @warn 'cos() function not found!';
    @return null;
  }

}
```

4. Then, create a file called `config.rb`. This file should contain the setting for Compass for your project, which should look as follows:

```
http_path = "/"
css_dir = "css"
sass_dir = "sass"
images_dir = "images"
javascripts_dir = "javascripts"
```

5. Run the following command in your console:

```
compass init
```

6. The command from the previous step should output a message like that shown here:

```
Congratulations! Your compass project has been created.
```

7. Finally, after inspecting the CSS generated in the `css/main.css` file, you will find that this code looks as follows:

```
/* line 5, ../sass/main.scss */
.test {
  cosine: 0.5403;
}
```

How it works...

In the *Installing Compass* recipe of *Chapter 1, Getting Started with Sass*, you can find the complete file structure of a Compass project. The `config.rb` file contains the configuration for Compass. You can change the paths for your files in this file. In this recipe, you set the `css_dir` and `sass_dir` options to point to the paths of your project files. Just like the Sass compiler, Compass only compiles `main.scss` and ignores the partials. Partials are Sass files whose filename start with an underscore (_). Read more about partials in the *Working with partials* recipe of *Chapter 1, Getting Started with Sass*.

There's more...

Instead of compiling your project with Compass, you can also use the Sass command with the `--compass` option. The *Installing Compass* recipe of *Chapter 1, Getting Started with Sass*, shows you how to do this.

You can also integrate Compass with other applications. In the *Adding Compass to your Ruby on Rails setup* recipe of *Chapter 14, Ruby on Rails and Sass*, you can read how to integrate Compass with Ruby on Rails.

See also

A complete list of integrations of Compass with other applications can be found at `http://compass-style.org/help/tutorials/integration/`.

Maintaining your applications with Compass

After installing Sass and Compass, you can use Compass to maintain your application. This recipe describes how to maintain your applications with Compass on the command line.

Getting ready

Install Compass as described in the *Installing Compass* recipe of *Chapter 1, Getting Started with Sass*.

How to do it...

Perform the following step to get grips on maintaining your applications with Compass:

1. Create a new Sass project, as described in the *Installing Compass* recipe of *Chapter 1, Getting Started with Sass*, by using the following command in your console:

   ```
   compass create
   ```

2. Then, create a `sass/application.scss` file that imports the `sass/_base.scss` partial file (see step 4 of this recipe). The SCSS code in the `sass/application.scss` file should look as follows:

```
@import "base";

@include global-reset; // Eric Meyer's reset 2.0 Global reset
rules.
@include establish-baseline; // set a default font-size and line-
height on your <html> tag.

a {
  @include hover-link;
}
```

3. The `sass/_base.scss` partial file mentioned in the previous step should contain a SCSS code like that shown here:

```
$font-color: #a9a9a9; // darkgray
@import "compass";
```

4. Now, you can edit the `sass/application.scss` file and compile your project by running the following command in your console:

   `compass compile`

5. The preceding command generates or rewrites the `stylesheets/application.css` file.

6. To remove the generated files and the Sass cache, you can run the following command:

   `compass clean`

7. Last, but not least, when you are happy with the results, you can run the following command to compile the compressed CSS code for production:

   `compass -e compile --force`

How it works...

In this recipe, you have learned to set up and maintain a project with Compass. The `sass/_base.scss` partial file imports the Compass core framework. You can add your custom mixins in the `sass/_base.scss` partial file too. Note that the `$font-color` variable used by Compass should be set before the `@import` statement.

After importing the `sass/_base.scss` partial file, the SCSS in the `sass/application.scss` file will use some of the mixins from Compass. The `@include global-reset;` code creates global reset rules for your style rules. You can read more about CSS Resets in the *Using a CSS Reset* recipe of *Chapter 9, Building Layouts with Sass.*

The `@include establish-baseline;` code sets a default font-size and line-height. You can read more about this in the *Creating a vertical rhythm for your site* recipe of *Chapter 8, Advanced Sass Coding*.

Finally, including the hover-link mixin of Compass sets some defaults for the hovering (mouse over) of the anchors in your project.

The `--force` option in the command of the last step enables Compass to overwrite existing files. Compass also supports a `--watch` option. Refer to the *Editing and debugging your Sass code in browser* recipe of *Chapter 2, Debugging Your Code*. You can run the following command in your console to get a complete overview of all the options supported by Compass.

There's more...

You can also use Compass without the command-line tools. An example can be found in the *Number Functions* recipe of *Chapter 5, Built-in Functions*, which shows you how to use some mathematical functions of Compass together with the Sass command-line compiler. You can use the `--compass` option of the compiler to do this. Note that you have to install Compass first, as described in the *Installing Compass* recipe of *Chapter 1, Getting Started with Sass*, before you can use the `--compass` option.

The Compass cosine function, as mentioned in the preceding, as used in the *Number functions* recipe of *Chapter 5, Built-in Functions*, is a built-in function similar to the functions described in the *Adding Custom Functions* recipe of *Chapter 5, Built-in Functions*. On the other hand, to reuse Compass mixins, you will have to import them explicitly in your code with the `@import` directive. You can do this by adding the following line of code at the start of your main SCSS project file:

```scss
@import "compass";
```

This imports the compass core framework, which includes the CSS3, Typography, and Utilities modules. To import only the CSS3 module, you can use the following SCSS code:

```scss
@import "compass/css3";
```

The Layout and Reset modules should be imported apart from the core modules.

See also

You can read more about Eric Meyer's reset rules at `http://meyerweb.com/eric/tools/css/reset/`.

Using Bootstrap with Compass

According to their website, Bootstrap is the most popular HTML, CSS, and JS framework for developing responsive, mobile-first projects on the Web.

Getting ready

You can read more about Bootstrap in *Chapter 12, Bootstrap and Sass*, of this book. Also, read the *Installing Sass for command line usage* recipe of *Chapter 1, Getting Started with Sass*, to learn more about Ruby and RubyGems.

In this recipe, version 3 of Bootstrap is used to show you how to use Bootstrap with Compass and Sass. In *Chapter 12, Bootstrap and Sass*, of this book, version 4 is used. Bootstrap 4 was still under development at the time of writing this book. Bootstrap 4 is not backward compatible with Bootstrap 3, but migrate guides will be available. Bootstrap 4 moved from Less to Sass, which means that you do not have to use the `bootstrap-sass` gem anymore.

How to do it...

The following steps will show you how to install `bootstrap-sass` and use it together with Compass:

1. Run the following command in your console to install Bootstrap for Sass:

   ```
   gem install bootstrap-sass
   ```

2. Then, create a new Bootstrap project for Compass by running the following command:

   ```
   compass create bootstrap-project -r bootstrap-sass --using bootstrap
   ```

3. The preceding command creates a new Compass project with the directory structure, as follows:

   ```
   ├── config.rb
   ├── fonts
   │   └── bootstrap
   │       ├── glyphicons-halflings-regular.eot
   │       ├── glyphicons-halflings-regular.svg
   │       ├── glyphicons-halflings-regular.ttf
   │       ├── glyphicons-halflings-regular.woff
   │       └── glyphicons-halflings-regular.woff2
   ├── javascripts
   │   ├── bootstrap
   │   ├── bootstrap.js
   │   ├── bootstrap.min.js
   │   └── bootstrap-sprockets.js
   ├── sass
   │   ├── _bootstrap-variables.scss
   │   └── styles.scss
   └── stylesheets
       └── styles.css
   ```

4. That's all the ways in which you can use Bootstrap with Sass, as described in
    Chapter 12, Bootstrap and Sass, and maintain it with Compass, as described
    in the *Maintaining your applications with Compass* recipe.

How it works...

Although Bootstrap's CSS code is originally written with Less; a version for Sass is available
too. You can use the Sass version of Bootstrap to integrate Bootstrap easily in your
Sass project.

In this recipe, you use the Compass `-r` and `--using` flags to create a new Compass project
with the files from `bootstrap-sass`. The files include the following files for Bootstrap:

*   `styles.sass`: The main project's Sass file imports Bootstrap and variables
*   `bootstrap-variables.sass`: This file will contain a copy of Bootstrap's Sass
    variables which you can override for customization.
*   `--using`: This flag installs Bootstrap dependencies

There's more...

The maintainers of the `bootstrap-sass` code create some script to automatically build the
Sass code from the Less code base. The preceding means that the `bootstrap-sass` code
does not use Compass mixins. Some `bootstrap-sass` mixins may even conflict with the
Compass' ones.

Secondly, Bootstrap requires the use of Autoprefixer. Autoprefixer adds vendor prefixes to
CSS rules using values from the Can I Use database (also, refer to the *Tuning vendor prefixes
from Compass stylesheets* recipe of this chapter). You can read more about Autoprefixer in
the *Using the autoprefixer plugin* recipe of *Chapter 16, Setting up a Build Chain with Gulp*.
Because the `bootstrap-sass` code does not use Compass mixins, as described earlier,
you cannot rely on Compass mixins for prefixing your code.

Blueprint was bundled with older versions of Compass. Blueprint is a CSS framework similar
to Bootstrap. Blueprint helped build the layout for your projects, but it has not kept up with
layout and responsive approaches like Bootstrap.

See also

*   You can find Bootstrap's documentation at `http://getbootstrap.com/`
*   Bootstrap for Sass can be downloaded at `https://github.com/twbs/
    bootstrap-sass`.
*   An overview of websites built with Bootstrap can be found at `http://expo.
    getbootstrap.com/`

7

Cross-Browser CSS3 Mixins

In this chapter, you will learn the following topics:

- ▶ Browser support
- ▶ Using vendor prefixes
- ▶ Cross-browser CSS3 with Compass
- ▶ The Can I Use database
- ▶ Applying progressive enhancement
- ▶ The -prefix-free library
- ▶ Mobile first strategies

Introduction

Web technologies change and develop every day. The **World Wide Web Consortium (W3C)** creates international standards for the **World Wide Web**(**WWW**). Web browsers implement these standards and techniques to create the best user experience for their users. Because people do not always use the newest web browser, CSS developers should support both old and new standards.

Also, browsers may differ and people may use many different types of devices to visit web pages. The recent growth of mobile internet and the overwhelming usage of cell phones and tablets to browse the Internet have given new techniques, such as responsive design, a real boost.

Sass can help you write maintainable and cross-browser CSS code.

Browser support

People do not always use the latest version of a web browser. In this recipe, you will learn why you can use mixins or mixin libraries to add cross-browser support to your multiple column layout.

Getting ready

To compile the SCSS of this recipe, you should have the Ruby Sass compiler installed. The *Installing Sass for command line usage* recipe of *Chapter 1, Getting Started with Sass*, describes how to install Ruby Sass on your system. You can inspect the final results in any modern web browser.

How to do it...

Perform the following steps to get grips on creating cross-browser CSS code:

1. Create your main project file called `main.scss`. This file should import the column partial file. So, `main.scss` should contain a SCSS code like that shown here:

```scss
$grid-gutter-width: 15px;

@import 'components/columns';

.columns {
  @include content-columns(3);
}
```

2. The column partial, the `components/_columns.scss` file, should contain the mixin that creates your content columns. The SCSS code in this file will look as follows:

```scss
// scss-lint:disable VendorPrefix

// CSS3 Content Columns

@mixin content-columns($column-count, $column-gap: $grid-gutter-width) {
  -webkit-column-count: $column-count;
  -moz-column-count: $column-count;
  column-count: $column-count;
  -webkit-column-gap: $column-gap;
  -moz-column-gap: $column-gap;
  column-gap: $column-gap;
}
```

The SCSS code of the preceding mixin originates from the Bootstrap Sass project (`https://github.com/twbs/bootstrap-sass/`).

3. Now, compile your project by running the following command in your console:

```
sass sass/main.scss main.css
```

4. Create an `index.html` file that will link the compiled `main.css` file from the previous step and contain the HTML markup code as follows:

```
<div class="columns">Lorem ipsum dolor sit amet, consectetuer
adipiscing elit. Aenean commodo ligula eget dolor. Aenean
massa. Cum sociis natoque penatibus et magnis dis parturient
montes, nascetur ridiculus mus. Donec quam felis, ultricies nec,
pellentesque eu, pretium quis, sem. Nulla consequat massa quis
enim. Donec pede justo, fringilla vel, aliquet nec, vulputate
eget, arcu. In enim justo, rhoncus ut, imperdiet a, venenatis
vitae, justo. Nullam dictum felis eu pede mollis pretium.
Integer tincidunt. Cras dapibus. Vivamus elementum semper nisi.
Aenean vulputate eleifend tellus. Aenean leo ligula, porttitor
eu, consequat vitae, eleifend ac, enim. Aliquam lorem ante,
dapibus in, viverra quis, feugiat a, tellus. Phasellus viverra
nulla ut metus varius laoreet. Quisque rutrum. Aenean imperdiet.
Etiam ultricies nisi vel augue. Curabitur ullamcorper ultricies
nisi. Nam eget dui. Etiam rhoncus. Maecenas tempus, tellus eget
condimentum rhoncus, sem quam semper libero, sit amet adipiscing
sem neque sed ipsum. Nam quam nunc, blandit vel, luctus pulvinar,
hendrerit id, lorem. Maecenas nec odio et ante tincidunt tempus.
Donec vitae sapien ut libero venenatis faucibus. Nullam quis ante.
Etiam sit amet orci eget eros faucibus tincidunt. Duis leo. Sed
fringilla mauris sit amet nibh. Donec sodales sagittis magna. Sed
consequat, leo eget bibendum sodales, augue velit cursus nunc,</
div>
```

5. Finally, open `index.html` in your browser. You will find that your columns look as follows:

Lorem ipsum dolor sit amet, consectetuer adipiscing elit. Aenean commodo ligula eget dolor. Aenean massa. Cum sociis natoque penatibus et magnis dis parturient montes, nascetur ridiculus mus. Donec quam felis, ultricies nec, pellentesque eu, pretium quis, sem. Nulla consequat massa quis enim. Donec pede justo, fringilla vel, aliquet nec, vulputate eget, arcu. In enim justo, rhoncus ut, imperdiet a, venenatis vitae, justo. Nullam dictum felis eu pede mollis pretium. Integer tincidunt.

Cras dapibus. Vivamus elementum semper nisi. Aenean vulputate eleifend tellus. Aenean leo ligula, porttitor eu, consequat vitae, eleifend ac, enim. Aliquam lorem ante, dapibus in, viverra quis, feugiat a, tellus. Phasellus viverra nulla ut metus varius laoreet. Quisque rutrum. Aenean imperdiet. Etiam ultricies nisi vel augue. Curabitur ullamcorper ultricies nisi. Nam eget dui. Etiam rhoncus. Maecenas tempus, tellus eget condimentum rhoncus, sem quam semper

libero, sit amet adipiscing sem neque sed ipsum. Nam quam nunc, blandit vel, luctus pulvinar, hendrerit id, lorem. Maecenas nec odio et ante tincidunt tempus. Donec vitae sapien ut libero venenatis faucibus. Nullam quis ante. Etiam sit amet orci eget eros faucibus tincidunt. Duis leo. Sed fringilla mauris sit amet nibh. Donec sodales sagittis magna. Sed consequat, leo eget bibendum sodales, augue velit cursus nunc,

How it works...

As you can see, in the SCSS code of the `content-columns` mixin, the CSS3 Multiple Column Layout Module requires the `-webkit` and `-moz` vendor prefixes. You can read more about vendor prefixes in the *Using vendor prefixes* recipe of this chapter. When vendor prefixes are required, you can use a single line declaration to set your properties. Mixins can solve this problem. Using the `content-columns` mixin enables you to set your columns with a line declaration and makes your code DRY (Don't Repeat Yourself).

When your requirements change and you have to drop or add a vendor prefix to the column properties, you should only change your `content-columns` mixin instead of each occurrence of a column property in your code.

Also, refer to the *Can I Use database* recipe of this chapter to find out which browsers support CSS columns with or without vendor prefixes.

There's more...

Older browsers do not support the CSS3 Multiple Column Layout Module at all. Browsers that do not support the CSS3 Multiple Column Layout Module will show your content in a single column. Because you can still read the text when displayed in a single column, the CSS columns degrade gracefully. You can read more about **graceful degradation** versus **progressive enhancement** in the *Applying progressive enhancement* recipe of this chapter.

The CSS3 Multiple Column Layout Module defines a `column-width` property too. The value of the `column-width` property is not an absolute value, but rather a minimum width. Given the column-width, the browser will calculate how many columns of at least that width can fit in the available space. When you define both the `column-count` and `column-width` properties, you can also use the shorthand `column` property. On using the shorthand `column` property, your CSS code could look like that shown here:

```
.columns {
  columns: 3 200px;
}
```

In the preceding code, the 3 value defines the maximum number of columns, and the 200px value sets the minimum width of these columns. Once the browser cannot render even two columns of the width set by the `column-width` property in the available space, the browser will display no columns at all.

Finally, note that the CSS columns are CSS columns responsive-friendly. In the *Mobile first strategies* recipe of this chapter, you can read how to make CSS more responsive-friendly using CSS media queries.

- ▶ You should read *The Guide to Responsive-Friendly CSS Columns* by Katy Decorah at `https://css-tricks.com/guide-responsive-friendly-css-columns/` to learn more about CSS columns.

- ▶ More about CSS columns can also be found at `https://developer.mozilla.org/en-US/docs/Web/Guide/CSS/Using_multi-column_layouts`.

- ▶ The `Lorem ipsum` dummy text for this recipe has been generated with the blind text generator, which can be found at `http://www.blindtextgenerator.com/lorem-ipsum`.

Using vendor prefixes

In this recipe, you will learn how to create cross-browser background gradients with Sass using vendor prefixes.

Getting ready

Also, read the *Writing mixins with arguments* recipe of *Chapter 3*, *Variables, Mixins, and Functions*. Of course, you will need the Ruby Sass compiler for this. The *Installing Sass for command line usage* recipe of *Chapter 1, Getting Started with Sass*, describes how to install Ruby Sass on your system.

How to do it...

Learn how to create cross-browser background gradients with Sass by performing the following steps:

1. Create your main project file called `main.scss`. This file should import the gradient partial file. So, the `main.scss` should contain a SCSS code like that shown here:

```scss
// scss-lint:disable ColorKeyword, ColorVariable

@import 'components/gradients';

header {
  @include gradient-horizontal(yellow, green);

  color: white;
  padding: 20px;
}
```

2. The gradient partial, the `components/_gradients.scss` file, should contain the mixin that creates your background gradient. The SCSS code in this file will look as follows:

```scss
// scss-lint:disable ColorKeyword, ColorVariable

@mixin gradient-horizontal($start-color: #555, $end-color: #333,
$start-percent: 0%, $end-percent: 100%) {
  background: $start-color; // Old browsers
  background: -moz-linear-gradient(left, $start-color $start-
percent, $end-color $end-percent); /* FF3.6+ */
  background: -webkit-gradient(linear, left top, right top, color-
stop($start-percent,$start-color), color-stop($end-percent,$end-
color)); /* Chrome,Safari4+ */
  background: -webkit-linear-gradient(left, $start-color $start-
percent,$end-color $end-percent); /* Chrome10+,Safari5.1+ */
  background: -o-linear-gradient(left, $start-color $start-
percent, $end-color $end-percent); /* Opera 11.10+ */
  background: -ms-linear-gradient(left, $start-color $start-
percent, $end-color $end-percent); /* IE10+ */
  background-image: linear-gradient(to right, $start-color $start-
percent, $end-color $end-percent); // Standard, IE10, Firefox 16+,
Opera 12.10+, Safari 7+, Chrome 26+
  background-repeat: repeat-x;
  filter: progid:DXImageTransform.Microsoft.
gradient(startColorstr='#{ie-hex-str($start-color)}',
endColorstr='#{ie-hex-str($end-color)}', GradientType=1); // IE9
and down
}
```

3. Now, compile your project by running the following command in your console:

```
sass sass/main.scss main.css
```

4. Create an `index.html` file that will link the compiled `main.css` file from the previous step and contain an HTML markup code like that shown here:

```
<header>Background gradients with Sass</header>
```

5. Finally, open `index.html` in your browser. You will find that your background gradient looks as follows:

How it works...

CSS3 introduced **vendor-specific rules** that offer you the possibility of writing some additional CSS applicable to only one browser. At first sight, this seems the exact opposite of what you want. What you want is a set of standards and practicalities that work the same with every browser and a standard set of HTML and CSS, which has the same effect and interpretation for every browser. These vendor-specific rules are intended to help us reach this utopia.

Vendor-specific rules provide us with early implementations of standard properties and alternative syntaxes. Last, but not least, these rules allow browsers to implement proprietary **CSS properties** that would otherwise have no working standards (and may never actually become standardized).

For these reasons, vendor-specific rules play an important role in many new features of CSS3. For example, **animation properties**, **border-radius**, and **box-shadow**; all are dependent on vendor-specific rules.

Vendors use the following prefixes:

- **WebKit**: `-webkit`
- **Firefox**: `-moz`
- **Opera**: `-o`
- **Internet Explorer**: `-ms`

In this recipe, the progressive enhancement strategy has been applied. You can read more about the progressive enhancement strategy for web development in the *Applying progressive enhancement* recipe of this chapter. In the *Writing mixins with arguments* recipe of *Chapter 3, Variables, Mixins, and Functions*, only the official W3C syntax for background gradients was used. Prefixes for older browsers can also be automatically added, as described in the *Automatically prefixing your code with Grunt* recipe of *Chapter 16, Setting up a Build Chain with Grunt*. The **postcss autoprefixer** only adds browser prefixes and does not support polyfills or nonstandard fallbacks. In the case of the background gradient used in this recipe, neither the fallback background color, nor the Filter syntax for older versions of the Microsoft Internet Explorer (IE) browser, is automatically added. So, even when running the postcss autoprefixer postprocessor, creating your own mixins for background gradients makes sense.

In the *Cross browser CSS3 with Compass* recipe of this chapter, you can read how to create the same cross-browser mixin with Compass.

There's more...

The SCSS code that adds the filter syntax for the IE browser version 9 and lower looks as follows:

```
filter: progid:DXImageTransform.Microsoft.
gradient(startColorstr='#{ie-hex-str($start-color)}',
endColorstr='#{ie-hex-str($end-color)}', GradientType=1);
```

Note the usage of the `ie_hex_string()` function in the code of the `gradient-horizontal()` mixin in the preceding. The Filter syntax of the IE browser requires color in the #AARRGGBB format. This format is used in Internet Explorer and .NET and Android development. The `ie_hex_string()` function translates colors into the #AARRGGBB format that IE understands.

In this recipe, only a horizontal gradient has been implemented. CSS3 also supports different directions for the gradients. In fact, the first argument of the `linear-gradient()` CSS function is an angle between 0 and 360 degrees. In the `gradient-horizontal()` mixin in this recipe, keywords were used to describe the angle of the gradient. So, the values `to top`, `to bottom`, `to left` and `to right` are translated into the angles `0deg`, `180deg`, `270deg`, and `90deg`, respectively.

Also, see the following image that illustrates an element with `background: linear-gradient(45deg, white, black);`:

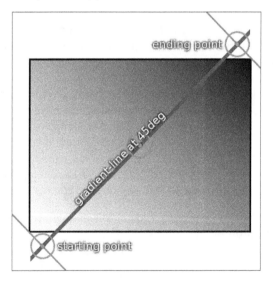

Finally, you should note that older syntaxes use a different definition of the angle of the gradient. This means that the background gradient becomes more complex when you have to support older browsers. So, for instance, the start angle of the `webkit-gradient` vendor prefixed code becomes `left top` instead of `left`.

- ▸ More information on the CSS background-image property can be found at `https://developer.mozilla.org/en/docs/Web/CSS/background-image`.

- ▸ Read more about the `linear-gradient()` syntax at `https://developer.mozilla.org/en-US/docs/Web/CSS/linear-gradient`.

- ▸ You can read more about gradient angles in the old and new syntaxes at `http://www.quirksmode.org/css/images/angles.html`.

Cross browser CSS3 with Compass

In the *Using vendor prefixes* recipe, you can read about how to create a cross-browser background gradient with Sass and Compass. In this recipe, you will learn how to create the same gradient by using the Compass CSS3 module.

Getting ready

The *Installing Sass for command line usage* recipe of *Chapter 1, Getting Started with Sass*, describes how to install Ruby Sass on your system. Also, study how to use Compass in *Chapter 6, Using Compass*. You should read the *Using vendor prefixes* recipe of this chapter first; it describes how to create the same cross-browser background gradient without using Compass.

How to do it...

See how Compass can help you to create cross-browser background gradient in the following steps:

1. Create your main project file called `main.scss`. This file should import the gradient partial file. So, `main.scss` should contain a SCSS code like that shown here:

    ```scss
    // scss-lint:disable ColorKeyword, ColorVariable

    @import 'components/gradients';

    header {
      @include gradient-horizontal(yellow, green);

      color: white;
      padding: 20px;
    }
    ```

2. The gradient partial, the `components/_gradients.scss` file, should contain the mixin that creates your background gradient. The SCSS code in this file will look as follows:

```scss
// scss-lint:disable ColorKeyword, ColorVariable

@import 'compass';

@mixin gradient-horizontal($start-color: #555, $end-color: #333,
$start-percent: 0%, $end-percent: 100%) {
  background-color: $start-color; // Old browsers
  @include filter-gradient($start-color, $end-color, horizontal);
// IE6-9
  @include background-image(linear-gradient(to right, $start-color
$start-percent, $end-color $end-percent));
}
```

3. Now, compile your project by running the following command in your console:

   sass --compass sass/main.scss main.css

4. Create an `index.html` file that will link the compiled `main.css` file from the previous step and contain an HTML markup code like that shown here:

   `<header>Background gradients with Sass</header>`

5. Finally, open `index.html` in your browser. You will find that your background gradient looks as follows:

How it works...

When using Compass as described in *Chapter 6, Using Compass*, you can also use the Compass image mixins to build your background gradients. In this recipe you have used both the `filter-gradient()` and the `background-image()` mixins. Also notice that the first argument of the `background-image()` mixin is a mixin call again. The `linear-gradient()` function creates a linear gradient using standard official or legacy syntax. This function must be included in one of the image module mixins to work properly.

There's more...

The CSS3 module of Compass provides cross-browser mixins for the CSS properties introduced in CSS3. These mixins automatically add vendor prefixes, as described in the *Using vendor prefixes* recipe of this chapter.

The Compass CSS3 module enables you to use a single line declaration for many properties that require vendor prefixes. In the *Tuning vendor prefixes from Compass stylesheets* recipe of *Chapter 6, Using Compass*, you can read about how to tune the vendor prefixes set by the mixins. Compass uses the Can I Use database, as described in the *Can I Use database* recipe of this chapter, to correlate browser support with browser usage statistics and browser versions for you.

Compass also provides CSS3 helper functions to build your own mixins. In the *Using the @if directive* recipe of *Chapter 8, Advanced Sass Coding*, you will find an example of how to use these functions.

See also

▶ The Ultimate CSS Gradient Editor created by Alex Sirota (iosart) enables you to create gradients with a Photoshop-like interface. This tool can generate SCSS code, which requires Compass and can be used in your projects. You can find the Ultimate CSS Gradient Editor at `http://www.colorzilla.com/gradient-editor/`.

▶ More information on the Compass CSS3 module can be found at `http://compass-style.org/reference/compass/css3/`.

▶ The Compass cross-browser helpers can be found at `http://compass-style.org/reference/compass/helpers/cross-browser/`.

The Can I Use database

The Can I Use database, which can be found at `http://caniuse.com/`, provides compatibility tables for the support of HTML5, CSS3, SVG, and other technologies in various browsers. In this recipe, you will learn to find out which vendor prefixes, as discussed in the *Using vendor prefixes recipe* of this chapter, you will have to use to support the browsers of your requirements.

Getting ready

For this recipe, you only need a web browser.

How to do it...

Use the following steps to learn how to use the Can I Use website to find out which vendor prefixes you will have to use to support your target browsers:

1. Open your web browser and navigate to `http://caniuse.com/#feat=multicolumn`.

2. Now, you will find the support table for the **CSS3 Multiple column layout**, which will look as follows:

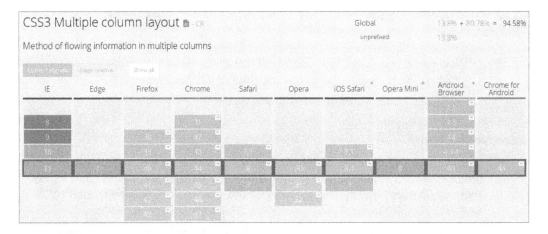

How it works...

The support table tells you that Internet Explorer version 8 and version 9 support the CSS3 Multiple column layout. These browsers are colored red. The table shows the latest version of the most used browsers. It also shows you if vendor prefixes are required for the looked up property or feature. Note that the information in the support table may differ when you look it up, because this information is updated frequently.

You can also look up the more complex CSS gradients. Point your browser to `http://caniuse.com/#feat=css-gradient` and inspect the results. As you can see, the Can I Use database also gives you some hits about how to support older browsers. You can also read that syntaxes used by browsers with prefixed support may be incompatible with that for proper support, which means that you will have to create your own mixins for CSS gradients depending on your unique requirements in most situations. In the *Using vendor prefixes* and *Cross browser CSS3 with Compass* recipes, you can read how to create cross-browser mixins for CSS gradients with or without Compass.

There's more...

The Can I Use database also contains global browser usage tables. These tables show which browsers and versions are most used worldwide.

For your project, you do not have to look up each property by hand. The autoprefixer, as described in the *Automatically prefixing your code with Grunt* recipe of *Chapter 16, Setting up a Build Chain with Grunt*, can automatically add vendor prefixes

You can also use the Compass to create your prefixed properties, as also described in the *Cross browser CSS3 with Compass* recipe of this chapter. Compass uses the very same data that drives the Can I Use website to correlate browser support with browser usage statistics and browser versions.

See also

▸ Also, other sources can provide you with information about CSS properties and features. The Web developer guide of the Mozilla Developer Network tells you how to use properties and which vendor prefixes are required. You can find the Web developer guide at `https://developer.mozilla.org/en-US/doc/Web/Guide`.

▸ The autoprefix tool that adds vendor prefixes to rules using the Can I Use database can be found at `https://github.com/postcss/autoprefixers`.

▸ The Compass framework can be found at `http://compass-style.org/`.

Applying progressive enhancement

In this recipe, you will read about progressive enhancement. Progressive enhancement is a web development approach, which is also described as a part of the Web Standards Curriculum by the W3C. You will also learn to know the differences between the progressive enhancement and graceful degradation approaches for web development.

Getting ready

In this recipe, you will work with CSS background gradients and CSS columns. These techniques are also described in the *Browser support*, *Mobile first strategies*, *Using vendor prefixes*, and *Cross-browser CSS3 with Compass* recipes of this chapter. You can read these recipes to learn more about CSS background gradients and CSS columns.

How to do it...

The following steps will show you how progressive enhancement works:

1. Create your main project file called `main.scss`. This file should import the gradient partial file. So, the `main.scss` should contain a SCSS code like that shown here:

```
// scss-lint:disable ColorKeyword, ColorVariable

@import 'components/gradients';

header {
  @include gradient-horizontal(yellow, green);

  color: white;
  padding: 20px;
}
```

2. The gradient partial, the `components/_gradients.scss` file, should contain the mixin that creates your background gradient. The SCSS code in this file will look as follows:

```
// scss-lint:disable ColorKeyword, ColorVariable

@mixin gradient-horizontal($start-color: #555) {
  background: $start-color; // Old browsers
}
```

3. Now, you can extend the mixin with the official W3 standard syntax for CSS gradients to build in more advanced functionalities for newer browsers:

```
// scss-lint:disable ColorKeyword, ColorVariable

@mixin gradient-horizontal($start-color: #555, $end-color: #333,
$start-percent: 0%, $end-percent: 100%) {
  background: $start-color; // Old browsers
  background-image: linear-gradient(to right, $start-color $start-
percent, $end-color $end-percent); // Standard
}
```

4. Now, compile your project by running the following command in your console:

```
sass sass/main.scss main.css
```

5. Create an `index.html` file that links the compiled `main.css` file from the previous step and contains an HTML markup code like that shown here:

```
<header>Background gradients with Sass</header>
```

How it works...

When you apply progressive enhancement, you should start by establishing a basic level of user experience first. All the browsers should be able to provide the basic level of user experience when rendering your website. More advanced functionalities will automatically be available to browsers that can use it. In the preceding code, you start with a red background color and add a gradient to those browsers that support the gradient syntax.

When reading the *Using vendor prefixes* recipe of this chapter, you should note that only adding the official W3 standard syntax for CSS gradients is a very simplified solution, because you can also use vendor prefixes and the filter syntax to support other or older browsers.

Another example: when you apply the progressive enhancement for your website's navigation, you could start with a simple list and add clipped submenus for only those browsers that support JavaScript or more advanced CSS features.

There's more...

The counterpart of progressive enhancement is graceful degradation. It is not always easy to see the differences between progressive enhancement and graceful degradation. While applying graceful degradation, you will start creating a certain level of user experience in more modern browsers and degrade gracefully to a lower level of user experience in older browsers.

Remember also the CSS columns, as described in the *Browser support* and *Mobile first strategies* recipes of this chapter. When your browser does not support CSS columns (or your screen is not wide enough to fit two or more columns), your layout will degrade gracefully into a single column layout.

The W3C's explanation of graceful degradation versus progressive enhancement tells you that graceful degradation often will be applied when you don't have time to finish a product with full progressive enhancement.

You should realize that old browsers run mostly on old hardware too. For instance, the calculation of gradients will take a lot of process time, so it slows down your website. For this reason, graceful degradation can be a viable strategy in many other situations.

See also

- A more complex use case of applying progressive enhancements has been excellently described at `https://css-tricks.com/progressive-enhancement-data-visualizations/`
- The W3C discusses the difference between graceful degradation and progressive enhancement in the Web Standards Curriculum, which can be found at `http://www.w3.org/wiki/Graceful_degradation_versus_progressive_enhancement`

The -prefix-free library

The -prefix-free library developed by Lea Verou is a small JavaScript library that runs client-side in your browser. The -prefix-free library lets you use only unprefixed CSS properties everywhere.

Getting ready

For this recipe, you only need a web browser.

How to do it...

Perform the following steps to see the -prefix-free JavaScript library in action:

1. Download the -prefix-free library at `http://leaverou.github.io/prefixfree/`.

2. Create an `index.html` HTML file, which includes a CSS stylesheet file with some standard unprefixed CSS3 properties. For instance, this CSS stylesheet file may contain the following CSS code:

    ```
    .columns {
      column-count: 3;
      column-gap: 15px; }
    ```

3. Include the `prefixfree.min.js` minified JavaScript file you have downloaded in the first step right after the stylesheets that you have included in the second step.

4. Finally, a section of your index.html HTML file should look like that shown here:

    ```
    <link rel="stylesheet" type="text/css" href="main.css" />
    <script src="prefixfree.min.js"></script>
    ```

5. Open the `index.html` file in your web browser and inspect the results.

How it works...

You can use the Can I Use website, as described in the The Can I Use database recipe of this chapter, to find some CSS3 properties that require a vendor prefix for your current browser. The code example of this book uses the unprefixed SCSS code (prefixes are removed from the mixin) from the *Browser support* recipe of this chapter. Both the Mozilla Firefox and the Google Chrome browsers require vendor prefixes for the CSS multiple column layout at the time of writing this book.

The -prefix-free library detects the current browser and adds the required browser's prefix to any CSS code, only when it's needed.

The -prefix-free library automatically detects which properties are available and need a prefix. The -prefix-free library doesn't have to keep lists of which prefixes to add for which features in contrast to the Can I Use database discussed in the *Can I Use database* recipe of this chapter, of which prefixes to add for which features. Because of the -prefix-free library does not use lists but is based on feature detection instead this solution is very future proof.

There's more...

For those users who do not support JavaScript the -prefix-free library requires JavaScript, so you can apply graceful degradation, as described in the *Applying progressive enhancement* recipe of this chapter.

Because the -prefix-free library runs client-side after the CSS code is loaded, some people detect or expect a **flash of unstyled content** (**FOUC**) for the pages using this library. Verou advices you to include prefixfree.js after the stylesheets to minimize FOUC.

You should also note that only the properties that require a prefix become unstyled. Using the -prefix-free library helps you keep your compiled CSS code clean and as small as possible. You do not have to add any unused vendor prefix code in your CSS code. Unused CSS code is an important cause of performance issues related to CSS.

See also

Chris Coyier of CSS-Tricks interviewed Lea Verou about the -prefix-free library in 2011. You can read this interview at `https://css-tricks.com/five-questions-with-lea-verou/`.

Mobile first strategies

Different definitions of mobile first strategies exist. Mobile first strategies were introduced by companies that created the designs for mobile devices before the desktop designs. First, mobile devices not only had small screens, but they also supported a limited set of CSS and JavaScript features.

Nowadays, you can use CSS media queries, as discussed in the *Media Queries with Breakpoint* recipe of *Chapter 8, Advanced Sass Coding*, to change your designs depending on the screen size of your user's device. When using CSS media queries to create responsive websites, the mobile first strategy is more like a way of organizing your code. In this recipe, you will learn how to organize your code using a mobile first strategy.

In this recipe, you will use a CSS media query that will set the height of the CSS columns depending on the width of the viewport. Read more about CSS columns in the *Browser support* recipe of this chapter.

Getting ready

Install the Ruby Sass compiler, as described in the *Installing Sass for command line usage* recipe of *Chapter 1, Getting Started with Sass*. In this recipe, CSS media queries are used. You can also read more about CSS media queries in the *Media Queries with Breakpoint* recipe of *Chapter 8, Advanced Sass Coding*, and the *Creating responsive grids* recipe of *Chapter 9, Building Layouts with Sass*.

How to do it...

The following steps will demonstrate you to apply a mobile first strategy when implementing a design:

1. Create your main project file called `main.scss`. This file should import the column partial file. So, `main.scss` should contain a SCSS code like that shown here:

```scss
$grid-gutter-width: 15px;

@import 'components/columns';

.columns {
  @include content-columns(3);
}
```

2. The column partial, the `components/_columns.scss` file, should contain the mixin that creates your content columns. The SCSS code in this file will look as follows:

```scss
// scss-lint:disable VendorPrefix

// CSS3 Content Columns

$breakpoint: 768px;

@mixin content-columns($column-count, $column-gap: $grid-gutter-width) {
  -webkit-column-count: $column-count;
  -moz-column-count: $column-count;
  column-count: $column-count;
  -webkit-column-gap: $column-gap;
  -moz-column-gap: $column-gap;
  column-gap: $column-gap;

  @media (min-width: $breakpoint) {
    height: 400px;
  }
}
```

3. Now, compile your project by running the following command in your console:

```
sass sass/main.scss main.css
```

4. Create an `index.html` file that links the compiled `main.css` file from the previous step and contains an HTML markup code like that shown here:

```
<div class="columns">Lorem ipsum dolor sit amet, consectetuer
adipiscing elit. Aenean commodo ligula eget dolor. Aenean
massa. Cum sociis natoque penatibus et magnis dis parturient
montes, nascetur ridiculus mus. Donec quam felis, ultricies nec,
pellentesque eu, pretium quis, sem. Nulla consequat massa quis
enim. Donec pede justo, fringilla vel, aliquet nec, vulputate
eget, arcu. In enim justo, rhoncus ut, imperdiet a, venenatis
vitae, justo. Nullam dictum felis eu pede mollis pretium.
Integer tincidunt. Cras dapibus. Vivamus elementum semper nisi.
Aenean vulputate eleifend tellus. Aenean leo ligula, porttitor
eu, consequat vitae, eleifend ac, enim. Aliquam lorem ante,
dapibus in, viverra quis, feugiat a, tellus. Phasellus viverra
nulla ut metus varius laoreet. Quisque rutrum. Aenean imperdiet.
Etiam ultricies nisi vel augue. Curabitur ullamcorper ultricies
nisi. Nam eget dui. Etiam rhoncus. Maecenas tempus, tellus eget
condimentum rhoncus, sem quam semper libero, sit amet adipiscing
sem neque sed ipsum. Nam quam nunc, blandit vel, luctus pulvinar,
hendrerit id, lorem. Maecenas nec odio et ante tincidunt tempus.
Donec vitae sapien ut libero venenatis faucibus. Nullam quis ante.
Etiam sit amet orci eget eros faucibus tincidunt. Duis leo. Sed
fringilla mauris sit amet nibh. Donec sodales sagittis magna. Sed
consequat, leo eget bibendum sodales, augue velit cursus nunc,</
div>
```

5. Finally, open `index.html` in your browser. Now, make your browser window smaller than 768 pixels and find that the text is not hidden by overflow.

How it works...

When your screen is less than 768 pixels wide or your browser does not support media queries, your content will only be divided into three columns; no height for the columns has been set. When you set the height of your columns, the element will expand horizontally to fit the content. So, for small screens, the text overflow becomes invisible. No height ensures that all the content is visible. The default situation for viewports smaller than the breakpoint of 768 pixels is true for mobile phones. Mobile phones have either small screens or don't support media queries.

Following the mobile first approach, you should only set the height of your columns for wider (nonmobile) screens.

For wider screens, the media query evaluates true and the height of the columns is set to a value of `400px`.

There's more...

Together with media queries, the CSS3 Multiple Column Layout Module enables you to create very responsible layouts. Although the CSS3 Multiple Column Layout Module can also be applied to the body element, one should use this module only to divide some elements of the design into columns. You can use other techniques to create responsive page layouts. In the *Implementing Semantic Layouts* recipe of *Chapter 12, Bootstrap and Saas*, you can read about Bootstrap's responsive grid.

Also, the CSS Grid Layout Module is very interesting for creating responsive page layouts, but at the time of writing this book, few web browsers support this module.

See also

- ▶ Bootstrap is a mobile first CSS framework. You can find it at `http://getbootstrap.com/`
- ▶ Read more about the CSS Grid Layout Module at `http://www.w3.org/TR/2015/WD-css-grid-1-20150806/`

8

Advanced Sass Coding

In this chapter, you will learn the following topics:

- ▶ Using @if
- ▶ Using @for
- ▶ Using @each
- ▶ Loops with @while
- ▶ Creating a vertical rhythm for your website
- ▶ Creating color contrast automatically
- ▶ Using icon fonts
- ▶ Image sprites with Compass
- ▶ Media queries with Breakpoint

Introduction

In this chapter, you will be introduced to some Sass statements that you probably already know from your experience with functional programming languages. Sass statements, such as `@if` or `@while`, help create dynamical and recursive Sass code.

You will also learn how to create a vertical rhythm or color contrast for your project by using Compass. In the last three recipes, we'll get grips on icon fonts, image sprites, and CSS media queries by making use of Sass.

Using @if

SassScript supports the **if-then-else** construct, which also can be found in most of the high-level programming languages. In this recipe, the conditional @if statement will be discussed.

Getting ready

The recipe uses SCSS code from a part of the Compass Image module. Read more about Compass in *Chapter 6, Using Compass*. Also, read the *Installing Sass for command line usage* recipe of *Chapter 1, Getting Started with Sass*.

How to do it...

Notice that the SCSS in this recipe does not use the @if statement directly. The code calls the background-with-css2-fallback() mixin with different parameters. The @if statements themselves are inside the background-with-css2-fallback() mixin, as explained in the *How it works...* section. Here is how we can do it:

1. Create a Sass file called main.scss that will contain an SCSS code like that shown here:

```
@import 'compass';

div.withfallback {
   @include background-with-css2-fallback(linear-gradient(top,
#0E1B31, #0A1322), #0E1B31);
}

div.withoutfallback {
   @include background-with-css2-fallback(linear-gradient(top,
#0E1B31,#0A1322));
}
```

2. Then, run the following command in your console:

```
sass --compass main.scss
```

3. The command from the previous step should output the compiled CSS as follows:

```
div.withfallback {
   background: #0E1B31;
   background: -webkit-gradient(linear, 50% 0%, 50% 100%, color-
stop(0%, #0e1b31), color-stop(100%, #0a1322)), #0E1B31;
   background: -moz-linear-gradient(top, #0e1b31,#0a1322), #0E1B31;
   background: -webkit-linear-gradient(top, #0e1b31, #0a1322),
#0E1B31;
```

```
    background: linear-gradient(to bottom, #0e1b31, #0a1322),
    #0E1B31; }

div.withoutfallback {
    background: -webkit-gradient(linear, 50% 0%, 50% 100%, color-
stop(0%, #0e1b31), color-stop(100%, #0a1322));
    background: -moz-linear-gradient(top, #0e1b31, #0a1322);
    background: -webkit-linear-gradient(top, #0e1b31, #0a1322);
    background: linear-gradient(to bottom, #0e1b31, #0a1322); }
```

How it works...

The @if statement will be followed by a condition and some SassScript between accolades. The SassScript will only be compiled into CSS code when the condition evaluates true.

In this recipe, the background-with-css2-fallback() mixin from the Compass Image module has been used. The SCSS code of this mixin looks as follows:

```
// Set any number of background layers, along with a fallback.
// The final argument will be output separately, first, as a css2
fallback.
@mixin background-with-css2-fallback($backgrounds...) {
@if length($backgrounds) > 1 or prefixed(-css2, $backgrounds) {
background: -css2(nth($backgrounds, -1));
}
@include background($backgrounds...);
}
```

In the preceding code, the background: -css2(nth($backgrounds, -1)); code only compiles into CSS code when the following conditional expression evaluates true:

```
@if length($backgrounds) > 1 or prefixed(-css2, $backgrounds)
```

You can use == (equal) and != (not equal) to test whether two values are the same or not. When testing two numerical values, you can also use the > (greater than), >= (greater than or equal to), < (less than), and <= (less than or equal to) comparison operators. In the preceding code, the length($backgrounds) function call returns a number that can be tested with the > operator for being greater than 1.

The or, and, and not logical operators can be used to test multiple conditions within a conditional expression. In the preceding conditional expression, the conditional expression evaluates true when only one or both conditions evaluate true.

Each @if statement can be followed by one or more @else if statements or an @else statement.

When the `@if` statement fails, the optional `@else` will be reached and the styles nested beneath it will be compiled into CSS code. The following SCSS code shows you an example of the if-then-else construct with the `@else if` statements in SASS:

```
@if x == 0 {
  color: red;
} @else if x < 10 {
  color: black;
} @else {
  color: green;
}
```

There's more...

The mixin used in this recipe is a part of the Compass Image module. You can read more about Compass in *Chapter 6, Using Compass*, of this book. Also, the `background()` mixin, which sets the background property with the required vendor prefixes, is a part of this image module. The `background-with-css2-fallback()` mixin creates background images with the required vendor prefixes and a default background color for older browsers. Also, read the *Using vendor prefixes* and *Cross-browser CSS3 with Compass* recipes of *Chapter 7, Cross-Browser CSS3 Mixins*.

Both the `prefixed()` and `-css2()` functions are a part of Compass Cross Browser Helpers.

The `background-with-css2-fallback` mixin can be called with an unlimited number of background parameters, due to the `$backgrounds...` variable argument. The final argument will be outputted separately, first as a CSS2 fallback. You can read more about variable arguments in the *Writing mixins with arguments* recipe of *Chapter 3, Variables, Mixins, and Functions*. Inside the mixin, the variable arguments are available as a list. So, you can use the `length()` and `nth()` list functions, as described in the *List functions* recipe of *Chapter 5, Built-in Functions*.

Finally, you should note that the `@if` control directive differs from the `if()` function used to create conditions assessments. Read more about conditions assessments in the *Conditional assignments* recipe of *Chapter 5, Built-in Functions*.

See also

▸ Read more about conditional statements in other programming languages at `https://en.wikipedia.org/wiki/Conditional_%28computer_programming%29`

▸ The documentation for the Compass Image module can be found at `http://compass-style.org/reference/com/pass/css3/images/`

▸ Read more about the Compass Cross Browser Helpers at `http://compass-style.org/reference/compass/helpers/cross-browser`

Using @for

In this recipe, you will learn how to create iterations by using for loops in Sass.

Getting ready

Read the *Installing Sass for command line usage* recipe of *Chapter 1, Getting Started with Sass*, to find out how to use Ruby Sass on the command line. If you are not familiar with for-loops already, try to study for-loops in other programming languages.

How to do it...

Learn how to use for loops in Sass by performing the following steps:

1. Create a Sass file called `iteration.scss` that will contain an SCSS code like that shown here:

   ```
   @for $i from 1 to 4 {
      .font-size-#{$i} { font-size: 0.8em * $i; }
   }
   ```

2. Then run the following command in your console:

   sass --compass iteration.scss

3. After running the command from the previous step, the following compiled CSS will be outputted in your console:

   ```
   .font-size-1 {
      font-size: 0.8em; }

   .font-size-2 {
      font-size: 1.6em; }

   .font-size-3 {
      font-size: 2.4em; }
   ```

How it works...

Those who are already familiar with using **for** loops in other programming languages won't have difficulty in understanding the SCSS code in this recipe. In contrast to other loops, such as the `@while` loop, discussed in the *Loops with @while* recipe of this chapter, for loops have a **loop variable** or **loop counter**. In SassScript, you can use the `@for` directive together with the `from` and `to` (or `through`) keywords to create **iterations**. The compiler repeats your code until the end value is reached. After each iteration, the loop variable will be increased by one. The format of a for loop will look like that shown here:

```
@for $loop-variable from $startvalue to $endvalue {}
```

Here, the `to` keyword can be replaced with the `through` keyword to include the end value. See also the example in the following *There's more...* section; with the `@for $i from 1 to 3{}` loop, the `.third` class has not been included in the output.

When the start value is higher than the end value, the loop variable will decrease instead of increase each iteration.

You can use the loop variable (`$loop-variable`) just like any other variable in Sass. In this recipe, `$loop-variable` was used to dynamically create both property names and values. To create the property names' variable interpolation, as described in the *Interpolation of variables* recipe of *Chapter 3, Variables, Mixins, and Function*, was used to create the names of the properties.

There's more...

You can also use Sass for loop together with the list functions to iterate over Sass lists. Read more about these list functions in the *List Functions* recipe of *Chapter 5, Built-in Functions*. The following example SCSS code will show you how to create a list of CSS classes:

```
$class-names: first, second, third;
$number: length($class-names);

@for $i from 1 through 3 {
  $class: nth($class-names, $i);
  .#{$class} {
     width: (100% / $number) * $i ;
   }
}
```

The preceding SCSS code will compile into CSS code like that shown here:

```
.first {
  width: 33.33333%; }

.second {
  width: 66.66667%; }

.third {
  width: 100%; }
```

In the *Using @each* recipe of this chapter, you can read about how to iterate over items of a list or map using the `@each` control directive.

See also

Read more about for loops in other programming languages at `https://en.wikipedia.org/wiki/For_loop`

Using @each

The @each control directive in Sass can be used to read the items of a list or map. In this recipe, you will learn how to use the @each control directive to dynamically create your CSS code.

Getting ready

You can use the Ruby Sass command-line compiler to compile the SCSS code into static CSS code. You can read about how to install and use the Ruby Sass command-line compiler in the *Installing Sass for command line usage* recipe of *Chapter 1, Getting Started with Sass*.

How to do it...

Perform the following steps to understand how to use the @each directive in Sass:

1. Create a Sass file called list.scss that will contain an SCSS code like that shown here:

```scss
$class-names: first, second, third;

@each $class in $class-names {
  .#{$class} {
    color: white;
  }
}
```

2. Then, run the following command in your console:

```
sass list.scss
```

3. The compiled CSS code from the previous step should look like that shown here:

```css
.first {
  color: white; }

.second {
  color: white; }

.third {
  color: white; }
```

How it works...

The `@each` directive in SassScript enables you to iterate over a list or map. Read more about lists and maps in the *List Functions* and *Maps Functions* recipes of *Chapter 5, Built-in Functions*. The `@each` loop has a form like that shown here:

```
@each $variable in <list or map>
```

In the `@each` loop, the `$variable` variable will be set to each item in the list or map.

You can also use multiple variables when iterating over a list of lists. Consider the following example to see how this works:

```scss
@each $class, $width in (small, 100px),(medium, 250px),(large, 750px)
{
  .#{$class} {
    width: $width;
  }
}
```

The preceding SCSS code compiles into CSS code as follows:

```css
.small {
  width: 100px; }

.medium {
  width: 250px; }

.large {
  width: 750px; }
```

Because SassScript treats maps as a list of lists, the preceding example can also be written as follows:

```scss
@each $class, $width in (small: 100px, medium: 250px, large: 750px) {
  .#{$class} {
    width: $width;
  }
}
```

There's more...

In this recipe, the same list of class names as in the *Using @for* recipe was used. In the *Using @for* recipe, the loop counter was used to dynamically create the values for the width property. You can add a loop counter in an `@each` loop yourself too. The following SCSS code will generate the same CSS code as in the *Using @for* recipe:

```scss
$class-names: first, second, third;
$number: length($class-names);
```

```scss
$i: 1;

@each $class in $class-names {
  .#{$class} {
      width: (100% / $number) * $i ;
  }
    $i: $i + 1;
}
```

In the preceding code, the `$i` variable holds the loop counter.

Loops with @while

In this recipe, you will learn how to create loops with the `@while` control directive in SassScript.

Getting ready

Read how to install and use the Ruby Sass command-line compiler in the *Installing Sass for command line usage* recipe of *Chapter 1, Getting Started with Sass*.

How to do it...

Learn how to use the `@while` directive in Sass by performing the following steps:

1. Create a Sass template called `list.scss`. This template should contain the following SCSS code:

    ```scss
    $class-names: first, second, third;
    $number: length($class-names);

    $i: 1;

    @while $i <= $number {
      $class: nth($class-names, $i);
      .#{$class} {
          width: (100% / $number) * $i ;
      }
        $i: $i + 1;
    }
    ```

2. Then run the following command in your console:

    ```
    sass list.scss
    ```

3.   The compiled CSS code from the previous steps will look like that shown here:

```
.first {
  width: 33.33333%; }

.second {
  width: 66.66667%; }

.third {
  width: 100%; }
```

How it works...

The `@while` control directive runs and compiles the SCSS code between the curly brackets until the condition returns `false`. In this recipe, a loop-variable (`$i`) is added to the loop. The `@while` loop in this recipe compiles the same output as the *Using @for* recipe in this chapter.

There's more...

Because you are able to change the loop counter inside the loop, the `@while` control directive can be used to achieve more complex looping than the `@for` statement is capable of. Read more about the `@for` control directive in the *using @for* recipe of this chapter. For instance, you can change the `$i: $i + 1;` declaration to `$i: $i + 2;`, resulting in only the first and third classes being compiled in your CSS code.

Creating a vertical rhythm for your website

In this recipe, you will learn how to use Compass to create a vertical rhythm for your website. A vertical rhythm in typography ensures that the text of your website text is aligned to the evenly spaced horizontal lines. The rhythm makes your website more cohesive and easier to read. The vertical rhythm calculates font size, line height, and margins/padding, and applies them to your CSS.

Getting ready

This recipe requires both Sass and Compass installed. Read the *Installing Sass for command line usage* and *Installing Compass* recipes of *Chapter 1, Getting Started with Sass*, to find out more about installing Sass and Compass.

How to do it...

The following steps help you to create a vertical rhythm for your projects:

1. Create your main project file called `main.scss` in the `sass` folder of your project. This file should contain an SCSS code like that shown here:

```scss
@import 'compass/typography/vertical_rhythm';

// Compass Vertical Rhythm Settings
$base-font-size: 20px; // Sets the base font size
$base-line-height: 36px; // Sets the base line height

// Set a default font-size and line-height on the <html> tag
@include establish-baseline;

h1 {
  @include adjust-font-size-to(45px);
}

h2 {
  @include adjust-font-size-to(30px);
}

aside {
  padding: rhythm(0.5);
  background-color: #000;
  color: #fff;
  float: right;
}
```

2. Now, compile your project by running the following command in your console:

   `sass --compass sass/main.scss main.css`

3. Create an `index.html` file that will link the compiled `main.css` file from the previous step and contain an HTML markup code like that shown here:

```html
<h1>Title</h1>
<h2>subTitle</h2>
<aside>Lorem ipsum dolor sit amet</aside>
<p>Lorem ipsum dolor sit amet, consectetuer adipiscing elit.
Aenean commodo ligula eget dolor. Aenean massa. Cum sociis natoque
penatibus et magnis dis parturient montes, nascetur ridiculus mus.
Donec quam felis, ultricies nec, pellentesque eu, pretium quis,
sem. Nulla consequat massa quis enim. Donec pede justo, fringilla
vel, aliquet nec, vulputate eget, arcu. In enim justo, rhoncus ut,
imperdiet a, venenatis vitae, justo. Nullam dictum felis eu pede
```

mollis pretium. Integer tincidunt. Cras dapibus. Vivamus elementum semper nisi. Aenean vulputate eleifend tellus. Aenean leo ligula, porttitor eu, consequat vitae, eleifend ac, enim. Aliquam lorem ante, dapibus in, viverra quis, feugiat a, tellus. Phasellus viverra nulla ut metus varius laoreet. Quisque rutrum. Aenean imperdiet. Etiam ultricies nisi vel augue. Curabitur ullamcorper ultricies nisi. Nam eget dui. Etiam rhoncus. Maecenas tempus, tellus eget condimentum rhoncus, sem quam semper libero, sit amet adipiscing sem neque sed ipsum. Nam quam nunc, blandit vel, luctus pulvinar, hendrerit id, lorem. Maecenas nec odio et ante tincidunt tempus. Donec vitae sapien ut libero venenatis faucibus. Nullam quis ante. Etiam sit amet orci eget eros faucibus tincidunt. Duis leo. Sed fringilla mauris sit amet nibh. Donec sodales sagittis magna. Sed consequat, leo eget bibendum sodales, augue velit cursus nunc,</p>

4. Finally, open `index.html` in your browser and find that the page looks as follows:

How it works...

The Sass Vertical Rhythm module is a set of functions and mixins that helps you calculate line heights, vertical padding, and margins values based on a base line height ($base-line-height) and base font size ($base-font-size) to conform to a baseline grid.

This recipe demonstrates how to use the functions and mixins of the Sass Vertical Rhythm module. First, the `establish-baseline()` mixin was called. This mixin creates an `html` selector at the beginning of your CSS code. The `html` selector sets the default font size and line height according to the values set by the $base-line-height and $base-font-size variables for your document. The compiled CSS code of the `establish-baseline()` mixin call looks as follows:

```
html {
  font-size: 125%;
  line-height: 1.8em; }
```

After setting the default font size and line height, you can use the `adjust-font-size-to()` mixin to adjust a block to have a different font size and line height to maintain the rhythm. The first argument of this mixin is the desired font size in pixels. The `adjust-font-size-to()` mixin also has a second and third option argument. The second parameter specifies how many multiples of the baseline rhythm each line of this font should use up. And the third parameter enables you to set a font size other than the base font size to adjust from. In this recipe, the `adjust-font-size-to()` mixin has been used to set the font size and line height of the `h1` selector, as follows:

```
h1 {
    @include adjust-font-size-to(45px);
}
```

The preceding SCSS code compiles into CSS code as follows:

```
h1 {
    font-size: 2.25em;
    line-height: 1.6em; }
```

Finally, the `rhythm()` function is used to set the padding of the `aside` selector. The `rhythm()` function allows you to quickly calculate multiple line heights' worth of margins and paddings without doing the math. The `rhythm()` function called in this recipe returns `0.9em`. `0.9em = 0.5 * 1.8em;`, `1.8em;` being the equivalent of `20px` set by the `$base-font-size: 20px;` declaration.

There's more...

The vertical rhythm code of Compass has some configurable variables. The most important variables are the `$base-font-size` and `$base-line-height` variables, as described already. Another interesting variable is the `$rhythm-unit` variable. This variable has a default value of `em` units, but can also be set to `px` or `rem` units.

`em` measure units are an alternative for pixels that seem to be more future proof. `em` units are based on the font size and are relative to their parent. em-based layouts react to the content when the user zooms or changes the default font size.

`rem measure units` or root `em` units are based or are relative to the font size set for the `html` element (*root*). Note that neither Internet Explorer version 8 and lower, nor the Opera Mini browser, supports `rem` units. For this reason, Compass creates fallback values in `px` units when using `rem` units as the rhythm-unit.

See also

▸ The documentation for the Sass Vertical Rhythm module can be found at `http://compass-style.org/reference/compass/typography/vertical_rhythm/`

▸ Also, read the *Vertical Rhythm with Compass* post by John Ferris at `http://atendesigngroup.com/blog/vertical-rhythm-compass` to get more grip on Vertical Rhythm

▸ The `Lorem ipsum` dummy text for this recipe has been generated with the blind text generator, which can be found at `http://www.blindtextgenerator.com/lorem-ipsum`

Creating color contrasts automatically

In this recipe, you will learn to find the right font color for a background color. High contrast plays an important role in web designing. Designs with high contrast help you meet **accessibility** standards. Color contrast is important for the **readability** and accessibility of text on the page. High contrast not only helps visibly disabled or color blind people, it also influences those with normal vision, as humans are naturally in favor of high-contrast color designs. This preference plays a role in the first impression of your website.

Getting ready

In this recipe, you will make use of both Sass and Compass. Read the *Installing Sass for command line usage* recipe of *Chapter 1, Getting Started with Sass*, to find out more about installing Sass and get the Ruby Sass compiler ready. Color contrast and other calculations are done with the functions and mixins built in Compass. So, read the *Installing Compass* recipe of *Chapter 1, Getting Started with Sass*, and all recipes of *Chapter 6, Using Compass*.

How to do it...

Learn how to automatically create color contrasts by using the Compass Utilities module:

1. Create your main project file called `main.scss`. This file should contain an SCSS code like that shown here:

```scss
@import 'compass/utilities/color/contrast';

@mixin create-colors-with-contrast($no-of-colors) {
  $frequency: 5 / $no-of-colors;
  @for $i from 1 through $no-of-colors {
    $red: sin($frequency * $i + 0) * (127) + 128;
    $green: sin($frequency * $i + 1) * (127) + 128;
    $blue: sin($frequency * $i + 3) * (127) + 128;
    $currentcolor: rgb(floor($red), floor($green), floor($blue));
```

```scss
    .color-#{$i} {
      @include contrasted($currentcolor);
    }
  }
}
```

```scss
@include create-colors-with-contrast(9);
```

2. Now, compile your project by running the following command in your console:

   sass --compass sass/main.scss main.css

3. Create an `index.html` file that will link the compiled `main.css` file from the previous step and contain an HTML markup code like that shown here:

```html
<body>
  <div class="color-1">Color 1</div>
  <div class="color-2">Color 2</div>
  <div class="color-3">Color 3</div>
  <div class="color-4">Color 4</div>
  <div class="color-5">Color 5</div>
  <div class="color-6">Color 6</div>
  <div class="color-7">Color 7</div>
  <div class="color-8">Color 8</div>
  <div class="color-9">Color 9</div>
</body>
```

4. Finally, open `index.html` in your browser. You will find that the page looks like that shown in the following image:

How it works...

Calculating the right amount of contrast is not always easy. Also, in your projects, you don't want to have to change all your font colors after changing the basic colors of your design. In this recipe, the `contrasted()` mixin from the Compass Utilities module will help you choose a color that can easily be seen against a colored background. This mixin sets the specified background color and calculates a dark or light contrasted text color.

The SCSS code in the `create-colors-with-contrast()` mixin of this recipe uses three normalized sine waves to calculate the red, green, and blue values of the automatically generated colors. To generate the colors, you will use the `@for` loop, as described in the Using *@for* recipe of this chapter.

The `contrasted()` mixin sets both the `background-color` and `color` properties for the CSS classes. The `background-color` property gets either `black` or `white` depending on the highest absolute difference between the compute of the brightness of the input color and the compute of the brightness of black (0) or white (1).

The `create-colors-with-contrast()` mixin calls the `sin()` mixin, which is a part of Compass too. Read more about the usage of trigonometric functions in the *Introspection Functions* recipe of *Chapter 5, Built-in Functions*. The `create-colors-with-contrast()` mixin also use the `rgb()` and `floor()` functions to calculate the values for the color channels. These are built-in functions of Sass. To learn more about these functions, you should read the *Color Functions* and *Number Functions* recipes, respectively, of *Chapter 5, Built-in Functions*.

There's more...

The `contrasted()` mixin mentioned previously calls the `contrast-color()` function, which in turn makes use of the `brightness()` function. In accordance with WCAG 2.0 (http://www.w3.org/TR/2008/REC-WCAG20-20081211/#relativeluminancedef), the `brightness()` function approximates how humans perceive the intensity of the different RGB components of a color. So, this function calculates the **brightness** or **luminance** of a color.

See also

> ▸ Read the *Accessible contrast with Less and Sass* post by Mike Riethmuller. Riethmuller talks about the different ways to calculate and measure the brightness of a color and find an appropriate text color for a particular background. You can find his post at http://madebymike.com.au/writing/accessible-contrast-with-l.ess-and-sass/.

▶ The formula to calculate the rainbow colors can be found at `http://www.markandey.com/2012/04/how-to-generate-rainbow-colors.html`.

▶ The CONTRAST-A-WEB V2.0 application allows you to experiment with color combinations, examine them under the aspect of accessibility guidelines, and create custom color palettes. You can find this online tool at `http://dasplankton.de/ContrastA/`.

Using icon fonts

In this recipe, the usage of icon fonts for your projects is discussed. As the name suggests, icon fonts are sets of icons defined as a font. Icon fonts can replace image icons in your projects. The main reason for using icon fonts instead of images and the reason they are discussed here is that icon fonts, just like any normal font, can be fully manipulated with CSS. In your project, you can set the size, color, and shadows of the used icon fonts with Sass. The primary reason for using icon fonts is to benefit the load time of your website; similar to sprite images, but with more styling options, only one HTTP request is needed to load them all. Icon fonts will look good on different resolutions and displays too. In this recipe, you will learn how to use the Font Awesome iconic font and toolkit with Sass.

Getting ready

Read the *Installing Sass for command line usage* recipe of *Chapter 1, Getting Started with Sass*, to find out more about installing Sass and get the Ruby Sass compiler ready.

How to do it...

Learn how to use icon font by performing the following steps:

1. Download and unzip the Font Awesome files into your working directory. You can find the zip file at `https://fortawesome.github.io/Font-Awesome/`.

2. Then, create a new project file called `main.scss`. This file should contain an SCSS code like that shown here:

```
$fa-font-path: 'font-awesome-4.4.0/fonts';
@import '../font-awesome-4.4.0/scss/font-awesome.scss';
```

3. Your file and directory structure should now look as follows:

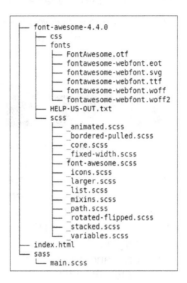

```
├── font-awesome-4.4.0
│   ├── css
│   ├── fonts
│   │   ├── FontAwesome.otf
│   │   ├── fontawesome-webfont.eot
│   │   ├── fontawesome-webfont.svg
│   │   ├── fontawesome-webfont.ttf
│   │   ├── fontawesome-webfont.woff
│   │   └── fontawesome-webfont.woff2
│   ├── HELP-US-OUT.txt
│   └── scss
│       ├── _animated.scss
│       ├── _bordered-pulled.scss
│       ├── _core.scss
│       ├── _fixed-width.scss
│       ├── _font-awesome.scss
│       ├── _icons.scss
│       ├── _larger.scss
│       ├── _list.scss
│       ├── _mixins.scss
│       ├── _path.scss
│       ├── _rotated-flipped.scss
│       ├── _stacked.scss
│       └── _variables.scss
├── index.html
└── sass
    └── main.scss
```

4. Now, compile your project by running the following command in your console:

```
sass  sass/main.scss main.css
```

5. Create an `index.html` file that will link the compiled `main.css` file from the previous step and contain an HTML markup code like that shown here:

```html
<span class="fa-stack fa-lg">
  <i class="fa fa-square-o fa-stack-2x"></i>
  <i class="fa fa-twitter fa-stack-1x"></i>
</span>
fa-twitter on fa-square-o<br>
<span class="fa-stack fa-lg">
  <i class="fa fa-circle fa-stack-2x"></i>
  <i class="fa fa-flag fa-stack-1x fa-inverse"></i>
</span>
fa-flag on fa-circle<br>
<span class="fa-stack fa-lg">
  <i class="fa fa-square fa-stack-2x"></i>
  <i class="fa fa-terminal fa-stack-1x fa-inverse"></i>
</span>
fa-terminal on fa-square<br>
<span class="fa-stack fa-lg">
  <i class="fa fa-camera fa-stack-1x"></i>
  <i class="fa fa-ban fa-stack-2x text-danger"></i>
</span>
fa-ban on fa-camera
```

6. Finally, load the `index.html` file in your browser. You will find that the result looks like the following image:

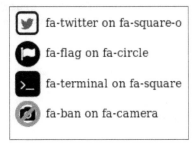

How it works...

The compiled CSS code of this recipe generates a CSS class for each icon. For the Twitter icon, the CSS code will look like that shown here:

```
.fa-twitter:before {
  content: "™"; }
```

As you can see, this class sets the `content` property. The `content` CSS property is used with the `::before` and `::after` pseudo-elements to generate content in an element. The `@font-face` CSS at-rule helps you specify online fonts to display text on web pages. The `@font-face` at-rule sets a URI, which loads the font file. The Font Awesome font files contains icons instead of characters, so when you set the `content` property to some character the matching icon will be displayed.

Just like sprites images, as described in the *Image sprites with Compass* recipe, loading the font file requires only one HTTP request for all the icons. As already mentioned, the appearance of the icons fonts can be fully manipulated with CSS. You can change the size and color of the icons with CSS. The appearance of images and image sprites can not be changed by CSS.

There's more...

The `@font-face` at-rule requires different declarations for the URI that loads different font files for full browser support. The Font Awesome SCSS code contains mixins to add cross-browser code for the `@font-face` at-rule. When inspecting the beginning of the compiled CSS code, you will find that this cross-browser code looks as follows:

```
@font-face {
  font-family: 'FontAwesome';
  src: url("font-awesome-4.4.0/fonts/fontawesome-webfont.
eot?v=4.4.0");
  src: url("font-awesome-4.4.0/fonts/fontawesome-webfont.
eot?#iefix&v=4.4.0") format("embedded-opentype"), url("font-
```

```
awesome-4.4.0/fonts/fontawesome-webfont.woff2?v=4.4.0")
format("woff2"), url("font-awesome-4.4.0/fonts/fontawesome-webfont.
woff?v=4.4.0") format("woff"), url("font-awesome-4.4.0/fonts/
fontawesome-webfont.ttf?v=4.4.0") format("truetype"), url("font-
awesome-4.4.0/fonts/fontawesome-webfont.svg?v=4.4.0#fontawesomeregul
ar") format("svg");
  font-weight: normal;
  font-style: normal; }
.fa {
  display: inline-block;
  font: normal normal normal 14px/1 FontAwesome;
  font-size: inherit;
  text-rendering: auto;
  -webkit-font-smoothing: antialiased;
  -moz-osx-font-smoothing: grayscale; }
```

Also, notice that the Compass Font Face module offers cross-browser support for the `@font-face` at-rule too. The mixin enables you to set the `@font-face` at-rule, as mentioned earlier, with a single line declaration. Read more about Compass in *Chapter 6, Using Compass*.

In this recipe, the original code of the Font Awesome repository was used. When you are building a Sass-powered Ruby application, you can also use the font-awesome-sass gem file (read more about Ruby gems in the *Installing Sass for command line usage* recipe of *Chapter 1, Getting Started with Sass*). Font-awesome-sass plays nicely with Ruby on Rails, Compass, Sprockets, and so on. In *Chapter 14, Ruby on Rails and Sass*, of this book, you can read how to build Sass-powered Ruby on Rails applications.

Font Awesome also plays very well with Bootstrap, but Bootstrap includes over 250 glyphs in font format from the Glyphicon Halflings set by default. Read more about Bootstrap in *Chapter 12, Bootstrap and Sass*.

Although loading the Font Awesome font file only requires a single HTTP request, loading all the icons, including CSS classes, still generates a lot of overhead when you only use some of these icons in your project. Fonticons, from the makers of Font Awesome, enable you to load only those icons that you really need.

See also

- ▶ Read more about the `content` property at `https://developer.mozilla.org/en/docs/Web/CSS/content`

- ▶ Information about the `@font-face` at-rule can be found at `https://developer.mozilla.org/en-US/docs/Web/CSS/%40font-face`

- ▶ Font-awesome-sass can be found at `https://github.com/FortAwesome/font-awesome-sass`

- The Glyphicon library, used by Bootstrap, can be found at `http://glyphicons.com/`
- You can find Fonticons at `https://fonticons.com/`
- Also, Fontastic enables you to create your icon fonts in seconds. You can find Fontastic at `http://fontastic.me/`

Image sprites with Compass

CSS sprite images is a technique that dates back many years. All the website's images are added to a single image, the sprite. If the browser requests an image, the sprite will be loaded as the background image. CSS is used to show the requested image containing a part of the sprite. Loading one big sprite, which can be cached, instead of several small images will reduce the number of HTTP requests needed by the browser to show the page. The fewer the HTTP requests, the faster the page will load.

Getting ready

For this recipe, you have to install both Sass and Compass. Read the *Installing Sass for command line usage* and *Installing Compass* recipes of *Chapter 1, Getting Started with Sass*.

You will also need some PNG images and to create a file and directory structure like that shown in the following image:

```
├── images
│   └── logos
│       ├── compass-logo-hover.png
│       └── compass-logo.png
├── index.html
└── sass
    └── main.scss
```

How to do it...

Learn how to create image sprites for your projects with Sass and Compass by following the steps as shown:

1. Create an `images/logos` folder in your project folder, which will contain some PNG image files. In the example code, two images of 423 x 88 pixels in the PNG format called `compass-logo.png` and `compass-logo-hover.png` are used.

2. After this, create your main project file called `main.scss`. This file should contain the following SCSS code:

```
@import 'compass/configuration';
$compass-options: (http-path: './');
```

```
@include compass-configuration($compass-options);

@import 'compass/utilities/sprites';
@import 'logos/*.png';
@include all-logos-sprites;

body {
  background-color: #000;
}

h1#logo {
  text-indent: -9999px;
  overflow: hidden;
  width: 423px;
  height: 88px;
  padding: 0;
  margin: 0 auto 18px;
}
```

3. Run the following command to compile your SCSS code into CSS code:

   ```
   sass --compass sass/main.scss main.css
   ```

4. Also, create an `index.html` file that will link the compiled `main.css` file and contain an HTML markup code like that shown here:

   ```
   <h1 id="logo" class="logos-compass-logo">Title</h1>
   ```

5. Now, open the `index.html` file in your favorite web browser and move your mouse over the logo to see the hover effect. The HTML page in your browser should look like that shown in the following image:

How it works...

In this recipe, the CSS Sprite Helpers for Compass was used. These helper functions require a special import like that shown here:

```
@import 'logos/*.png';
```

Importing your PNG files in the `images/logos` folder automatically generates a sprite image file in the `images` folder.

Also, the special `all-logos-sprites` mixin call should get your attention. This mixin call automatically generates the CSS code for your sprites based on the file names of the images in your `images/logos` folder.

The name of the `compass-logo-hover.png` PNG file ends with the `-hover` extension. The Sprite Helpers use this extension to compile the `:hover` pseudo classes like that shown here:

```
.logos-compass-logo:hover, .logos-compass-logo.compass-logo-hover {
    background-position: 0 0; }
```

The Sprite Helpers set the path to the sprite image file to the wrong path by default. In this recipe, the Sass configuration utilities were used to correct this path to the sprite image. The following lines of SCSS code show you how to correct the path:

```
@import 'compass/configuration';
$compass-options: (http-path: './');
@include compass-configuration($compass-options);
```

There's more...

The CSS Sprite Helpers for Compass automatically compile your CSS classes for the image sprites. When inspecting the compiled CSS code and the used HTML code, you will find that additional CSS classes create some overhead. The compiled CSS code contains CSS classes, such as the `.logos-sprite` and `.logos-compass-logo` CSS classes. This also means that your HTML code should contain the `.logos-compass-logo` CSS class.

Because the `h1` selector already has a unique identifier, the `id="logo"` declaration, you may not have to use the additional `.logos-compass-logo` CSS class. The Sprite Helpers also enable you to have control over what selectors are generated.

You can use the following SCSS code to set the background sprite image on the `h1#logo` selector:

```
h1#logo {
    @include logos-sprite(compass-logo);
}
```

The preceding SCSS code into CSS code as follows:

```
h1#logo {
    background-position: 0 -88px; }
    h1#logo:hover, h1#logo.compass-logo-hover {
        background-position: 0 0; }
```

Notice that you do not have to explicitly set the `:hover` pseudo class selector. In your HTML code, you can use an HTML code like that shown here:

```
<h1 id="logo">Title</h1>
```

Data URIs are the most used alternatives for sprite images now. Data URIs should be used sparingly, as testing has revealed that, on some mobile views, a data URI is on an average 6x slower than using a binary source. You can read more about data URIs in the *Extending Sass with Compass helper functions and more* recipe of *Chapter 6, Using Compass*. When you are using Sprite to show icons on your website, you should consider using icon fonts, as described in the *Using icon fonts* recipe of this chapter.

See also

- A useful tutorial on how to use CSS Sprite Helpers for Compass can also be found at `http://compass-style.org/help/tutorials/spriting/`

- Read more about the Sass configuration utilities for Compass at `http://compass-style.org/help/documentation/sass-based-configuration-options/`.

- You can also add the Sprite configuration to your `config.rb` file; read more about configuring the paths in your `config.rb` file at `https://www.webfoobar.com/node/10`

- Also, **SpriteMe** (`http://spriteme.org/`) can help you create sprites for your projects

Media queries with Breakpoint

CSS media queries play an important role nowadays in web development. Media queries are used to create **responsive designs**. The Breakpoint Sass plugin makes writing media queries in Sass super simple. In this recipe, you can read how to install and use Breakpoint in your project.

Getting ready

First, you should install Ruby Sass on your system. You can read how to install it in the *Installing Sass for command line usage* recipe of *Chapter 1, Getting Started with Sass*. This recipe also tells you more about installing gems. Gems are Ruby packages. In this recipe, you will install the Breakpoint gem to use Breakpoint in your projects.

How to do it...

The following steps demonstrate you how to create responsive designs with ease by using the Breakpoint library:

1. Run the following command in your console to install the Breakpoint gem and make Breakpoint available for Sass:

    ```
    sudo gem install breakpoint
    ```

2. Then, create a Sass template called `mediaqueries.scss`, which will contain an SCSS code like that shown here:

    ```scss
    @import 'breakpoint';

    $breakpoint: 768px;

    .half {
      width: 100%;

      @include breakpoint($breakpoint) {
        width: 50%;
        float: left;
      }
    }
    ```

3. Compile the SCSS code from the second step into CSS code by running the following command in your console:

    ```
    sass -r breakpoint mediaqueries.scss
    ```

4. Now, you should find a compiled CSS code like that shown here in your console:

    ```css
    .half {
      width: 100%; }
      @media (min-width: 768px) {
        .half {
          width: 50%;
          float: left; } }
    ```

How it works...

Breakpoint is designed to allow you to write most common media queries as quickly as possible. By default, it assumes that your most common media queries are the `min-width` media queries or the `min-)width`/`max-width` media query pairs. So, the `breakpoint(768px)` call compiles into the `@media (min-width: 768px)` CSS code, while the `breakpoint(768px 1024px)` call compiles into the `@media (min-width: 768px) and (max-width: 1024px)` CSS code.

There's more...

In the *Creating a vertical rhythm for your website* recipe of this chapter, the elastic measure units `em` and `rem` for CSS properties were discussed. Elastic measure units are also useful to build responsive layouts and grids, as described in the *Creating responsive grids* recipe of *Chapter 9, Building Layouts with Sass*. Grids and layouts with `em`-based media queries have breakpoints that scale with your font size.

Breakpoint can automatically rewrite your nonem-based media queries into `em`-based media queries by declaring `$breakpoint-to-ems: true;`.

When you add the `$breakpoint-to-ems: true;` declaration at the beginning of the `mediaqueries.scss` Sass template used for this recipe, you will find that your compiled CSS will look like that shown here:

```
.half {
  width: 100%; }
  @media (min-width: 48em) {
    .half {
      width: 50%;
      float: left; } }
```

Notice that all modern web browsers have a consistent zoom behavior nowadays.

Also, read the *Mobile first strategies* recipe of *Chapter 7, Cross-Browser CSS3 Mixins*, to get more grip on media query usage for your projects.

See also

- ▶ A full documentation on Breakpoint is available on Breakpoint Wiki, which can be found at `https://github.com/at-import/breakpoint/wiki`.
- ▶ Also, read *The EMs have it: Proportional Media Queries FTW!* article by Lyza Gardner. This article can be found at `http://blog.cloudfour.com/the-ems-have-it-proportional-media-queries-ftw/`.

9
Building Layouts with Sass

In this chapter, you will learn the following:

- ▶ Using a CSS Reset
- ▶ Importing and organizing your files
- ▶ Building a grid with grid classes
- ▶ Creating responsive grids
- ▶ Building a semantic grid with mixins
- ▶ Applying the grid on your design
- ▶ Integrating a vertical navigation menu in your layout
- ▶ Creating grids with semantic.gs
- ▶ Using Compass Layout Module

Introduction

In the recipes in this chapter, you will learn how to create a layout for your website or web application with Sass. The grid forms the basics of the layout. Grids help web designers and developers to work together and make deploying responsive layouts easier.

In the course of time, different ways to deploy layouts on the web saw the light. For years, tables have been (mis)used to build HTML layouts. Newer techniques leverage the CSS float to arrange elements. The CSS `float` property is a positioning property that keeps HTML elements in the flow of the document instead of applying a text wrap on it. Other layouts are built with the `display` property set to `inline-block`. HTML elements with the `display` property set to `inline-block` are positioned like lines of text. The Bootstrap CSS framework, as we will see in *Chapter 12, Bootstrap and Sass,* uses the float technique, but Bootstrap 4, as described in *Chapter 12, Bootstrap and Sass,* also ships with an opt-in, flexbox-based grid system and components. An example of the inline-block technique can be found at `http://cardinalcss.com`.

Even the CSS `display: table` declaration can be used to build a responsive layout, as can be seen at `https://github.com/mdo/table-grid`, but in this chapter you will build a grid layout with the CSS3 flexbox module.

Every technique mentioned previously has its pros and cons. Saying that you should prefer one above the other is not easy. Some people predict the CSS flexbox module as the most modern, and so preferred technique, to build your layouts.

The Bootstrap team says:

> *The future is now—switch a Boolean variable and recompile your CSS to take advantage of a flexbox-based grid system and components.*

The recipes in this chapter will show you how to build a grid layout with flexible boxes, but do not necessarily advise you to do so. The CSS Flexible box module is intended to describe the spatial position of child elements in relation to their parent, but flexible boxes are also intended to position only single UI elements and not the entire page layout.

When using flexible boxes for page layouts, the browsers have to do a lot of repainting that can result in bad, slow, or unexpected rending of elements, which have also been described at `http://jakearchibald.com/2014/dont-use-flexbox-for-page-layout/`. On the other hand, others such as Paul Irish claim the opposite, you can read more about that at `http://updates.html5rocks.com/2013/10/Flexbox-layout-isn-t-slow`. The cons of the flexbox layouts are that it dramatically reduces the complexity of fluid grids. When choosing a technique, you should always carefully consider the pros and cons, and make sure you are optimizing for the real bottlenecks.

Finally, you will notice that the flexbox module has been intended to lay out major regions of an application. The **CSS3 Grid Layout** module in contrast to the flexbox module can be applied on a high-level HTML element such as header, footer, and main. At the time of writing this book, only a few browsers support the Grid Layout module.

Besides the flexbox layout, this chapter pays attention to CSS Resets, organizing your Sass code and files, importing files, and how to build a navigation menu for your site.

Using a CSS Reset

When talking about **cascade** in CSS, there will no doubt be a mention of the browser default settings getting a higher precedence than the author's preferred styling. When writing Sass code, the compiled CSS code will overwrite the browser's default styling. In other words, anything that you do not define in your Sass code will be assigned a default styling, which is defined by the browser. This behavior plays a major role in many cross-browser issues. To prevent these sorts of problems, you can perform a **CSS Reset**, or a CSS Reset alternative such as **Normalize.css**.

Getting ready

In this recipe, you will use `Normalize.css` as an alternative for other CSS Resets. You can download `Normalize.css` at `https://necolas.github.io/normalize.css/`. After downloading the file you can compile your code with the Ruby Sass compiler. The *Installing Compass* recipe of *Chapter 1, Getting Started with Sass* describes how to install Compass for command line usage on your system.

How to do it...

Perform the the following step to use Normalize.css as an alternative for other CSS Resets in your Sass code:

1. Download the `normalize.css` file at `https://necolas.github.io/normalize.css/`.

2. Rename the `normalize.css` to `_normalize.scss` and then create the file and directory structure like that shown in the following figure:

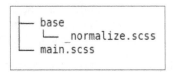

3. Your `main.scss` can now import the `_normalize.scss` partial file by declaring the following line of code:

   ```
   @import 'base/normalize';
   ```

4. As you will see now, when you compile your project by running the command like that shown in the following code, the compiled CSS code will start with the CSS code from `normalize.css`:

   ```
   sass main.scss
   ```

How it works...

CSS resets the overwrite of the default styling rules of the browser and creates a starting point for styling. This starting point looks and acts the same on all (or most) browsers. In this book, `Normalize.css v3.0.2` is used. `Normalize.css` is a modern, HTML5-ready alternative to CSS Resets. It lets browsers render all elements more consistently and makes them adhere to modern standards.

In this recipe, you had to rename the original CSS file. You should prepend an underscore to the file name and change the file extension to make it a Sass partial file. The preceding prevents Sass from compiling the file into CSS. Read more about partials in the *Working with partials* recipe of *Chapter 1, Getting Started with Sass*. Also notice that changing the file extension from `.css` to `.scss` will prevent Sass from creating a regular CSS `@import` declaration instead of importing and processing the file, as explained in the *Importing and organizing your files* recipe of this chapter. You should always import the reset code at the beginning or top of your style rules.

Bootstrap 4, as described in *Chapter 12, Bootstrap and Sass*, uses an extended version of `Normalize.css` called **Reboot**.

There's more...

When you start a project, you should also think about the CSS Reset that you will have to use. Writing a CSS Reset yourself seems like reinventing the wheel again. On the other hand, using a random CSS Reset code without any research may cause unwanted effects or unnecessary process time for your project. Your choice should depend on using HTML5 or not, the browsers that you will have to support, and so on. At `http://www.cssreset.com/`, you can find and download the most popular CSS Resets, including `Normalize.css`. To make a motivated choice, you can read the *Which CSS Reset Should I Use?* section on that website, too. Download the CSS file (with the `.css` extension) of the CSS Reset of your choice and save this file into your working directory. Rename it as shown in this recipe. You can use the Ruby Sass compiler to see how the CSS Reset compiles into your final CSS code.

The oldest and most famous browser reset is Eric Meyer's CSS Reset. When you use Compass as described in *Chapter 6, Using Compass*, you can directly apply Meyer's CSS Reset by using the Compass Reset module. The module applies the global reset to your stylesheet by simply importing it.

Use Meyer's CSS Reset with compass by declaring the following `@import` statement at the beginning of your code:

```
@import 'compass/reset';
```

See also

Read more about Eric Meyer's CSS Reset at `http://meyerweb.com/eric/tools/css/reset/`.

Importing and organizing your files

In the *Working with partials* recipe of *Chapter 1, Getting Started with Sass,* you can read about the `@import` directive in Sass. The `@import` directive enables you to have as many files as you want in your development environment and this will compile to a single file in production. When your project grows, the number of files will also grow. In this recipe, you will learn how to use and organize these files.

Getting ready

In this recipe, you only will compile a single Sass template into CSS code to demonstrate the use of the `@import` directive. You can compile this template by using the Ruby Sass compiler. Read the *Installing Sass for command line usage* recipe of *Chapter 1, Getting Started with Sass,* to find out how to install Ruby Sass.

How to do it...

The following steps will learn you how to import files and organize your files:

1. Create a Sass template called `imports.scss`. The `imports.scss` file should contain the following lines of SCSS code:

    ```scss
    @import 'file.css';
    @import 'file' screen;
    @import 'http://sass-lang.com/file.scss';
    @import url(file.scss);
    ```

2. Then run the following command in your console to compile it into CSS code:

    ```
    sass imports.scss
    ```

3. Finally, you will find that the SCSS code from Step 1 compiles into static CSS code like that shown in the following:

    ```css
    @import url(file.css);

    @import "file" screen;

    @import "http://sass-lang.com/file.scss";

    @import url(file.scss);
    ```

How it works...

The syntax of the `@import` directive in Sass is similar to the `@import` at-rule in CSS. So Sass should only process Sass templates and leave other `@import` at-rules intact. When you import a Sass template, you do not explicitly have to set the file extension; the compiler automatically searches for files with the `.scss` and `.sass` extension and processes these files.

As you can see when evaluating the compiled CSS code in Step 3, all other declarations compile into a regular CSS `@import` at-rule.

The `@import 'file.css';` declaration will not be processed due to the `.css` extension. The second declaration contains the `screen` media query. At compile time, there is no context to evaluate the media query so this declaration also compiles into a CSS `@import` at-rule. Also, file names that are in the `url()` form, or start with `http://`, will compile into CSS `@import` at-rules.

Remember that Sass will ignore files that begin with underscores until you specifically import them. These files are called partials. In this book, the so-called 7-1 pattern has been used to organize the Sass templates. Note that you may not include a partial and a non-partial with the same file name in the same directory. You can read more about partials in the 7-1 pattern in the *Working with partials* recipe of *Chapter 1, Getting Started with Sass*.

There's more...

Although you mostly use the `@import` directives at the beginning of your style document, Sass also allows you to nest a Sass with the `@import` directive inside of a style rule.

When your `_nested.scss` partial file contains the SCSS like that shown as follows:

```
p {
color: red
}
```

You can compile the following SCSS code:

```
#library {
  @import 'nested';
}
```

The previous code compiles into CSS code as follows:

```
#library p {
  color: red; }
```

- Read more about the CSS `@import` at-rule, which allows you to import style rules from other stylesheets, at `https://developer.mozilla.org/en/docs/Web/CSS/@import`.

- You can read more about the 7-1 pattern developed by Hugo Giraudel at `http://sass-guidelin.es/#the-7-1-pattern`.

- Read why you should not use Sprockets directives in Asset Pipeline to combine your Sass files at `http://blog.pivotal.io/labs/labs/structure-your-sass-files-with-import`.

- Matt Stauffer wrote a quick blog post about Nesting Sass @imports, with BEM. You can find Stauffer's post at `https://mattstauffer.co/blog/nesting-sass-imports-with-bem`.

- The Sass globbing plugin allows you to import many Sass or SCSS files in a single import statement. You can find this plugin at `https://github.com/chriseppstein/sass-globbing`.

- And finally the Sass CSS Importer plugin, which enables you to import a CSS file into Sass, can be found at `https://github.com/chriseppstein/sass-css-importer`.

Building a grid with grid classes

Grid-based layouts divide your design into a collection of rows with equal-sized columns. Content and graphical elements can be organized according to this layout. Grids help in creating a logical and formal structure for designs. They prevent inconsistencies between the original design and the final implementation in HTML as designers and developers work with the same grid.

Grids are also helpful in **responsive design**, because the grid's columns can easily be rearranged to fit different screen widths.

Grids are formed by rows and columns. A grid with 12 columns can be easily adopted for different screen sizes. In this recipe, CSS classes are used to set the width of the grid items.

There are 12 classes for a grid of 12 columns, where each class has a width that spans a number of columns. The total items that span the columns in a row should be equal to the total number of columns in the grid. So, when your grid has 12 columns, a row can contain, for instance, three items that span four columns, or one item that spans one column and one item that spans 11 columns.

Getting ready

The code used in this recipe is based on the **CSS3 Flexible box** module, using the same naming conventions as Bootstrap. Read more about Bootstrap in *Chapter 12, Bootstrap and Sass*. Notice that Bootstrap 4 also has opt-in flexbox support.

Though it will be interesting to inspect the compiled code, the best way to test the grid you will construct in this recipe will be to use it in your browser. Notice that the code in this recipe uses the official W3C syntax for flexboxes, so you should use a browser that supports this syntax. You can find out which browsers support the Flexible box layout at http://caniuse. com/#feat=flexbox.

Also, the box-sizing property, as described in the *There's more...* section, should be supported by your browser. In the *How it works...* section of this recipe, you can read how to add support for older browsers, too.

 If you are not familiar with the CSS Flexible box module already, it's strongly recommended that you read more about it before you start this recipe. An excellent article titled *A Complete Guide to Flexbox* can be found at http://css-tricks.com/snippets/css/a-guide-to-flexbox/.

Of course, you will have to compile the Sass code of the recipe. Read *Chapter 1, Getting Started with Sass* to find out how to install Sass on your system. Also read the *Using vendor prefixes* recipe of *Chapter 7, Cross-Browser CSS3 Mixins*.

How to do it...

Now, build a flexbox grid yourself by performing the following steps:

1. Firstly, create a Sass file called sass/main.scss and write down the SCSS code shown here into this file:

    ```
    @import 'utils/variables';
    @import 'base/normalize';
    @import 'base/base';
    @import 'layout/grid';
    ```

    The file shown previously contains the CSS Reset as already described in the *Using a CSS Reset* recipe of this chapter. In the section of this recipe, you can read about setting the box-sizing property to make a calculation of widths inside your grids more easily. The base/_base.scss file only sets the box-sizing property.

2. Create a Sass partial file called `utils/_variables.scss` and write down the SCSS code into this file:

```scss
// variables;

$half-gutter-width: .5rem !default;
$gutter-compensation: -.5rem !default;
$outer-margin: 2rem !default;
$grid-columns: 12 !default;
$border-color: #ff6347 !default; // tomato
```

3. Also, create the `layout/_grid.scss` partial file and write down the SCSS code for the grid into it:

```scss
// mixins

@mixin grid () {
  padding-right: $outer-margin;
  padding-left: $outer-margin;
}

@mixin row() {
  box-sizing: border-box;
  display: flex;
  flex-direction: row;
  flex-wrap: wrap;
  margin-right: $gutter-compensation;
  margin-left: $gutter-compensation;
}

@mixin make-columns($grid-columns: $grid-columns) {
  @for $i from 1 through $grid-columns {
    .col-#{$i} {
      flex-basis: ((100% / $grid-columns) * $i);
      max-width: ((100% / $grid-columns) * $i);
    }
  }
}

// the grid

.grid {
  @include grid();
}
```

```scss
.row {
  @include row();
}

[class^="col-"],
[class*=" col-"] {
  border: 2px solid $border-color;
  box-sizing: border-box;
  display: flex;
  flex-direction: column;
  flex-grow: 0;
  flex-shrink: 0;
  padding-left: $half-gutter-width;
  padding-right: $half-gutter-width;
}

@include make-columns($grid-columns);
```

4. Now run the following command in your console to compile the SCSS code from Step 3 into CSS code:

   ```
   sass sass/main.scss main.css
   ```

5. Then, create an HTML file named `index.html` and include the `main.css` file into it by adding the following lines of HTML code to the head section:

   ```html
   <link rel="stylesheet" type="text/css" href="main.css" />
   ```

6. Now write the following snippet of HTML code into the body of the `index.html` file to make the grid visible in your browser:

   ```html
   <div class="grid">
       <div class="row">
           <div class="col-12"> </div>
       </div>
       <div class="row">
           <div class="col-6"> </div>
           <div class="col-6"> </div>
       </div>
       <div class="row">
           <div class="col-4"> </div>
           <div class="col-4"> </div>
           <div class="col-4"> </div>
       </div>
   </div>
   ```

7. Finally, load the `index.html` file in your browser and you will find that it will look as shown in the following screenshot:

How it works...

You have created separate files for variables, mixins, and even the grid code. As already mentioned, the code used in this recipe is inspired by the flexbox grid library. The code has been simplified to keep the recipe clear and understandable.

In this recipe, you will use a `@for` loop directive as described in the *Using the @for directive* recipe of *Chapter 8, Advanced Sass Coding*, to create the grid classes. In contrast to more semantic grid systems, such as the grid described in the *Building a semantic grid with mixins* recipe of this chapter, the SCSS code in this recipe compiles into 12 grid classes. Some of these grid classes might never be used for your project. The compiled CSS code contains more code than possibly needed; on the other hand, you can easily apply the grid for your designs and reuse the CSS code.

The general properties for the `col-*` classes are set with the `[class^="col-"]`, `[class*=" col-"]` selectors. These attribute selectors reduce the size of the CSS or make an additional base class unnecessary. Some developers avoid attribute selectors because they have a negative influence on performance. The partial attribute selector performance is indeed worse for Microsoft's Internet Explorer web browser. Also note that the overall performance of the CSS code never depends on a single selector, and calculations are complex. When optimizing your CSS code, removing unused selectors will have a more significant effect on performance.

If you resize the browser window when looking at the results of this recipe, you will find that the flexbox grid already acts in a fluid manner. When the size of the grid changes, the grid items resize too and the aspect ratios are kept intact. To create a responsive design, you probably also want to change the size of your grid items depending on the screen size. In the *Creating responsive grids* recipe of this chapter, you will learn how to use CSS media queries to create a responsive grid.

The Sass code in this recipe does not add browser prefixes for properties to support older browsers. Of course, you can write your own set of mixins to add these vendor prefixes to your `flex-*` and `box-sizing` properties, but a better alternative in this situation seems to use a mixin library with support for the CSS3 flexbox module. Notice that you can read more about the `box-sizing` property of the **CSS Box** model at the end of this section.

Compass has a flexbox module that provides prefixing support for the three versions of flexbox that have been implemented by browsers since 2009. Compass has also got a `box-sizing()` mixin for cross-browser changing of the box model. Read more about Compass in *Chapter 6, Using Compass*. In the *Implementing semantic layouts* recipe of *Chapter 12, Bootstrap and Sass*, you can read how to create cross-browser flexbox layouts leveraging the Bootstrap library.

Alternatively, you can use the autoprefixer to add cross-browser prefixes to your CSS code. In contrast to the Sass compiler, autoprefixer is a postprocessor for your CSS. The autoprefixer checks the Can I Use database. Read the *Automatically prefixing your code with Grunt* recipe of *Chapter 16, Setting up a Build Chain with Grunt* to find out how to use the autoprefixer.

The `-prefix-free` project enables you to use unprefixed CSS properties. Because the `-prefix-free` project code runs at the client side, some people claim that you shouldn't use it for production. Client-side code has a negative effect on end-user performance in many cases.

On the other hand, Lea Vera, the author of the `-prefix-free` project says, *-prefix-free detects which features need a prefix and only adds it if needed*. With the `-prefix-free` library, you can use smaller CSS files without any prefix and you don't have to update your code when some new browsers become available. Also read *The -prefix-free library* recipe of *Chapter 7, Cross-Browser CSS3 Mixins*.

There are also prefix plugins available for some text editors.

There's more...

In this section, you will learn how to use the `box-sizing` property of the CSS Box model.

Using the box-sizing property with Sass

When building grids and layouts, it is useful to pay some attention to the `box-sizing` property. The `box-sizing` property sets the CSS Box model and is used to calculate the width and height of an element. The default value of the `box-sizing` property is `content-box`; this model does not take borders and padding into account when calculating dimensions. On the other hand, the border-box model calculates dimensions that includes borders and padding. The difference between these two models can be easily made clear with a simple example. Consider the following SCSS code:

```
// scss-lint:disable VendorPrefix

// Box sizing
@mixin box-sizing($boxmodel) {
  -webkit-box-sizing: $boxmodel;
  -moz-box-sizing: $boxmodel;
```

```scss
    box-sizing: $boxmodel;
}

$background-color: #000; // black
$border-color: #f00; // red
$font-color: #fff; // white

.container {
  &.fit {
    @include box-sizing(border-box);
  }

  > div {
    @include box-sizing(inherit);
    background-color: $background-color;
    border: 5px $border-color solid;
    color: $font-color;
    float: left;
    padding: 10px;
    width: 50%;
  }
}
```

The compiled CSS code of the preceding SCSS code can be applied to the following HTML snippet:

```html
<div class="container">
  <div>col 1</div>
  <div>col 2</div>
</div>
<div class="container fit">
  <div>col 3</div>
  <div>col 4</div>
</div>
```

When you load the preceding code into your browser, it will look like what is shown in the following screenshot:

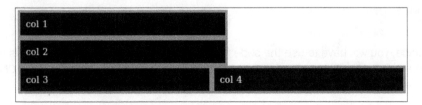

As you can see in the preceding screenshot, the last two columns of 50% width fit in the same row. Neither the padding nor the border sizes of this column influences the total width of these columns due to the border-box model. So the border-box model makes the calculation of column sizes for your layouts easier, because of which you may ignore the padding and border sizes in your calculations.

See also

- More information about the Compass `box-sizing()` mixin can be found at `http://compass-style.org/reference/compass/css3/box_sizing`

- Bottlenecks in CSS performance are tested and described at `http://benfrain.com/css-performance-revisited-selectors-bloat-expensive-styles/`

- An online service that prefixes your CSS code can be found at `http://prefixr.com/`

- The autoprefixer can be found at `https://github.com/postcss/autoprefixer/`

- The `-prefix-free` project can be found at `http://leverou.github.io/prefixfree/`

- You can read an interview with Lea Vera, author of the `-prefix-free` project, by Chris Coyier of CSS-tricks.com at `http://css-tricks.com/five-questions-with-lea-verou/`

- The Can I Use database can be found at `http://caniuse.com/`

Creating responsive grids

CSS media queries make it possible to only apply style rules when a certain condition is true. For responsive designs, the screen width can be used as a condition to evaluate the media queries. A typical media query looks like the following:

```
@media (min-width: 768px) {
  //style rules
}
```

The style rules inside the preceding media query will only be applied when the screen's width (viewport) is equal to or wider than 768 pixels.

Getting ready

In this recipe, you will have to use the code from the *Building a grid with grid classes* recipe of this chapter. You also will have to use the command line Ruby Sass compiler. Read *Chapter 1, Getting Started with Sass*, to find out how to install Sass on your system.

How to do it...

Perform the following steps to create a responsive grid yourself:

1. Copy the files from the *Building a grid with grid classes* recipe of this chapter into your working directory. You should end up with a file and directory structure like that shown in the following figure:

```
├── index.html
└── sass
    ├── base
    │   ├── _base.scss
    │   └── _normalise.scss
    ├── layout
    │   └── _grid.scss
    ├── main.scss
    └── utils
        └── _variables.scss
```

2. Then, change the `make-columns()` mixin to the `sass/layout/_grid.scss` file by adding a `$grid` parameter. Finally, the `make-columns()` mixin should look like that shown in the following SCSS code:

```scss
@mixin make-columns($grid, $grid-columns: $grid-columns) {
  @for $i from 1 through $grid-columns {
    .col-#{$grid}-#{$i} {
      flex-basis: ((100% / $grid-columns) * $i);
      max-width: ((100% / $grid-columns) * $i);
    }
  }
}
```

3. Also, remove the `make-columns()` mixin call at the end of the `sass/layout/_grid.scss` file.

4. Next, create a `sass/main.scss` file that will contain the following SCSS code:

```scss
@import 'utils/variables';
@import 'base/normalize';
@import 'base/base';
@import 'layout/grid';

// the responsive grid
$basefontsize: 16;
$sm-breakpoint: (768 / $basefontsize) *1em;
$grid-columns: 4;
```

```
@include make-columns(xs);

@media (min-width: $sm-breakpoint) {
  @include make-columns(sm);
}
```

5. Then, compile the `sass/main.scss` file by running the following command in the console:

    sass sass/main.scss main.css

6. In the next code, you will find part of the compiled CSS code that contains the styles for the columns of the grid. The other styles for the grid, including flexbox properties, are not shown:

```
.col-xs-1 {
  flex-basis: 25%;
  max-width: 25%; }

.col-xs-2 {
  flex-basis: 50%;
  max-width: 50%; }

.col-xs-3 {
  flex-basis: 75%;
  max-width: 75%; }

.col-xs-4 {
  flex-basis: 100%;
  max-width: 100%; }

@media (min-width: 48em) {
  .col-sm-1 {
    flex-basis: 25%;
    max-width: 25%; }

  .col-sm-2 {
    flex-basis: 50%;
    max-width: 50%; }

  .col-sm-3 {
    flex-basis: 75%;
    max-width: 75%; }

  .col-sm-4 {
    flex-basis: 100%;
    max-width: 100%; } }
```

7. Now write down the following HTML code into the `index.html` file:

```html
<div class="grid">
<div class="row">
    <div class="col-xs-2 col-sm-3">col-xs-2 col-sm-3</div>
    <div class="col-xs-2 col-sm-1">col-xs-2 col-sm-1</div>
</div>
</div>
```

8. In your browser, the previous code should look like that shown in the following figure:

col-xs-2 col-sm-3	col-xs-2 col-sm-1

9. Finally, resize your browser so that the screen width is smaller than 40em (~640 pixel) and you will find that each column gets 50% of the width of the grid now.

How it works...

In this recipe, you created two grids: the `xs` (extra small) grid with the `col-xs-*` classes, and the `sm` (small) grid with the `col-sm-*` classes for screen sizes wider than `40` em. Notice that the breakpoint has been set in `em` units instead of pixels. The `em` units let the media queries appropriately respond to a change in font size, such as when the user magnifies the page. Modern browsers do not require media queries in (r)em values for correct zooming; viewports do not depend on font sizes and earlier bugs about the zooming behavior have already been fixed. Also, Bootstrap 4 defines its breakpoint in pixel values again. Also realize that pixels provide absolute control and consistent rendering across every browser. Designers used to think and operate in pixels.

There's more...

To make the code act in a mobile-first manner, the `.make.-cols(xs);` mixin call is not wrapped in any media query. You can also use this strategy for other style rules. Start with the default style rules without media queries and add more or other style rules for wider screen sizes with media queries, which set the `min-width` condition. The mobile-first strategy refers to earlier times when mobile browsers did not support JavaScript or the full range of CSS (or CSS3) rules. This strategy is still true, and the browser loads the default-style rules first. Other style rules are loaded and applied if the browser supports them. The mobile-first strategy also prevents the browser from loading features and style rules that are never used in the situation where bandwidth and processing power are limited.

See also

▸ An insight into responsive design fundamentals can be found at
https://developers.google.com/web/fundamentals/layouts/

▸ Read more about the mobile-first strategy at http://www.uxmatters.com/mt/
archives/2012/03/mobile-first-what-does-it-mean.php

Building a semantic grid with mixins

In the *Building a grid with grid classes* recipe of this chapter, you can read how to build a grid
with CSS grid classes. Using these grid classes on the div elements breaks the semantic
nature of HTML5. In this recipe, you will learn how to keep the HTML5 semantic tags intact
when deploying a grid.

Getting ready

In this recipe, you will have to use the code from the *Building a grid with grid classes* and
Creating responsive grids recipes of this chapter. You will use the Ruby Sass compiler as
described in *Chapter 1, Getting Started with Sass,* to compile your CSS code.

How to do it...

Learn how to set up a semantic grid by performing the step beneath:

1. Leverage the SCSS code from the *Building a grid with grid classes* and *Creating
   responsive grids* recipes, and edit the sass/layout/_grid.scss file so that
   it contains the following SCSS code:

```scss
@mixin set-span($col-number) {
  flex-basis: ((100% / $grid-columns) * $col-number);
  max-width: ((100% / $grid-columns) * $col-number);
}

@mixin grid-item($span, $unit) {
  @if $unit == xs {
    @include set-span($span);
  } @else if $unit == sm {
    @media (min-width: $sm-breakpoint) {
      @include set-span($span);
    }
  }
}
```

2. The SCSS code in the `sass/main.scss` file should look like that shown in the following:

```scss
@import 'utils/variables';
@import 'base/normalize';
@import 'base/base';
@import 'layout/grid';

article {
  @include grid-item(4,xs);
  @include grid-item(2,sm);
}
```

3. Then, compile the `sass/main.scss` file by running the following command in the console:

```
sass sass/main.scss main.css
```

4. Finally, the compiled CSS code should look like that shown in the following:

```css
article {
  flex-basis: 100%;
  max-width: 100%; }
  @media (min-width: 48em) {
    article {
      flex-basis: 50%;
      max-width: 50%; } }
```

How it works...

The Sass compiler does not group equal media queries; this is why the loop in the *Building a grid with grid classes* recipe was called inside a media query, as can be seen in the following snippet of SCSS code:

```scss
@media (min-width: $sm-breakpoint) {
  @include make-columns(sm);
}
```

When each iteration of the loop creates a class that includes the corresponding media query, the compiled CSS will become inefficient and contain many unnecessary media queries. The result of the preceding code is that the mixins of the flexbox grid library do not define media queries. Moreover, the original `make-column()` mixin always creates a class.

To solve the issue in the preceding code, the `make-column()` mixin has been split up into two new mixins as follows:

```
@mixin set-span($col-number) {
  flex-basis: ((100% / $grid-columns) * $col-number);
  max-width: ((100% / $grid-columns) * $col-number);
}

@mixin grid-item($span, $unit) {
  @if $unit == xs {
    @include set-span($span);
  } @else if $unit == sm {
    @media (min-width: $sm-breakpoint) {
      @include set-span($span);
    }
  }
}
```

Now you can call the `set-span()` mixin to set the flexbox properties without defining a class. To solve the media query issue, a `grid-item()` helper mixin has been created. The `grid-item()` helper mixin sets the required media query based on the `$span` input parameter and the already defined `$*-breakpoint` variables. Notice that media queries are still not grouped, but the number of media queries will be limited when you have to generate all the grid classes.

There's more...

Building your grid with responsive mixins instead of CSS classes helps you to write more semantic HTML code. Also notice that grid items should still be wrapped in a row and a row, in turn, should have a grid as its parent. The need for these wrappers to set the flexbox properties will mean you can't build a pure semantic layout.

The `semantic.gs` grid system enables you to build pure semantic grids. You can read more about `semantic.gs` in the *Building semantic grids with semantic.gs* recipe of this chapter.

See also

▸ A post CSS processor such as CSS MQPacker can pack the same CSS media query rules into one media query rule. CSS MQPacker can be found at `https://github.com/hail2u/node-css-mqpacker`. Also read the *Automatically prefixing your code with Grunt* recipe of *Chapter 16, Setting up a Build Chain with Grunt* to find out how to integrate postprocessors in your build process using **PostCSS**.

▸ More information on the semantic grid system can also be found at `http://semantic.gs/`.

▶ On the HTML5 Doctor website at `http://html5doctor.com/`, you will find an easy-to-understand HTML5 sectioning element flowchart to help you get to grips with some of the semantic elements in HTML5.

Applying the grid on your design

In this recipe, you will learn how to build a layout using the flexbox code you have already built in the preceding recipes of this chapter.

Getting ready

Read *Chapter 1, Getting Started with Sass* to find out how to compile your CSS code using Ruby Sass. You will reuse the code from the *Building a grid with grid classes* recipe of this chapter.

How to do it...

You need to perform the following steps to apply the grid on your design:

1. Copy the files of the *Building a grid with grid classes* recipe of this chapter into your working directory. Your file and directory structure should look like that shown in the following figure:

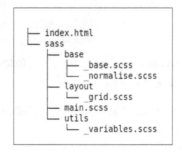

2. Now edit the `sass/layout/_grid.scss` file. Write down the following SCSS code at the end of this file:

```scss
@mixin make-cols($grid) {
  @for $col-number from 1 through $grid-columns {
    @include make-column($grid, $col-number);
  }
}

@include make-cols(xs);
```

```scss
@media (min-width: $sm-breakpoint) {
  @include make-cols(sm);
}

@media (min-width: $md-breakpoint) {
  @include make-cols(md);
}

@media (min-width: $lg-breakpoint) {
  @include make-cols(lg);
}
```

3. The `Main Body` part in the HTML code in Step 5 contains an unordered list (`ul`). This list gets grid classes to lay it out. Use the following SCSS at the end of the `sass/main.scss` file to set the colors and other styling elements of the items on the list:

```scss
.blocks {
  padding: 0;

  li {
    background-color: $blocks-background-color;
    border: 2px solid;
    color: $blocks-font-color;
    font-size: 3em;
    height: 100px;
    padding: 10px;
  }
}
```

4. Compile the `sass/main.scss` file by running the following command in the console:

   sass sass/main.scss main.css

5. Finally, create an `index.html` file and write the following HTML code into it:

```html
<div class="grid">
    <header class="row">
    <h1 class="col-xs-12">Flexbox Grid System</h1>
    </header>

    <div class="row">
    <!-- Main Body -->
        <section class="col-xs-12 col-sm-9">
        <ul class="row blocks">
        <li class="col-xs-12 col-sm-6 col-md-4">1</li>
        <li class="col-xs-12 col-sm-6 col-md-4">2</li>
        <li class="col-xs-12 col-sm-6 col-md-4">3</li>
        <li class="col-xs-12 col-sm-6 col-md-4">4</li>
        <li class="col-xs-12 col-sm-6 col-md-4">5</li>
```

```
<li class="col-xs-12 col-sm-6 col-md-4">6</li>
<li class="col-xs-12 col-sm-6 col-md-4">7</li>
<li class="col-xs-12 col-sm-6 col-md-4">8</li>
<li class="col-xs-12 col-sm-6 col-md-4">9</li>
</ul>
</section>

<aside class="col-xs-12 col-sm-3">
<h2>Sidebar</h2>
<nav>
<ul class="row">
<li class="col-xs-12">Item 1</li>
<li class="col-xs-12">Item 2</li>
<li class="col-xs-12">Item 3</li>
</ul>
</nav>
</aside>
</div>
</div>
```

6. Load the `index.html` file in your browser and you will see what it will look like in the following screenshot:

Also, resize your browser window to see the effect of the media queries. The previous figure shows the layout for screens (viewports) between 768 pixels (48em) and 960 pixels (60em) wide.

How it works...

The SCSS code of this recipe with different grids for different screen sizes is defined. For each grid, there are a set of classes that set the column span for the grid items. The naming of the grid classes is equal to that in Bootstrap 3. In *Chapter 12, Bootstrap and Sass,* you can read about Bootstrap 4; the small grid of Bootstrap 4 starts at a screen width of 544 pixels instead of 768 pixels.

This recipe also shows you that a grid row can be easily nested. The `<ul class="row blocks">` element defines a nested row. In the small (sm), medium (md), and large (lg) grids, this nested row has a 9 divided by 12 equals 75 percent of the screen width due to the `col-sm-9` class of its parent.

In the *Building a semantic grid with mixins* recipe of this chapter, you can read how to use mixins to set the properties of a grid item. Leveraging the mixins from this recipe, which are not included in the Less code you have downloaded, you could also use the following SCSS code to style the block structure:

```
.row.blocks li {
  .grid-item(12,xs);
  .grid-item(6,sm);
  .grid-item(4,md);
}
```

The compiled CSS of the preceding SCSS code will make the repeated usage of the `col-xs-12 col-sm-6` and `col-md-4` classes in the list of blocks unnecessary, which will help you to keep your HTML clean and readable.

There's more...

As already mentioned, the SCSS code declarations in the recipe only contain the official and unprefixed W3C syntax for the flexbox properties. You should use the autoprefixer, as described in the *Automatically prefixing your code with Grunt* recipe of *Chapter 16, Setting up a Build Chain with Grunt*, to prefix your code.

Adding the browser prefixes, as described in the preceding steps, does not add flexbox support for older browsers, such as Internet Explorer below version 9. For older browsers that don't support flexbox, you can create a fallback. Tools such as Modernizr can be used to check for flexbox support. In the *Reusing Bootstrap's grid* recipe of *Chapter 12, Bootstrap and Sass*, you can read how to compile Bootstrap's grid into a single CSS file. Because the flexbox grid code uses the same naming conventions for grid classes as that of Bootstrap, you could also consider using Bootstrap's grid as a fallback for Internet Explorer 8. Notice that Bootstrap 4 itself has already got optional flexbox support.

▸ Modernizr can be found at `http://modernizr.com/`

▸ Read more about conditional stylesheets by Paul Irish at `http://www.paulirish.com/2008/conditional-stylesheets-vs-css-hacks-answer-neither/`

Integrating a vertical navigation menu in your layout

In this recipe, you will learn how to integrate a menu into a layout. Both the menu and the layout are built with the CSS3 Flexible box module.

Getting ready

In this recipe, you will integrate this navigation menu in the example layout created in the *Applying the grid on your design* recipe of this chapter. Read the preceding recipes mentioned in this chapter before you start is recommended. Use a flexbox-ready browser to inspect the results of this recipe. You can check for support for the flexbox module of your browser at `http://caniuse.com/#feat=flexbox`. The SCSS is compiled with Ruby Sass on the command line. Read the *Installing Sass for command line usage* recipe of *Chapter 1, Getting Started with Sass* to find out how to use Ruby Sass.

How to do it...

The following steps will show you how to integrate a vertical navigation menu into the layout you have created before in the the Applying the grid on your design recipe:

1. Start by copying the files of the *Applying the grid on your design* recipe of this chapter.

2. Then, create a `sass/components/_navigation.scss` file and write the following SCSS code into it:

```scss
nav#mainmenu > ul {
  list-style: none;
  margin: 0;
  padding: 0;
  background: purple;
  display: flex;
  flex-direction: column;

  @media all and (min-width: $sm-breakpoint) {
    justify-content: space-around;
```

```
      flex-direction: row;
    }

    @media all and (min-width: $md-breakpoint) {
      justify-content: flex-end;
    }

    li {
      padding: 20px;

      a {
        color: white;

        &:hover{
          color: red;
        }
      }
    }
  }
}
```

3. Next, import the `sass/components/_navigation.scss` file from Step 2 in the `sass/main.scss` file of your project.

4. Compile the `sass/main.scss` file by running the following command in the console:

    `sass sass/main.scss main.css`

5. Open the `index.html` file you copied from the *Applying the grid on your design* recipe. Write the following HTML code between the `<header>` and `<div class="row">` tags:

    ```
    <nav id="mainmenu" class="row" role="navigation">

        <ul class="col-xs-12">
          <li><a href="">Menu item 1</a></li>
          <li><a href="">Menu item 2 (long text)</a></li>
          <li><a href="">Three</a></li>
        </ul>

    </nav>
    ```

6. Finally, save the modified index .html file and load it into your browser. The result should look similar to what is shown in the following screenshot:

How it works...

The navigation menu uses the same breakpoints set by the $sm-bsreakpoint and $md-breakpoint variables in the sass/utils/_variables.scss file as the layout grid. For small screens, the menu items stack due to the flex-direction: column; declaration and, for wider screens, the menu becomes horizontal due to the flex-direction: row; declaration. Finally, for large screens, the menu moves to the right of the page due to the justify-content: flex-end; declaration.

There's more...

As already mentioned several times in this chapter, the flexbox syntax requires vendor prefixes for better browser compatibility. Read *Chapter 7, Cross-Browser CSS3 Mixins* to find out more about vendor prefixes. Of course, you can also run the autoprefixer, as described in the *Automatically prefixing your code with Grunt* recipe of *Chapter 16, Setting up a Build Chain with Grunt,* or use Compass; see *Chapter 6, Using Compass,* to declare your flexbox properties.

See also

▸ You can read more about flexbox in the CSS specifications at http://www.w3.org/TR/css3-flexbox/

▸ The Compass flexbox module provides prefixing support for the three versions of flexbox that have been implemented by browsers since 2009. You can find more about this module at http://compass-style.org/reference/compass/css3/flexbox/

Creating grids with semantic.gs

HTML5 introduced many new semantic HTML tags, such as footer, header, section, among others; nevertheless, many modern CSS grid systems are built with non-semantic div tags and CSS classes. Critics even say that building your grids with div tags does not differ from the old-school table layouts. The semantic.gs mixins library provides you with a simple manner to build a 12-column semantic grid. Grids can be used as the skeleton of a responsive website.

Using grids in web design will help both the web designer and the web developer to prevent inconsistencies from occurring between the original design and the final implementation in HTML.

Getting ready

For this recipe, you have to download the latest version of the semantic.gs mixins, which can be found at `https://github.com/tylertate/semantic.gs/zipball/master`. After editing the Sass files with a text editor, you can test the result in your browser. Use the Ruby Sass compiler as described in *Chapter 1, Getting Started with Sass,* to compile your CSS code.

How to do it...

In this recipe, you will rebuild the example that is also shown on the home page of the semantic.gs website. The media queries in the example code are changed so that the compiled CSS code will follow the mobile-first approach:

1. Download the files of the semantic.gs library from `https://github.com/tylertate/semantic.gs/zipball/master` and unzip it in the `sass` folder of your project.

2. After unzipping the files, you should end up with a file and directory structure like that shown in the following:

```
├── index.html
└── sass
    ├── main.scss
    └── tylertate-semantic.gs-c2aa77c
        ├── changelog.md
        ├── examples
        ├── js
        ├── LICENSE.txt
        ├── README.md
        └── stylesheets
```

3. Use your favorite editor to edit the `sass/main.scss` file, and write down the following SCSS code into this file:

```scss
$column-width: 60;
$gutter-width: 20;
$columns: 12;
$total-width: 100%;

@import 'semantic.gs/stylesheets/scss/grid';

header {
    @include column(12);
}

article {
    @include column(12);
}

aside {
    @include column(12);
}

@media (min-width: 960px) {

    article {
        @include column(9);
    }

    aside {
        @include column(3);
    }

}
```

4. Compile the `sass/main.scss` file by running the following command in the console:

   sass sass/main.scss main.css

5. Create and edit the `index.html` file, which should contain the following HTML code:

```html
<!doctype html>
<html lang="en">
<head>
  <meta charset="utf-8">
```

```
    <title>Creating Grids with Semantic.gs</title>
    <meta name="description" content="Creating Grids with Semantic.
gs">
    <meta name="author" content="Bass Jobsen">

    <link rel="stylesheet" type="text/css" href="main.css" />

</head>

<body>
<header>This is a header</header>
<article>This is an article</article>
<aside>This is an aside</aside>

</body>
</html>
```

6. Finally, load the `index.html` file in your browser. You will find that the `aside` element float on the right-hand side of the article as expected.

How it works...

The semantic.gs mixins provide you with an easy way to build a responsive grid without classes, and that is it. It is good to realize that using a grid does not have to break the semantic structure of your website.

Creating a responsive layout with the semantic.gs mixins is easy and straightforward. You can set the number of columns with the `$columns` variable; also, the column width and the gutter size are set by variables.

You will also notice that the grid had some limitations. In the recipe, the column size of the compiled CSS is fixed, although the columns stack for screen widths taller than 960 pixels will be set to 960 (12 x (`$column-width` + `$gutter-width`)). The gutter is set with the margin property. This issue can be partly solved by setting the `$total-width` variable to 100%. After that the column widths (and margins) are also calculated as a percentage of the total available width and the grid becomes fluid.

There's more...

The semantic.gs mixins use the `float` CSS property to layout the grid columns, just like Bootstrap, although Bootstrap 4 has got opt-in flexbox support too. Bootstrap, as discussed in this chapter, builds its grid with `div` HTML elements and classes. Bootstrap 4 also includes Sass variables and mixins to quickly generate semantic layouts.

You can download Bootstrap's source files, including the Sass files, at `http://getbootstrap.com/`. Notice the following example code uses Bootstrap version 4. After that, you can import `bootstrap's SCSS code` into your `main.scss` project file. Write down the following SCSS code into the `main.scss` file:

```scss
@import 'scss/variables';
@import 'scss/mixins';
@import 'scss/grid';

$breakpoint: 960px;

// Reset the box-sizing
*,
*:before,
*:after {
  box-sizing: border-box;
}

r {
  @include make-container();
}

.row {
  @include make-row();
}

header {
  @include make-col();
  @include make-col-span(12);
}

article {
  @include make-col();
  @include make-col-span(12);
  @media (min-width: $breakpoint) {
    @include make-col-span(9);
  }
}

aside {
  @include make-col();
  @include make-col-span(12);
  @media (min-width: $breakpoint) {
    @include make-col-span(3);
  }
}
```

The compiled CSS code of the preceding SCCS code can be used with the `index.html` file you have created in this recipe. Notice that you still will have to wrap the layout in `<div class="container"><div class="row">` to use the CSS code. Also, the `box-sizing: border-box;` declaration is required. As you will see, the result will be a layout similar to that already created with the semantic.gs mixins.

When reusing Bootstrap's code for your projects, you should keep in mind that you will have to prefix your properties, too. Also see *Chapter 12, Bootstrap and SASS*, for more information about Bootstrap and the prefixing of CSS properties.

See also

▶ On the semantic.gs website at `http://semantic.gs/`, you can find other examples of how to build the fluid, nested, and responsive layout with the semantic.gs mixins

▶ More information about Bootstrap can be found at `http://www.getbootstrap.com/`

Using Compass Layout Module

In this last recipe, you can read about the Compass Layout Module. Compass is an open-source CSS framework for Sass. You can read more about Compass in *Chapter 6, Using Compass*. The code in this recipe demonstrates how to use the Compass Layout Module to generate fixed, fluid, and elastic grid-images on-the-fly using CSS3 gradients.

Getting ready

Read *Chapter 6, Using Compass*, to learn more about Compass. Also read the *Installing Sass for command line usage* recipe of *Chapter 1, Getting Started with Sass*. This recipe uses the SCSS you have used for the *Creating grids with semantic.gs* recipe.

How to do it...

Learn how to use the Compass Layout Module by performing the following steps:

1. Copy the files from the *Creating grids with semantic.gs* recipe into your working directory.

2. Then, edit the `sass/main.scss` file and make sure it contains the following SCSS after that:

```
@import 'semantic.gs/stylesheets/scss/grid';
@import 'compass/layout/grid-background';
```

```scss
$column-width: 60;
$gutter-width: 20;
$columns: 12;
$total-width: 960px;

$grid-background-total-columns: $columns;
$grid-background-column-width: $column-width * 1px;
$grid-background-gutter-width: $gutter-width * 1px;


body {
  @include column-grid-background();
}

header {
  @include column(12);
}

article {
  @include column(12);
}

aside {
  @include column(12);
}

@media (min-width: 960px) {

  article {
    @include column(9);
  }

  aside {
    @include column(3);
  }

}
```

3. Compile the `sass/main.scss` file by running the following command in the console:

    sass --compass sass/main.scss main.css

4. Finally, load the `index.html` file in your browser and you will find that it will look like the following screenshot:

How it works...

The grid images are created by CSS3 gradient images. Read the *Using vendor prefixes* recipe of *Chapter 7, Cross-Browser CSS3 Mixins,* to learn more about CSS3 gradients and Sass. The code-compiled CSS code generates background images for the `body` selector. As you can see, you can use these grid images for testing both horizontal and vertical grids.

There's more...

The Compass Layout Module also contains mixins and functions to build sticky footers and to style absolutely positioned elements such that they will stretch to fill their positioning parent. You cannot use this module to build a complete (grid-based) page layout. Earlier versions of Compass ship with Blueprint CSS. Blueprint does not support the responsive approaches that are essential to web design nowadays.

Compass removed Blueprint CSS since version 0.13. Compass recommends you to use Susy to build your grid systems now. You can read more about Susy in *Chapter 10, Building Grid-based Layouts with Susy and Sass.*

See also

▶ Read more about the Compass Layout Module at `http://compass-style.org/reference/compass/layout/stretching/`

▶ The official website of Blueprint CSS can be found at `http://www.blueprintcss.org/`. Notice last updated on May 14, 2011

10
Building Grid-based Layouts with Susy and Sass

In this chapter, you will learn the following topics:

- ▸ Installing and configuring Susy
- ▸ Defining containers and columns
- ▸ Mobile first and responsive grids
- ▸ Preventing subpixel rounding errors
- ▸ Generating asymmetric layouts

Introduction

In this chapter, you will learn how to build a custom grid layout with Susy. Susy is a custom layout engine for Sass. You can use Susy to create fast, responsive, fully customizable grids in CSS without touching your HTML markup code. More information on Susy can be found at `http://susydocs.oddbird.net/`.

Installing and configuring Susy

In this recipe, you will learn how to install Susy on your system for command line usage and configure it to create grid-based layouts with ease. The Susy layout toolkit for Sass itself comes in the form of a Ruby Gem, which is an easy-to-install software package. You can read more about Ruby Gems in the *Installing Sass for command line usage* recipe of *Chapter 1, Getting Started with Sass*.

Getting ready

The only requirement for Susy is Sass. You should remember that Susy was built to be part of the Compass ecosystem, so it works well together with Compass. Read the *Installing Sass for command line usage* and *Installing Compass* recipes of *Chapter 1, Getting Started with Sass*, to learn how to install both Sass and Compass on your system. It's also recommended to pair Susy with tools, such as Breakpoint and Vertical Rhythms. Breakpoint has been discussed in more detail in the *Media Queries with Breakpoints* recipe of *Chapter 8, Advanced Sass Coding*. Finally, also read more about the Compass Vertical Rhythm module in the *Creating a vertical rhythm for your website* recipe of *Chapter 8, Advanced Sass Coding*.

How to do it...

Perform the following steps to install Susy on your system for command line usage:

1. Run the following command on your command line to install Susy on your system:

   gem install susy

2. The preceding command requires administrator rights for some systems. Use the sudo command for global installing with administrator rights.

3. Create a Sass file called susytest.scss, which will contain an SCSS code like that shown here:

   ```scss
   @import 'susy';

   $susy: (
     columns: 12,
     gutters: .25,
     gutter-position: inside,
   );

   body {
     @include container(60em);
   }
   ```

```scss
section {
  @include span(9 of 12);
}

nav {
  @include span(3 of 12);
}
```

4. Now, you can compile the SCSS from the previous step into CSS code by running the following command in your console:

sass -r susy susytest.scss

5. The command from the third step will output a CSS code like that shown here in your console:

```css
body {
  max-width: 60em;
  margin-left: auto;
  margin-right: auto; }
  body:after {
    content: " ";
    display: block;
    clear: both; }

section {
  -moz-box-sizing: border-box;
  -webkit-box-sizing: border-box;
  box-sizing: border-box;
  width: 75%;
  float: left;
  padding-left: 0.83333%;
  padding-right: 0.83333%; }

nav {
  -moz-box-sizing: border-box;
  -webkit-box-sizing: border-box;
  box-sizing: border-box;
  width: 25%;
  float: left;
  padding-left: 0.83333%;
  padding-right: 0.83333%; }
```

How it works...

You can build grids of all kinds with Susy. The basic Susy layout is composed using two simple mixins like that shown here:

```
@include container; // establish a layout context
@include span(<width>); // lay out your elements
```

To configure Susy for your specific needs, you should create a special `$susy` variable. The `$susy` variable stores your settings in a Sass Map. Read more about maps in Sass in the *Map functions* recipe of *Chapter 5, Built-in Functions*. The options in the `$susy` variable overwrite Susy's default settings. In this recipe, the `columns`, `gutters`, and `gutter-position` options are set. These settings create a grid with 12 equal-sized columns. The gutters are constructed with the `padding` property, half the size of the gutter on both the sides of the column, due to the `gutter-position` option being set to `inside`. The size of the gutter is set to the `gutters` option times the width of the column. As you can see, the `box-sizing` property has been set to `border-box` automatically. Read more about the `box-sizing` property in the *Building a grid with grid classes* recipe of *Chapter 9, Building Layouts with Sass*.

Take a look at these calculations:

The width of each column is *100% / 12 = 8.3333%*

Then *guttersize = 0.25 * (columnwidth - guttersize) = 0.25 * (8.3333 - guttersize).*

So *guttersize = 0.25 * 8.3333 / 1.25 = 1.666%* and the `padding-left` and `padding-right` properties should be set to *1.666% / 2 = 0.8333%.*

Working with percentages here may cause fractional pixel values, such as `20.5`. Read the *Preventing subpixel rounding errors* recipe of this chapter to learn more about factional pixel value rounding errors in older browsers.

Depending on your configuration options, you can create grids of all kinds with Susy. Other configuration options are discussed in the other recipes of this chapter. All the columns of the grid in this recipe have the same width. In the *Generating asymmetric layouts* recipe of this chapter, you can read about asymmetric layouts with a grid that has columns of different widths.

There's more...

Instead of a Sass map for your setting, you can also use Susy's shorthand syntax. These two definitions are interchangeable. The shorthand syntax for this recipe will look as follows:

```
$shorthand: 12 1/4 fluid float inside;
```

In this recipe, you used Susy on the command line. You can also use Susy with Compass. Run the following command to add Susy to your current project:

```
compass install susy
```

In the *Using Susy with Ruby on Rails* recipe of *Chapter 14, Ruby on Rails and Sass*, you can read how to use Susy to build your grid-based layouts when developing a Ruby on Rails app.

See also

▶ A complete overview of the global Susy settings can be found at `http://susydocs.oddbird.net/en/latest/settings/`.

▶ You can build grids of all kinds with Susy. Define your grid using any unit of measurement (ems, pixels, percentages, inches, and so on) and then determine how and when you want that grid to respond to the viewport. You can find a few examples of grids with different container styles at `http://susy.oddbird.net/demos/grid-types/`.

Defining containers and columns

When using Susy to create a grid-based layout, you should define a container element that holds the grid. After this, you should define your columns or elements that span a certain number of columns inside the container. In this recipe, you will learn how to create a grid for your layout using Susy.

Getting ready

Read the *Installing and configuring Susy* recipe of this chapter and the *Installing Sass for command line usage* recipe of *Chapter 1, Getting Started with Sass*, to find out how to get both Sass and Susy ready on your system. In this recipe, you will rebuild the layout from the *Applying the grid to your design* recipe of *Chapter 9, Building Layouts with Sass*, using the Susy layout toolkit instead of the Flexible box code and mixins.

How to do it...

Perform the following steps to find out how to rebuild the layout of the *Applying the grid to your design* recipe of *Chapter 9, Building Layouts with Sass* by using Susy:

1. Firstly, create the file and directory structure as follows:

```
├── index.html
└── sass
    ├── base
    │   └── _normalize.scss
    ├── main.scss
    └── utils
        └── _variables.scss
```

2. Secondly, declare the special `$susy` variable in the `utils/_variables.scss` partial file that holds your susy configuration. Your SCSS code should look as follows:

```scss
// susy
$susy: (
  columns: 12,  // The number of columns in your grid
  gutters: 1/4, // The size of a gutter in relation to a single column
  gutter-position: inside,
);
```

3. Then, write down the following SCSS code in the `main.scss` file:

```scss
@import 'utils/variables';
@import 'base/normalize';
@import 'susy';

body {
  @include container();
  padding: gutter();
}

header {
  @include span(12);
  background-color: $header-background-color;
  color: $header-font-color;
}

section {
  @include span(9);
}

aside {
  @include span(3);
}
```

4. Notice that the `@import 'base/normalize'` import statement in the preceding code imports a CSS Reset, as described in the *Using a CSS Reset* recipe of *Chapter 9, Building Layouts with Sass*.

5. After this, you should create the `index.html` file that will contain the HTML code for your design. This file should contain an HTML markup code like that shown here:

```
<header>
<h1>Powered by Susy</h1>
</header>

<!-- Main Body -->
    <section>
        <ul class="blocks">
            <li>1</li>
            <li>2</li>
            <li>3</li>
            <li>4</li>
            <li>5</li>
            <li>6</li>
            <li>7</li>
            <li>8</li>
            <li>9</li>
        </ul>
    </section>

    <aside>
    <h2>Sidebar</h2>
    <nav>
        <ul>
            <li>Item 1</li>
            <li>Item 2</li>
            <li>Item 3</li>
        </ul>
    </nav>
    </aside>
```

6. Now, you should compile the Sass code into CSS by running the following command in your console:

```
sass -r susy sass/main.scss main.css
```

7. Now, make sure that the `index.html` file from the fourth step links the `main.css` file you have created in the previous step. The `head` section should contain the following line of HTML code:

```
<link rel="stylesheet" type="text/css" href="main.css" />
```

8. Finally, load the `index.html` file. The result should look as follows:

How it works...

In this recipe, the `container()` mixin was applied to body, the element of your HTML code. This means that your HTML does not have an unnecessary element to hold your grid. In the `utils/_variables.scss` partial file, the number of grid columns has been set to 12 by declaring `$grid-columns: 12;`. The `$susy Sass Map`, which contains your Susy settings, is also declared in the `utils/_variables.scss` partial file. Read the *Installing and configuring Susy* recipe of this chapter to learn more about the settings to configure Susy.

In the `main.scss` file, the columns' span for the HTML elements of your layout is set by calling the `span()` mixin. The `span()` mixin is called with the number of columns the element should span.

The element should span 3 of 12 columns, so the SCSS code should look as follows:

```
aside {
    @include span(3);
}
```

There's more...

When you compare the result of the recipe with that from the *Applying the grid on your design* recipe of *Chapter 9, Building Layouts with Sass*, you will find that the list in the main content area isn't styled.

The following steps will show you how to style the list element in the main content area so that it looks like the blocks from the *Applying the grid to your design* recipe.

Firstly, create a file called `elements/_blocks.scss`. This file should contain the following SCSS code:

```scss
.blocks {
  padding: 0;

  li {
    @include span(4);
    background-color: $blocks-background-color;
    border: 2px solid;
    color: $blocks-font-color;
    font-size: 3em;
    height: 100px;
    list-style-type: none;
    padding: 10px;
  }
}
```

The `$blocks-background-color` and `$blocks-font-color` variables in the preceding code are declared in the `sass/utils/_variables.scss` file.

Then, add the `nest` keyword to the `span()` mixin for the `section` element that represents the main content area of your design. The mixin call should now look as follows:

```scss
section {
  @include span(9 nest);
}
```

Finally, add the `elements/_block.scss` file to @import the declaration at the beginning of the `main.scss` file. You should import `_block.scss` after importing the Susy library.

Recompile your CSS code. You will find that the result in your browser looks as follows:

Mobile first and responsive grids

In this recipe, you will learn how to create mobile first and responsive grids with Susy. These grids first code the layout for small devices—the situation that none of the media queries evaluates to. Design changes and possible additional features are added for larger screens. The strategy for mobile first code is also explained already in the *Mobile first strategies* recipe of *Chapter 7, Cross-Browser CSS3 Mixins*.

Getting ready

This recipe uses the code from the *Defining containers and columns* recipe of this chapter. So, read this first and code the source code to your current working directory. Install both Sass and Susy, as described in the *Installing and configuring Susy* recipe of this chapter and the *Installing Sass for command line usage* recipe of *Chapter 1, Getting Started with Sass*. Finally, you can test the result in any modern browser that supports CSS media queries. Also, read the *Media Queries with Breakpoint* recipe of *Chapter 8, Advanced Sass Coding*, and the *Creating responsive grids* recipe of *Chapter 9, Building Layouts with Sass*, to learn more about CSS media queries.

How to do it...

The following steps will show you how to make the grid from the *Defining containers and columns* recipe of this chapter responsive:

1. Copy the source code of the *Defining containers and columns* recipe into your current working directory. Your file and directory structure should look as follows:

    ```
    ├── index.html
    └── sass
        ├── base
        │   └── _normalize.scss
        ├── main.scss
        └── utils
            └── _variables.scss
    ```

2. Secondly, open the file the `main.scss` file and edit the SCSS code for the `section` and `aside` selectors. After this, your SCSS code should look like that shown here:

    ```
    @include susy-breakpoint($lg-breakpoint) {
      section {
        @include span(9 nest);
      }
    ```

```scss
aside {
  @include span(3);
}
}
```

3. Then, open the `elements/_blocks.scss` file and edit the SCSS code. You should change the code for the column span of the `li` selectors. Give them a different span depending on the screen width of your device. Also, add a call to the `susy-clearfix` mixin for the `ul` selector. Finally, the SCSS code should look as follows:

```scss
.blocks {
padding: 0;

li {

    background-color: $blocks-background-color;
    border: 2px solid;
    color: $blocks-font-color;
        font-size: 3em;
    height: 75px;
    list-style-type: none;
    padding: 10px;

    @include susy-breakpoint($sm-breakpoint) {
      @include span(6);
    }

    @include susy-breakpoint($md-breakpoint) {
      @include span(4);
    }
  }

  @include susy-clearfix;
}
```

4. Recompile your CSS code by running the following command in your console:

    sass -r susy sass/main.scss main.css

5. Open the `index.html` file in your favorite browser and resize your window to see the effect of the media queries on the look of your design. For a screen width between 768 and 960 pixels, your layout should look as follows:

How it works...

In responsive designs, the breakpoint defines when your design changes or adopts to the current screen size. CSS media queries are used to apply some styles only when the media query evaluates true.

Susy comes with the `susy-breakpoint()` breakpoint mixin by default. Alternatively, you can use the breakpoint gem, as discussed in the *Media Queries with Breakpoint* recipe of *Chapter 8*, *Advanced Sass Coding*, to help with writing media queries.

When calling the `susy-breakpoint()` breakpoint mixin with only one parameter, this parameter sets the `min-width` value of your media query.

The breakpoint value in this recipe is declared in the `utils/_variables.scss` file. The following SCSS code sets the breakpoint value using the elastic measure em, a value for the pixel equivalents:

```
$basefontsize: 16px;
$sm-breakpoint: (768px / $basefontsize) * 1em;
$md-breakpoint: (960px / $basefontsize) * 1em;
$lg-breakpoint: (1024px / $basefontsize) * 1em;
```

In the *Creating a vertical rhythm for your website* recipe of this chapter, the elastic measure units, em and rem, for CSS properties were discussed. Elastic measure units are also useful to build responsive layouts and grids, as described in the *Creating responsive grids* recipe of *Chapter 9, Building Layouts with Sass*. Grids and layouts with the em-based media queries have breakpoints that scale with your font size.

The layout created in this recipe has two main columns with navigation on the right-hand side only for screens wider than the largest breakpoint, the equivalent of 1,024 pixels. The blocks in the main area respond to two breakpoints; when the first breakpoint is reached, the blocks show up in two columns. After the second breakpoint, a third column will be added. In the mobile (first) situation, none of the breakpoints evaluates true, so the navigation is under the content and the blocks are displayed in a single column under each other.

The clearfix() mixin clears the float property of an element after it has been rendered without the need for additional markup and guarantees that your elements will only float in their own row.

There's more...

In this recipe, the susy-breakpoint() breakpoint mixin was called with only one parameter. This parameter is a number followed by a unit, such as 768 px or 40 em. These calls compile into a CSS media query declaration with min-width set to the value of the parameter, such as @media (min-width: 40em) {}. Instead of a single value, you can also use media query shorthand created with the susy-query() mixin.

The susy-query() mixin can be used to create more complex media queries. Consider a CSS code like that shown here:

```
@include susy-media((
   min-height: 30em,
   orientation: landscape,
)) { /*...*/ }
```

The preceding SCSS code compiles into CSS code as follow:

```
@media (min-height: 30em) and (orientation: landscape) { /*...*/ }
```

The susy-breakpoint() breakpoint mixin also has an optional second and third argument.

The second argument defines a layout in the form of the shorthand, as described in the *Installing and configuring Susy* recipe of this chapter. When setting both the first and second parameters for the susy-breakpoint() breakpoint mixin, it acts as a shortcut for changing layout settings at different media-query breakpoints. In the *Generating asymmetric layouts* recipe of this chapter, you will find the mixin. The with-layout() mixin can be used for this too.

▸ More about units can be found in the *Why Ems?* Article by Chris Coyier. You can find it at `https://css-tricks.com/why-ems/`.

▸ Also, read the *Clearing Floats: An Overview of Different clearfix Methods* article by Nick Salloum to learn more about clearing floats. You can find Salloum's article at `http://www.sitepoint.com/clearing-floats-overview-different-clearfix-methods/`.

Preventing subpixel rounding errors

Fractional pixel values may cause rounding issues in older browsers. This recipe shows you how Susy can prevent you from these rounding errors.

Getting ready

Install Susy, as described in the *Installing and configuring Susy* recipe of this chapter. Of course, you will also need the Ruby Sass compiler, so read the *Installing Compass* recipe of *Chapter 1, Getting Started with Sass*.

How to do it...

After performing the steps beneath you should understand how to prevent subpixel rounding errors in your designs:

1. Write down the following SCSS code in your `main.scss` project file:

```
@import 'susy;

$susy: (
  columns: 3,
  gutters: 0,
  output: float,
);

body {
  @include container();
}

section {
  @include span(2 first);
}
aside {
  @include span(1 last);
}
```

2. Compile the Sass template from the first step into CSS code by running the following command in your console:

```
sass -r susy main.scss
```

3. Now, you will find a CSS code like that shown here outputted in your console:

```
body {
  max-width: 100%;
  margin-left: auto;
  margin-right: auto; }
  body:after {
    content: " ";
    display: block;
    clear: both; }

section {
  width: 66.66667%;
  float: left; }

aside {
  width: 33.33333%;
  float: right;
  margin-right: 0; }
```

4. Then, change the value of the `output` setting in the `$susy` configuration variable from `float` to `isolate`.

5. Compile your code again by repeating the command from the second step. You will find that the compiled code looks as follows:

```
body {
  max-width: 100%;
  margin-left: auto;
  margin-right: auto; }
  body:after {
    content: " ";
    display: block;
    clear: both; }

section {
  width: 66.66667%;
  float: left;
  margin-left: 0;
  margin-right: -100%; }
```

```
aside {
  width: 33.33333%;
  float: left;
  margin-left: 66.66667%;
  margin-right: -100%; }
```

How it works...

When working with fluid layout in the preceding section, your percentages may possibly create subpixels. Subpixels are fractional pixel values, such as `25.5`. These subpixels may cause some troubles for older browsers. Nowadays, all the modern browsers use subpixel rendering to visually represent fractions of a pixel. Subpixel rendering prevents your layouts from breaking and mesh up due to subpixel rounding errors.

For older browsers, the isolate technique prevents you from subpixel rounding errors. CSS isolation is not easy to understand. The developers of Susy describe it as follows:

> *"Every float is positioned relative to its container, rather than the float before it. It's a bit of a hack, and removes content from the flow, so I don't recommend building your entire layout on isolated floats, but it can be very useful as a spot-check when rounding errors are really causing you a headache."*

When using the `isolate` value output mode, you will have to declare the position of the elements in the grid by adding `at <position>` to the parameter of the `span()` mixin call. For the first and last elements of a row you can use the `first` and `last` keywords. An example of the usage of the `at <position>` parameter can be found in the *Generating asymmetric layouts* recipe of this chapter.

There's more...

Currently, the `output` setting of Susy only accepts two values. The default `float` value creates a grid layout with the floating technique, while the `isolate` value generates CSS code for the isolate technique, as described in this recipe.

Future versions of Susy may possibly also support output for other techniques, such as the Flexible box technique, as explained in *Chapter 9, Building Layouts with Sass*, of this book.

See also

▶ The Browser Rounding and Fractional Pixels article by Alex Kilgour includes a table that shows how different browsers and browser versions handle subpixel values. You can find Kilgour's article at `http://cruft.io/posts/percentage-calculations-in-ie/`.

▶ CSS isolation was originally a part of Zen Grids. Zen Grid implementation has been written in Sass too. You can find Zen Grids at `http://zengrids.com/`.

Generating asymmetric layouts

With asymmetric layouts, you can create something unique and different that attracts attention. Most grid-based layouts are in some way symmetrical, because of the equal size columns of the grid. In this recipe, you will learn how to create asymmetric grids with columns of different widths, and how apply your designs to them.

Getting ready

First, install both Sass and Susy. Read the *Installing and configuring Susy* recipe of this chapter to find out how to do this.

How to do it...

Learn how to create asymmetric layout with Susy by performing the following steps:

1. Create a file and directory structure, which should look as follows:

```
├── index.html
└── sass
    ├── base
    │   └── _normalise.scss
    ├── main.scss
    └── utils
        └── _variables.scss
```

2. Secondly, open the file the `main.scss` file and edit the SCSS code so that your SCSS code looks as follows:

```scss
@import 'utils/variables';
@import 'base/normalise';
@import 'susy';

body {
  @include container();
  padding: gutter();
}

header {
  background-color: $header-background-color;
  color: $header-font-color;
}
```

```scss
section {
  article {
    &:first-child {
      @include span(1 first);
    }
    &:nth-child(2) {
      @include span(1 at 2);
    }
    &:nth-child(3) {
      @include span(1 at 3);
    }
    &:nth-child(4) {
      @include span(1 at 4);
    }
    &:last-child {
      @include span(1 last);
    }
  }
  @include susy-clearfix;
}

footer {
  @include with-layout(3) {
    div {
      @include span(1);
    }
  }
}
```

3. Then, declare a special `$susy` variable in the `utils/_variables.scss` partial file, which will hold your susy configuration. Your SCSS code should look as follows:

```scss
// susy configuration
$susy: (
  columns: 1 1 2 3 5,
  gutters: 1/4,
  gutter-position: inside,
  output: isolate,
  debug: (
    image: show-columns,
    color: blue
  ),
);
```

4. Compile your CSS code by running the following command in your console:

   `sass -r susy sass/main.scss main.css`

5. Open the `index.html` file in your browser. You will see that your layout looks as follows:

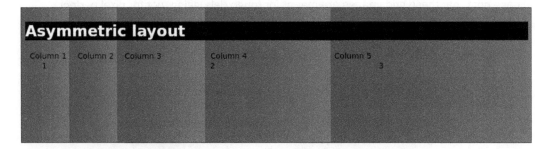

How it works...

As you can see, in the declaration of the special `$susy` variable in the `utils/_variables.scss` partial file, the `columns` setting does not specify the number of columns, but a list of column sizes. The third column of this list has twice the width of the first, and the fifth column has five times this width.

Asymmetric grids, as defined previously, required the `output` setting to be set to `Isolate`. In the `isolate` output mode, you will have to specify the position of each element in the grid using the `at <position>` syntax, as also described in the *Preventing subpixel rounding errors* recipe of this chapter.

The position of the `section` elements has been set using the `:first-child`, `:last-child`, and `:nth-child()` pseudo-element selectors. When you have to create a large or flexible number of columns, you can also use a -loop, as described in the *Using @for* recipe of *Chapter 8, Advanced Sass Coding*, to create your positions with the `:nth-child()` pseudo class selectors.

Finally, the `with-layout()` mixin was used to create a three-column layout for the `footer` element. The `with-layout()` mixin temporarily sets defaults for a section of your code.

There's more...

When inspecting the result of this recipe in your browser, you will see the blue backgrounds of the five columns. These background colors used to visualize the grid are initialized by the `debug` setting in the `$susy` configuration variable and are not a part of the design. Please note that these grid images are meant for rough debugging, not for pixel perfect measurements. This function is very similar to the grid images provided by the Compass layout module, as described in the *Using the Compass layout module* recipe of *Chapter 9, Building Layouts with Sass*.

See also

▶ Get inspired to use asymmetric layouts by reading the article at `https://webdesignviews.com/asymmetrical-layout-in-web-design/`

▶ Pseudo class selectors are explained in more detail at `http://www.sitepoint.com/web-foundations/css3-pseudo-classes/`

11
Foundation and Sass

In this chapter, you will learn the following topics:

- ▸ Installing Foundation CLI
- ▸ Integrating Foundation in a Compass project
- ▸ Creating semantic grids with Foundation
- ▸ Building off-canvas menus with Sass and JavaScript
- ▸ Using Foundation 6 with WordPress and Sass

Introduction

In this chapter, you can read about **Foundation 6 for Sites**. Foundation for Sites can be compiled with both Ruby Sass and LibSass. In the first recipe, you will read about how to install Foundation CLI (command-line interface). The starter project ships with a Gulp build chain and compiles with node-sass, a Node port of LibSass.

Installing Foundation CLI

In this recipe, you will learn how to install Foundation on the command line using npm.

Getting ready

To install Foundation CLI, you should have **Node.js** installed on your system. Read the *Installing Sass for command line usage* recipe of *Chapter 1, Getting Started with Sass*, to learn about Node.js and npm.

If you have Foundation 5 CLI installed, you should remove it before installing Foundation 6 CLI by running the following command in your console:

```
gem uninstall foundation
```

How to do it...

The following steps will show you how to install Foundation:

1. Run the following command on your command line to install Foundation on your system:

   ```
   npm install --global foundation-cli
   ```

2. The preceding command requires administrator rights for some systems. Use the `sudo` command for global installing with administrator rights.

3. Once you've installed the CLI, use the `new` command to start making a new project:

   ```
   foundation new
   ```

   Answer the questions, as shown in the following image:

```
$ foundation new
? What are you building today? A website (Foundation for Sites)
? What's the project called? recipe1
? Which template would you like to use? Basic Template: includes a Sass compiler


        ./|        ,
     , /|/  \/| /|      Thanks for using ZURB Foundation for Sites!
     /|/       |/ |      ---------------------------------------------
    |__|         |__|    Let's set up a new project.
    \__|  ^^   ^^  |__/   It shouldn't take more than a minute.
      |  -[o]--[o]- |
      |     __,     |
      |     ...     |
      _____/


Downloading the project template...
Done downloading!

Installing dependencies...
```

4. The command in the previous step creates a new folder called `recipe1`. This folder contains a file and directory structure like that shown here:

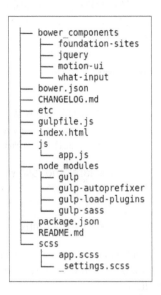

```
├── bower_components
│   ├── foundation-sites
│   ├── jquery
│   ├── motion-ui
│   └── what-input
├── bower.json
├── CHANGELOG.md
├── etc
├── gulpfile.js
├── index.html
├── js
│   └── app.js
├── node_modules
│   ├── gulp
│   ├── gulp-autoprefixer
│   ├── gulp-load-plugins
│   └── gulp-sass
├── package.json
├── README.md
└── scss
    ├── app.scss
    └── _settings.scss
```

5. Run the following command in your console:

   foundation build

6. Now, you can open the `index.html` file in your browser, which will show you the Sass basic template of Foundation 6.

7. After this, modify some variables in the `scss/_settings` file and run the build command again in your console:

   foundation build

8. The preceding command recompiles the CSS files; you can inspect the results in your browser again by reloading the `index.html` file.

How it works...

Foundation CLI uses npm and bower to install the required plugin files for your project. It also generates a `Gulpfile.js` file used by Gulp to compile your SCSS code with node-sass. The *Using the sass-gulp plugin with Gulp* recipe in *Chapter 1, Getting Started with Sass*, describes how to use Gulp with node-sass to compile your Sass code into CSS code. Read also the *Automatically prefixing your code with Grunt* recipe of *Chapter 16, Setting up a Build Chain with Grunt*, to learn more about how to set up build chains to compile your project.

The Sass code of Foundation contains a `_setting.scss` file; it contains all the Sass variables for the styles of the compiled CSS code. A copy of this file can be found in the `scss/_settings` file of the project. The settings file is imported in the `scss/app.scss` file with the following `@import` declaration: `@import 'settings';`. Because the Sass compiler first looks into the current path, the local `scss/_settings` file gets precedence over the original the `bower_components/foundation_sites/scss/settings_settings` file, which enables you to update Foundation without overwriting your changes in the local `scss/_settings` file.

You can also inspect the `scss/app.scss` file. This file is your main project file and is very similar to the `bower_components/foundation_sites/scss/foundation.scss` file. Notice that the `scss/app.scss` file also imports the `foundation.scss` file.

The first line in the `scss/app.scss` file declares the following line of code:

```
@charset 'utf-8';
```

The preceding declaration explicitly specifies the encoding of your stylesheet.

Sass does not support conditional imports. Foundation solves this with conditional mixin calls. These conditional mixin calls also enable you to (re)use only the mixins of a component without generating any other output.

The Sass file for each component of Foundation contains mixins and a special mixin, which generates the predefined CSS class. In your custom code, you can import the button mixins as follows:

```
@import 'components/button';
```

After the preceding import, you can call (`@include`) the button mixins in your own code. To generate the predefined button CSS classes, you should also call the special `foundation-button` mixin. So, to generate the predefined CSS classes in your compiled CSS code, you should use an SCSS code like that shown here:

```
@import 'components/button';
@include foundation-button;
```

The `scss/app.scss` file of the demo app calls all of the Foundation CSS classes generating mixins. When compiling a project for production, you should @include only the mixins that are really needed to prevent unused CSS code. The `foundation.scss` file itself also contains a special `@mixin foundation-everything($flex: false)` mixin, which enables you to compile the complete CSS code of Foundation once. The `$flex` parameter enables you to compile Foundation with Flex-box support or not.

The `foundation.scss`-file also sets some global variables and styles, so you always should @include it in your project, unless you explicitly call these styles, as follows:

```
// Sass utilities
@import 'util/util';

// Global variables and styles
@import 'global';
```

There's more...

Mac users, who prefer a GUI over the command line interface, can try **Yeti Launch**. Yeti Launch is a Mac app for quickly setting up blank projects for any of the three Foundation frameworks. Notice that only Foundation for Sites is described in this book. You can use **Foundation for Email** and **Foundation for Apps** in a very similar manner. All three types of Foundation have their own Sass code base.

In the *Utilizing Yeoman* recipe in *Chapter 16, Setting up a Build Chain with Grunt*, you can read how to set up a build chain for Bootstrap 4 with Yeoman. A Yeoman generator for Foundation 6 for Sites is also available.

See also

▶ Read more about installing Foundation 6 at `http://foundation.zurb.com/sites/docs/installation.html`

▶ Learn more about Foundation for Emails at `http://foundation.zurb.com/emails.html`

▶ Learn more about Foundation for Apps at `http://foundation.zurb.com/apps.html`

▶ A Yeoman generator for Foundation 6 for Sites can be found at `https://github.com/bassjobsen/generator-foundation6`

▶ Brunch is a HTML5 build tool. A Brunch skeleton for Foundation 6 for Sites can be found at `https://github.com/bassjobsen/brunch-foundation6`

Integrating Foundation in a Compass project

Compass is an open source CSS Authoring Framework. In *Chapter 6, Using Compass*, of this book, you can read about how to set up your Sass projects with Compass. In this recipe, you will learn how to easily integrate Foundation 6 into your Compass project workflow.

Getting ready

Read the *Installing Compass* recipe in *Chapter 1, Getting Started with Sass,* to find out how to install Compass on your system. In this recipe, you will use bower. Bower is a package manager for the Web; it is used for managing frontend components. Run the following command in your console to install Bower:

```
npm install -g bower
```

How to do it...

For this recipe, you should perform the following steps:

1. Create a new Compass project, as already described in the *Maintaining your applications with Compass* recipe of *Chapter 6, Using Compass,* by running the following command in your console:

   ```
   compass init
   ```

2. Then, use bower to install Foundation for Sites by running the following command in your console:

   ```
   bower install foundation-sites
   ```

3. Create a local copy of Foundation's `settings` file as follows:

   ```
   cp bower_components/foundation-sites/scss/settings/_settings.scss
   sass/_settings.scss
   ```

4. After performing the first three steps, you should end up with a file and folder structure like that shown here:

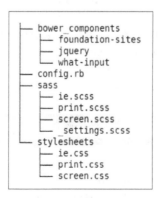

```
├── bower_components
│   ├── foundation-sites
│   ├── jquery
│   └── what-input
├── config.rb
├── sass
│   ├── ie.scss
│   ├── print.scss
│   ├── screen.scss
│   └── _settings.scss
└── stylesheets
    ├── ie.css
    ├── print.css
    └── screen.css
```

5. Now, open the `config.rb` file with your text editor and write down the following line of code into it:

   ```
   add_import_path "bower_components/foundation-sites/scss/"
   ```

6. Then, edit the `sass/screen.scss` file so that it contains an SCSS code like that shown here:

```
/* Welcome to Compass.
 * In this file you should write your main styles. (or centralize
your imports)
 * Import this file using the following HTML or equivalent:
 * <link href="/stylesheets/screen.css" media="screen, projection"
rel="stylesheet" type="text/css" /> */
@import "settings";
@import "compass/reset";

$grid-column-gutter: 30px;
// Import Foundation's Flex grid
@import "grid/_flex-grid";
@import "grid/_column";



#main {
  @include flex-grid-row;
  section {
    @include flex-grid-column(9);
  }

  aside {
    @include flex-grid-column(3);
  }
}
```

7. Now, you can compile your project by running the following command in your console:

    `compass compile`

8. Finally, inspect the compiled CSS code in the file. You will find that the grid code looks as follows:

```
/* line 14, ../sass/screen.scss */
#main {
  max-width: 75rem;
  margin-left: auto;
  margin-right: auto;
  display: flex;
  flex-flow: row wrap;
}
/* line 16, ../sass/screen.scss */
#main section {
```

```
        flex: 0 0 75%;
        padding-left: 0.9375rem;
        padding-right: 0.9375rem;
        max-width: 75%;
    }
    /* line 20, ../sass/screen.scss */
    #main aside {
        flex: 0 0 25%;
        padding-left: 0.9375rem;
        padding-right: 0.9375rem;
        max-width: 25%;
    }
```

How it works...

Using Compass is useful when you already have a code base that requires Compass' mixins and functions. The result of this recipe shows you that you can easily combine Compass with Foundation because Foundation also requires the autoprefixer post processor for full browser support. The autoprefixer adds vendor prefixes to CSS rules using values from the Can I Use database. You can read more about the autoprefixer in the *Automatically prefixing your code with Grunt* recipe of *Chapter 16, Setting up a Build Chain with Grunt*.

In this recipe, you built a grid using the optional Flexbox grid of Foundation. Older browsers, such as IE8, do not support the Flexbox module at all and other browsers require vendor prefixes for Flexbox support. Compass has its own built-in methods for vendor prefixes, as described in the *Tuning vendor prefixes from Compass stylesheets* recipe of *Chapter 6, Using Compass*. Because Foundation does not use the Compass mixins and functions for vendor prefixes, the compiled code in this recipe does not contain any vendor prefix.

There's more...

To solve the vendor-prefixing problem described in the previous section, you can consider using another solution to bundle both Compass and Foundation in your project. Reconsider the code of the *Installing Foundation CLI* recipe of this chapter. By default, Foundation CLI installs Gulp and compiles the Sass code with the `gulp-sass` plugin. The `gulp-sass` plugin uses node-sass, which in turn is a Node binding for LibSass. Compass uses internal functions of Ruby Sass and does not work together with LibSass. The `gulp-compass` plugin can solve this issue because it compiles your code with Ruby Sass. You can replace `gulp-sass` with `gulp-compass` by performing the following steps:

1. Run the following command in your console:

    ```
    npm install gulp-compass --save-dev
    ```

2. Then, replace the Sass task in the `Gulpfile.js` file as follows:

```
gulp.task('sass', function() {
  return gulp.src('scss/app.scss')
    .pipe($.compass({
      sass: 'scss',
      css: 'css',
      import_path: sassPaths
    }))
    .on('error', function(error) {
      // Would like to catch the error here
      console.log(error);
      this.emit('end');
    })
    .pipe($.autoprefixer({
      browsers: ['last 2 versions', 'ie >= 9']
    }))
    .pipe(gulp.dest('css'));
});
```

See also

▶ The official website of Compass can be found at `http://compass-style.org/`

▶ Find out which browsers support the W3C Flexible Box Layout Module at `http://caniuse.com/#feat=flexbox`

▶ Read more about the `gulp-compass` plugin at `https://www.npmjs.com/package/gulp-compass`

▶ The official website of Bower can be found at `http://bower.io/`

Creating semantic grids with Foundation

Foundation 6 has a 12-column grid and predefined grid classes by default. You can also use the grid mixins to apply the grid to selectors without predefined classes to generate semantic CSS for individual grid columns. In this recipe, you will learn how to use these grid mixins.

Getting ready

In this recipe, you will rebuild the layout from the *Applying the grid on your design* recipe of *Chapter 9, Building Layouts with Sass*, using Foundation 6. Another way to implement the same layout with Sass can be found in the *Mobile first and responsive grids* recipe of *Chapter 10, Building Grid-based Layouts with Susy and Sass*, the *Implementing Semantic layouts* recipe of *Chapter 12, Bootstrap and Sass*, and the *Semantic grids with Neats* recipe of *Chapter 13, Meeting the Bourbon Family*.

Read the *Installing Foundation CLI* recipe of this chapter before starting; you will need it for the first step of this recipe.

How to do it...

For this recipe, you should perform the following steps:

1. Install Foundation 6 for Sites, as already described in the *Installing Foundation CLI* recipe, by running the following command in your console:

   foundation new

2. Then, copy the `utils/_variables.scss` and `base/_normalize.scss` files from the *Applying the grid to your design* recipe of *Chapter 9*, *Building Layouts with Sass*, into the `scss` folder of your project created in the first step.

3. Edit the `app.scss` file so that it contains an SCSS code like that shown here:

```scss
@charset 'utf-8';

@import 'settings';
@import 'foundation';
@import 'grid/grid';

@include foundation-global-styles;
@include foundation-typography;

@import 'utils/variables';


header {
  @include grid-column-row;
  background-color: $header-background-color;
  color: $header-font-color;
}

#main {
  @include grid-row;
  section {
    @include grid-column(9);
  }

  aside {
    @include grid-column(3);
  }
}
```

4. The `index.html` file of your project should contain the following HTML code:

```html
<header>
<h1>Powered by Foundation 6</h1>
</header>


<!-- Main Body -->
<div id="main">
     <section>
     <ul class="blocks">
     <li>1</li>
     <li>2</li>
     <li>3</li>
     <li>4</li>
     <li>5</li>
     <li>6</li>
     <li>7</li>
     <li>8</li>
     <li>9</li>
     </ul>
     </section>

     <aside>
     <h2>Sidebar</h2>
     <nav>
     <ul>
     <li>Item 1</li>
     <li>Item 2</li>
     <li>Item 3</li>
     </ul>
     </nav>
     </aside>
</div>
```

5. Load the `index.html` file from the fourth step in your browser. You will find that it looks as follows:

How it works...

In this recipe, you used the grid mixins of Foundation to build a semantic grid. As already described in the *Installing Foundation CLI* recipe, the predefined CSS classes are not compiled in the CSS code, as the `foundation-grid` mixin is not included in the SCSS code.

Foundation also supports an optional Flexbox grid. You can implement this in a similar manner by using the `flex-grid-*` mixins from the `grid/_flex-@include grid.scss` file. An example of using the Flexbox mixins can be found in the *Creating a Compass project* recipe of this chapter.

There is more...

As you can see, the list in the main section of the HTML file stays unstyled. You can style this list with the block grid. Foundation's block grid gives you a way to evenly split the contents of a list within the grid. Elements in a row of the block grid stay evenly spaced irrespective of the screen size. The mixins for the block grid have been integrated into the grid code since Foundation 6. You can use the `grid-layout($n, $selector);` mixin with $n (the number of elements in a row) to generate a block grid.

Perform the following steps to style the list of the main section of the layout using the block grid:

1. Create a new file called `elements/_blocks.scss` and let `app.scss` import this file.

2. Edit the `elements/_blocks.scss` file so that it contains an SCSS code like that shown here:

```scss
.blocks {
  @include grid-row-nest();
  @include grid-layout(1,'li');
  @include breakpoint(medium) {
    @include grid-layout(3,'li');
  }
  li {

    background-color: $blocks-background-color;
    border: 2px solid;
    color: $blocks-font-color;
    font-size: 3em;
    height: 75px;
    list-style-type: none;
    padding: 10px;
  }
}
```

3. After recompiling the CSS code, your layout should look as follows:

Powered by Foundation 6			
1	2	3	**Sidebar** • Item 1 • Item 2 • Item 3
4	5	6	
7	8	9	

Notice that, here, the block grid is nested inside an element of the main grid, which spans nine columns. The `@include grid-row-nest();` mixin call inverts the margins of the nested block grid, so it fits inside the column.

The `@include breakpoint(medium);` mixin is used to create a mobile first solution; it compiles into `@media` a rule. For screen sizes smaller than the breakpoint, the block grid only has one element per row set by the `@include grid-layout(1,'li');` declaration. For wider screens, the number of elements in a row will rise to three due to the `@include grid-layout(3,'li');` declaration. Read more about mobile first strategies and CSS media queries in the *Mobile first strategies* recipe of *Chapter 7, Cross-Browser CSS3 Mixins*.

See also

- ▶ Read more about the Foundation grid component at `http://foundation.zurb.com/sites/docs/grid.html`

- ▶ Documentation for the Flexbox grid can be found at `http://foundation.zurb.com/sites/docs/flex-scss/grid.html`

- ▶ More information on using CSS media queries in Foundation can be found at `http://foundation.zurb.com/sites/docs/media-queries.html`

Building off-canvas menus with Sass and JavaScript

Foundation comes with a module for off-canvas menus. Off-canvas menus are positioned outside the viewport and slide in when activated. In this recipe, you will learn how to set up an off-canvas menu for your Foundation project. Off-canvas menus require both CSS and JavaScript code.

Getting ready

For this recipe, you have to create a new Foundation project, as described in the *Installing Foundation CLI* recipe of this chapter. You will use the same styles as used before in the *Creating semantic grids with Foundation* recipe of this chapter to create an example of an off-canvas menu. The off-canvas requires JavaScript too. An explanation on JavaScript usage is beyond the scope of this book.

How to do it...

The following steps will show you how to create an off-canvas menu for your projects:

1. Copy the files of the *Creating semantic grids with Foundation* recipe into your project folder.

2. Now, edit and change the `app.scss` file to import the off-canvas code. The content of this file should look as follows:

    ```scss
    @charset 'utf-8';

    @import 'settings';
    @import 'foundation';
    @import 'motion-ui';

    @include foundation-global-styles;
    @include foundation-typography;
    @include foundation-off-canvas;
    @include foundation-title-bar;


    @include motion-ui-transitions;
    @include motion-ui-animations;

    @import 'utils/variables';
    @import 'elements/blocks';


    header {
      @include grid-column-row;
      background-color: $header-background-color;
      color: $header-font-color;
    }

    #main {
      @include grid-row;
    ```

```scss
section {
  @include grid-column(12);
}

aside {
  @include grid-column(3);
}
}
```

3. Then, modify the `index.html` file so that the HTML code looks as follows:

```html
<div class="off-canvas-wrapper">
    <div class="off-canvas-wrapper-inner" data-off-canvas-wrapper>
        <div class="off-canvas position-right" id="offCanvas" data-off-canvas data-position="right">
            <aside class="off-canvas-content" data-off-canvas-content>
            <h2>Sidebar</h2>
            <nav>
            <ul>
            <li>Item 1</li>
            <li>Item 2</li>
            <li>Item 3</li>
            </ul>
            </nav>
            </aside>


        </div>
        <div id="main" data-off-canvas-content>

        <header class="title-bar">
        <h1 class="title-bar-left">Powered by Foundation 6</h1>
            <div class="title-bar-right">
                <button class="menu-icon" type="button" data-open="offCanvas"></button>
            </div>
        </header>

            <section>
            <ul class="blocks">
            <li>1</li>
            <li>2</li>
            <li>3</li>
            <li>4</li>
            <li>5</li>
```

```
        <li>6</li>
        <li>7</li>
        <li>8</li>
        <li>9</li>
        </ul>
        </section>

    </div>
    </div>
```

4. Recompile the CSS code by running the `gulp` command in your console.

5. Notice that the `index.html` file also has to load the required JavaScript code as follows:

```
<script src="bower_components/jquery/dist/jquery.js"></script>
<script src="bower_components/what-input/what-input.js"></script>
<script src="bower_components/foundation-sites/dist/foundation.
js"></script>
<script src="js/app.js"></script>
```

6. Then, load the `index.html` file from the fourth step in your browser. You will find that it looks as follows:

How it works...

The mixins of the off-canvas menus' module cannot be applied to a selector as usable. These mixins create the predefined classes for the elements of the off-canvas structure. Also, the JavaScript requires these classes and other predefined HTML attributes.

Basically, the HTML code for an off-canvas menu on the right-hand side of your page may look as follows:

```
<div class="off-canvas-wrapper">
  <div class="off-canvas-wrapper-inner" data-off-canvas-wrapper>
    <div class="off-canvas position-left" id="offCanvas" data-off-
canvas>
      <!-- your off canvas menu here -->
    </div>
    <div class="off-canvas-content" data-off-canvas-content>
    <!-- your main content here -->
    </div>
  </div>
</div>
```

The off-canvas should have a unique ID, so it can be targeted. In the preceding code, the ID is set using the `id="offCanvas"` attribute. A button can target this ID as follows:

```
<button type="button" class="button" data-toggle="offCanvas">Open
Menu</button>
```

There's more...

As mentioned before, applying mixins to selectors to create more semantic HTML code does not make much sense due to the required class names.

The base lines' styles for the off-canvas menus can be set with the `off-canvas-basics` mixin, as shown here:

```
@include off-canvas-basics;
```

The preceding mixin compiles into CSS code for the `html` and `body` selectors and also generates the predefined and required classes.

Of course, you can change the look and feel of the off-canvas menus by changing the variables in the `_settings.scss` file or by extending it with your own SCSS code.

See also

Read more about off-canvas menus at `http://foundation.zurb.com/sites/docs/off-canvas.html`

Using Foundation 6 with WordPress and Sass

WordPress is a popular **content management system** (**CMS**) installed on more than 60 million websites. In this recipe, you will learn how to use Foundation 6 with WordPress and Sass.

Getting ready

This recipe requires a web server with PHP and MySQL and WordPress installed. In this recipe, you will use the JointsWP theme; it does include Gulp and is optimized for a Gulp-based workflow. You should have Node.js installed to use Gulp. Read the *Using the sass-gulp with Gulp* recipe of *Chapter 1, Getting Started with Sass*, to learn how to install Node.js, which includes npm, on your system.

How to do it...

In the following steps you will meet the JointsWP theme for WordPress websites. JointsWP makes it possible to use Foundation and Sass for your WordPress projects, perform the following steps to understand how this works:

1. Download the JointsWP theme from `http://jointswp.com/`. Of course, you have to download the Sass version of the theme.

2. Unzip the Zip file downloaded in the first step into the `wordpress/wp_content/themes` folder of your WordPress project.

3. Then, navigate to the unzipped theme directory and run the following command in your console:

   ```
   npm install
   ```

   ```
   gulp
   ```

4. Now, you can activate the JointsWP theme in your WordPress dashboard.

5. Your WordPress website should look as follows:

Test   Sample Page

Template: Sticky

Posted on January 7, 2012 by themedemos - Uncategorized

This is a sticky post.

There are a few things to verify:

- The sticky post should be distinctly recognizable in some way in comparison to normal posts. You can style the `.sticky` class if you are using the post_class() function to generate your post classes, which is a best practice.
- They should show at the very top of the blog index page, even though they could be several posts back chronologically.
- They should still show up again in their chronologically correct postion in time, but without the sticky indicator.
- If you have a plugin or widget that lists popular posts or comments, make sure that this sticky post is not always at the top of those lists

Search for:

Search...

Search

Recent Posts

Hello world!
Markup: HTML Tags and Formatting
Markup: Image Alignment
Markup: Text Alignment
Markup: Title With Special Characters

Recent Comments

Mr WordPress on Hello world!
John Doe on Edge Case: No

How it works...

Running the `gulp style` command on the console will compile all of your Sass files from your `assets/sass` directory into the `assets/css` directory. It will create a minified and nonminified file; by default, the theme will add the nonminified file to a queue. The `assets/sass/styles.scss` file, which compiles into the `asssets/css/styles.css` file, will import Foundation and the other custom partials. The theme contains a local copy of `_settings.scss`, Foundation's file. You can run the `bower update` command to update Foundation safely without overwriting your changes.

You can write down your customizations and SCSS for WordPress classes in the `asssets/sass/_main.scss` file.

There is more...

The JointsWP theme also supports off-canvas menus, as described in the *Building off-canvas menus with Sass and JavaScript* recipe of this chapter. The theme menu will use off-canvas for small screens and display in the header for wider screens. You should edit the `header.php` file to replace the off-canvas menus with a responsive or off-canvas top bar. Explaining PHP code is beyond the scope of this book.

The Gulp build chain of the theme also compiles and bundles your custom JavaScript and Foundation's JavaScript files. The JavaScript part is also beyond the scope of this book, but you should note that the off-canvas menus of the theme require JavaScript.

See also

- ▸ WampServer is a Windows web development environment. It allows you to create web applications with Apache2, PHP, and a MySQL database. Read more about WampServer at `http://www.wampserver.com/`

- ▸ AMPPS is a WAMP, MAMP, and LAMP stack of Apache, MySQL, MongoDB, PHP, and Perl & Python. AMPPS enables you to focus more on using applications rather than maintaining them. You can download AMPPS at `http://ampps.com/download`

- ▸ *Famous 5-Minute Install* for WordPress can be found at `https://codex.wordpress.org/Installing_WordPress#Famous_5-Minute_Install`

- ▸ Read more about theme development for WordPress at `https://codex.wordpress.org/Theme_Development`

12

Bootstrap and Sass

In this chapter, you will learn the following topics:

- ▶ Downloading and installing Bootstrap
- ▶ Customizing Bootstrap with variables
- ▶ Configuring Bootstrap using variables
- ▶ Making custom buttons
- ▶ Making custom cards
- ▶ Making custom navbars
- ▶ Extending components using @extend
- ▶ Using Bootstrap mixins and classes
- ▶ Extending the mixins with your own mixins
- ▶ Implementing semantic layouts with Bootstrap
- ▶ Using WordPress with Bootstrap and Sass

Introduction

Bootstrap, formerly Twitter's Bootstrap, is the most popular HTML, CSS, and JavaScript framework to develop responsive, mobile-first projects on the web. You can use Bootstrap to build responsive websites and applications. This framework helps you to develop faster and more efficient applications using proven CSS code and components.

Bootstrap uses a responsive grid with 12 columns and many other reusable components.

In this chapter, you will learn more about Bootstrap's CSS. Bootstrap 4 is built with LibSass and Grunt. Using Sass as a preprocessor for the CSS code makes Bootstrap's code reusable and extendable. In this chapter, you will learn how to customize and extend Bootstrap by using Sass.

At the time of writing this book, Bootstrap 4 was not officially released. One of the most important changes in Bootstrap 4 is that it moved from Less to Sass. Bootstrap now compiles faster than ever, thanks to LibSass, and joins an increasingly large community of Sass developers. Other important changes are the improved grid system and opt-in flexbox support.

Some of Bootstrap's components require JavaScript; Bootstrap ships with jQuery plugins for these components. Configuring and extending these plugins is out of the scope of this book.

Bootstrap 4 comes with its own HTML reset module called Reboot. Reboot is based on **Normalize.css**, but gives you more opinionated resets, such as `box-sizing: border-box` and margin tweaks. Read more about **Normalize.css** in the *Using a CSS Reset* recipe of *Chapter 9, Building Layouts with Sass*.

Finally, Bootstrap 4 drops support for the Internet Explorer version 8 browser (IE8). Those who still need IE8 support should keep using Bootstrap 3. Dropping IE8 support allows you to swap pixel values for elastic measure `em` and `rem` values, where appropriate, to make responsive typography and component sizing even easier. In the *Creating a vertical rhythm for your site* recipe of *Chapter 8, Advanced Sass Coding*, the elastic measure `em` and `rem` units for CSS properties were discussed. Grids and layout with `em`-based media queries have breakpoints that scale with your font size; you can read more about that in the *Creating responsive grids* recipe of *Chapter 9, Building Layouts with Sass*.

The code used for the recipes in this chapter is based on the alpha version 4 of Bootstrap. Version 4 of Bootstrap was expected to be released in 2016. Of course, the code of the alpha version will differ from the official release, but when you understand how to configure and recompile the alpha code, you should be able to understand and use the code of the final version.

Downloading and installing Bootstrap

In this recipe, you will learn how to install Bootstrap and start your first project.

Getting ready

You can download the required files from `http://getbootstrap.com/getting-started/#download`. Choose the source version at this page, which includes the Sass source files, too.

For this recipe, you should have Node.js and Grunt installed on your system. You can read how to install Node.js and the Node.js package manager in the *Installing Grunt* recipe of *Chapter 16, Setting up a Build Chain with Grunt*.

After installing Node.js, which includes npm, you can install Grunt by running the following command:

```
npm install -g grunt-cli
```

Both Grunt and Gulp are JavaScript task runners; read the *Introduction* of *Chapter 16, Setting up a Build Chain with Grunt*, to learn more about the differences between them.

How to do it...

You need to perform the following steps:

1. Download the ZIP archive that contains the Bootstrap source files and unzip this file into your working directory. Alternatively, run the following command in your console:

   ```
   npm install bootstrap
   ```

2. Navigate into the `bootstrap` root directory and then run the following command in your console:

   ```
   npm install
   ```

3. Now, you can compile Bootstrap by running the following command in your console:

   ```
   grunt dist
   ```

4. Finally, the compiled CSS code can be used in your HTML by adding the following line of code in your HTML code:

   ```
   <link rel="stylesheet" type="text/css" href="dist/bootstrap.css">
   ```

How it works...

Bootstrap will be compiled with LibSass by default, but you can opt into traditional Ruby Sass by setting the `TWBS_SASS` environment variable. Run the following command to compile Bootstrap with Ruby Sass:

```
TWBS_SASS=sass grunt sass-compile
```

Notice that you have to run Bundler to install all Ruby dependencies before using Ruby Sass.

The Grunt `dist` command invokes the node-sass task, among others. The node-sass task compiles the Sass files from the directory into CSS. Read more about node-sass in the *Using the Sass-gulp plugin with Gulp* recipe of *Chapter 1, Getting Started with Sass*. The compiled CSS code will be saved in the `dist/css/bootstrap.css` file, and a minified copy of this code will be saved in the `dist/css/bootstrap.min.css` file.

Since version 3.2 of Bootstrap, the build process also runs the autoprefixer postprocessor. Read more about the autoprefixer in the *Automatically prefixing your code with Grunt* recipe of *Chapter 16, Setting up a Build Chain with Grunt*.

There's more...

You can also install Bootstrap with Bower by running the following command:

```
bower install bootstrap
```

Bower is a package manager that is optimized for frontend development. The Grunt task not only compiles the Sass code, but also bundles the required JavaScript plugins. Bootstrap components such as the navigation bar will not work without these plugins. Also, notice that the JavaScript plugins depend on **jQuery**.

See also

- ▸ The official Bootstrap website can be found at `http://getbootstrap.com`
- ▸ More information on Node.js can be found at `http://nodejs.org/`
- ▸ Read more about Bower at `http://bower.io/`
- ▸ Finally get informed about and download jQuery at `https://jquery.com/`

Customizing Bootstrap with variables

In the `scss` directory of your Bootstrap installation, you will find the `_variables.scss` partial file. This file is the sole place to edit and customize Bootstrap.

Getting ready

Download and install Bootstrap as described in the *Downloading and installing Bootstrap* recipe of this chapter.

How to do it...

Perform the steps beneath to learn how to customize Bootstrap by modifying the Sass variables:

1. Create an `index.html` file that loads the `dist/css/bootstrap.css` file from your Bootstrap installation folder and contains the HTML code similar to what is shown here:

```
<!doctype html>
<html lang="en">
<head>
  <meta charset="utf-8">
```

```
    <title>Customizing Bootstrap with variables</title>
    <meta name="description" content="Customizing Bootstrap with
variables">
    <meta name="author" content="Bass Jobsen">
    <link rel="stylesheet" type="text/css" href="bootstrap-4/dist/
css/bootstrap.css">
</head>
<body><br><br>
    <!-- Standard button -->
    <button type="button" class="btn btn-default">Default</button>

    <!-- Provides extra visual weight and identifies the primary
action in a set of buttons -->
    <button type="button" class="btn btn-primary">Primary</button>

    <!-- Indicates a successful or positive action -->
    <button type="button" class="btn btn-success">Success</button>

    <!-- Contextual button for informational alert messages -->
    <button type="button" class="btn btn-info">Info</button>

    <!-- Indicates caution should be taken with this action -->
    <button type="button" class="btn btn-warning">Warning</button>

    <!-- Indicates a dangerous or potentially negative action -->
    <button type="button" class="btn btn-danger">Danger</button>

    <!-- Deemphasize a button by making it look like a link while
maintaining button behavior -->
    <button type="button" class="btn btn-link">Link</button>
</body>
</html>
```

2. Load the `index.html` file from Step 1 in your browser, and it will look like what is shown in the following screenshot:

3. Then, open the `_variables.scss` file in the `scss` directory in a text editor and change the brand color variables. After you make the changes, these variables should have the following values assigned to them:

    ```
    $brand-primary:        orchid !default;
    $brand-success:        palegoldenrod !default;
    $brand-info:           olive !default;
    $brand-warning:        turquoise !default;
    $brand-danger:         thistle !default;
    ```

4. Run the following command in your console:

    grunt dist

5. Finally, reload the `index.html` file in your browser and you will find that the buttons now look like what is shown in the following screenshot:

How it works...

All the colors that define Bootstrap's look and feel are declared in the `_variables.scss` partial file. The other Bootstrap Sass code uses these variables. As you are changing the default color values, you will influence all the code, including the buttons, as you can see in this recipe.

There's more...

When you directly edit the original `_variables.scss` file, your customizations can be overwritten when upgrading Bootstrap.

One way to solve the problem shown in the preceding code is to create a separate file that will contain your customized variables. This file should be imported before importing the original variables file. This is similar to the copy of the `_settings.scss` file for Foundation as described in the *Installing Foundation CLI* recipe of *Chapter 11, Foundation and Sass*.

All of Bootstrap's variables are declared with the `!default` keyword, which means that you can easily overwrite them by declaring a new value before the declaration of the default value. Also read the *Declaring variables with !default* recipe of *Chapter 3, Variables, Mixins, and Functions*.

In a situation where you need to create a new file for your custom variables, the statement at the beginning of your `bootstrap.scss` may look like the following:

```
// Core variables and mixins
@import "custom-variables";
@import "variables";
@import "mixins";
```

The preceding code means that you have to create a new partial file called `_custom-variables.scss`, and it should contain the SCSS code like that shown here:

```
$brand-primary:         orchid;
$brand-success:         palegoldenrod;
$brand-info:            olive;
$brand-warning:         turquoise;
$brand-danger:          thistle;
```

Now you only have to add the `@import` for the `_custom-variables.scss` file to the `bootstrap.scss` file after updating Bootstrap.

Note that since Bootstrap 3.2, the autoprefixer postprocessor has been added to the default build process of Bootstrap. The autoprefixer postprocessor was added to automatically add vendor prefixes to the CSS properties, which means that running the autoprefixer is required for cross-browser support.

Compiling Bootstrap or the project file

When you add your customizations in a separate project file, which imports the `bootstrap.scss` file and compiles it with the command line Ruby Sass compiler, the autoprefixer does not run.

The autoprefixing problem can be solved by using the default build process for your modified code. Add the `@import "custom-variables"` line of code to the original `bootstrap.scss` file as described earlier. Or, alternatively, change the Grunt.js file so that it compiles your new project file instead of the original `bootstrap.scss` file. You should repeat both these solutions each time you update your Bootstrap source code. You can run the following command in your console to compile Bootstrap after the preceding changes take place:

grunt dist

Running the autoprefixer postprocessor with Gulp is also described in the *Automatically prefixing your code with Grunt* recipe of *Chapter 16, Setting up a Build Chain with Grunt*, and you can read more about vendor prefixes in the *Using vendor prefixes* recipe of *Chapter 7, Cross-Browser CSS3 Mixins*.

Finally, when you change the default colors, as described in the *Configuring Bootstrap using variables* recipe of this chapter, your buttons may look like that shown in the following screenshot:

See also

In the *Making Custom Buttons* recipe of this chapter, you can learn how to create your own custom buttons by using Bootstrap's mixins.

Configuring Bootstrap using variables

Bootstrap 4 comes with opt-in flexbox support. You can enable flexbox support by switching a Boolean variable and recompiling your CSS. In this recipe you will learn how to do this.

Getting ready

As already mentioned, enabling flexbox support is as simple as switching a Boolean variable and recompiling your CSS. So, first read the *Downloading and installing Bootstrap* and the *Customizing Bootstrap using variables* recipes of this chapter. In this recipe, you also will make use of the page inspector of your browser.

There are two main ways to open the **Inspector**:

> ▸ Without an element selected: Choose the **Inspector** option from the **Web Developer** menu or the equivalent keyboard shortcut

> ▸ With an element selected: Right-click an element on a web page and select **Inspect Element**

How to do it...

You can not only use Sass variables to customize Bootstrap, you can also use some variables to configure it. The following steps will show you how to use a single Sass variable to turn the optional flexbox support on:

1. Create an `index.html` file that loads the `dist/css/bootstrap.css` file from your Bootstrap installation folder and contains the HTML code similar to what is shown here:

```
<div class="container">
  <div class="row">
```

```
<div class="col-sm-4">
  One of three columns
</div>
<div class="col-sm-4">
  One of three columns
</div>
<div class="col-sm-4">
  One of three columns
</div>
    </div>
  </div>
</div>
```

2. Load the `index.html` file from Step 1 in your browser and open the page source inspector of your browser. Select the first `<div class="col-sm-4">` element. Now find that the styles for this element look like that shown in the following screenshot:

```
.col-sm-4 ☐ {                    _grid-framework.scss:27 @(min-width: 544px)
    width: 33.3333%;
}
.col-sm-1, .col-sm-2,            _grid-framework.scss:23 @(min-width: 544px)
.col-sm-3, .col-sm-4,
.col-sm-5, .col-sm-6, .col-sm-7, .col-sm-8, .col-sm-9, .col-sm-10,
.col-sm-11, .col-sm-12 ☐ {
    float: left;
}
.col-xs-1, .col-xs-2, .col-xs-3, .col-xs-4,          bootstrap.css:null
.col-xs-5, .col-xs-6, .col-xs-7, .col-xs-8,
.col-xs-9, .col-xs-10, .col-xs-11, .col-xs-12, .col-sm-1, .col-sm-2,
.col-sm-3, .col-sm-4, .col-sm-5, .col-sm-6, .col-sm-7, .col-sm-8,
.col-sm-9, .col-sm-10, .col-sm-11, .col-sm-12, .col-md-1, .col-md-2,
.col-md-3, .col-md-4, .col-md-5, .col-md-6, .col-md-7, .col-md-8,
.col-md-9, .col-md-10, .col-md-11, .col-md-12, .col-lg-1, .col-lg-2,
.col-lg-3, .col-lg-4, .col-lg-5, .col-lg-6, .col-lg-7, .col-lg-8,
.col-lg-9, .col-lg-10, .col-lg-11, .col-lg-12, .col-xl-1, .col-xl-2,
.col-xl-3, .col-xl-4, .col-xl-5, .col-xl-6, .col-xl-7, .col-xl-8,
.col-xl-9, .col-xl-10, .col-xl-11, .col-xl-12 ☐ {
  ☑ position: relative;
  ☑ min-height: 1px;
  ☑ padding-right: 0.9375rem;
  ☑ padding-left: 0.9375rem;
}
```

3. Then, open the `_variables.scss` file in a text editor and change the value of the `$enable-flex` variable to `true`.

4. Run the following command in your console to recompile your CSS code:

grunt dist

5. Finally, reload the `index.html` file in your browser and inspect the page source again. Now you will find that your styles for the `<div class="col-sm-4">` look like that shown in the following screenshot:

```
.col-sm-4 ⬡ { bootstrap.css:null @(min-width: 544px)
  ▸ flex: 0 0 33.3333%;
}
.col-xs-1, .col-xs-2, .col-xs-3,      bootstrap.css:null
.col-xs-4, .col-xs-5, .col-xs-6,
.col-xs-7, .col-xs-8, .col-xs-9, .col-xs-10,
.col-xs-11, .col-xs-12, .col-sm-1, .col-sm-2,
.col-sm-3, .col-sm-4, .col-sm-5, .col-sm-6,
.col-sm-7, .col-sm-8, .col-sm-9, .col-sm-10,
.col-sm-11, .col-sm-12, .col-md-1, .col-md-2,
.col-md-3, .col-md-4, .col-md-5, .col-md-6,
.col-md-7, .col-md-8, .col-md-9, .col-md-10,
.col-md-11, .col-md-12, .col-lg-1, .col-lg-2,
.col-lg-3, .col-lg-4, .col-lg-5, .col-lg-6,
.col-lg-7, .col-lg-8, .col-lg-9, .col-lg-10,
.col-lg-11, .col-lg-12, .col-xl-1, .col-xl-2,
.col-xl-3, .col-xl-4, .col-xl-5, .col-xl-6,
.col-xl-7, .col-xl-8, .col-xl-9, .col-xl-10,
.col-xl-11, .col-xl-12 ⬡ {
    position: relative;
    min-height: 1px;
    padding-right: 0.9375rem;
    padding-left: 0.9375rem;
}
```

How it works...

Bootstrap comes with a responsive grid of 12 columns. By default, Bootstrap uses the CSS `float` property to arrange the elements of the grid. The CSS `float` property is a positioning property that keeps HTML elements in the flow of the document instead of applying a text wrap on them. After compiling the code, your CSS code includes an extensive set of prebuilt classes for quickly creating grid columns. In this recipe, the `col-sm-4` class has been used to create blocks that span four grid columns on the small (`sm`) grid.

There are five grid tiers, one for each responsive breakpoint: extra small (`xs`), small (`sm`), medium (`md`), large (`lg`) , and extra large (`xl`). Each of these grids, except the extra small one, is collapsed by default and becomes horizontal when viewport width passes the breakpoint. The extra small grid is always horizontal. If you do not use the extra small grid classes, the columns are stacked for screen widths below the smallest breakpoint.

Also read the *Building a grid with grid classes* and *Creating responsive grids* recipes of *Chapter 9, Building Layouts with Sass*, to find out how to create responsive grid classes. And the *Mobile-first strategies* recipe of *Chapter 7, Cross-Browser CSS3 Mixins*, explains how to use CSS media queries to create responsive websites with the mobile-first strategy.

When you enable flexbox support by switching a Boolean variable, the same grid classes as described previously are compiled into your CSS, but the grid will use the CSS Flexible box module instead of the CSS `float` property technique to arrange the elements. The cons of the flexbox layout is that it dramatically reduces the complexity of fluid grids but, on the other hand, older browsers do not support the CSS Flexible box module at all.

There's more...

In this recipe, you have learned how to configure flexbox support by switching a Boolean variable. Bootstrap 4 contains some other customization options too. Instead of relegating style embellishments such as gradients, transitions, shadows, and more, to a separate stylesheet such as Bootstrap 3, all those options move into Sass variables. The list of options declared in the `_variables.scss` file looks like that shown in the following:

```
// Options
//
// Quickly modify global styling by enabling or disabling optional
features.

$enable-flex:               false !default;
$enable-rounded:            true !default;
$enable-shadows:            false !default;
$enable-gradients:          false !default;
$enable-transitions:        false !default;
$enable-hover-media-query:  false !default;
$enable-grid-classes:       true !default;
```

Every time you change a variable in the previous code, you will have to recompile your CSS code as described in the *Customizing Bootstrap with variables* recipe of this chapter. The *Customizing Bootstrap with variables* recipe also shows you how your buttons will look when the `$enable-rounded` variables have been set to `false`.

When using Bootstrap's source Sass files, you have the option of using Sass variables and mixins to create custom, semantic, and responsive page layouts, as described in the *Implementing semantic layouts with Bootstrap* recipe of this chapter. If you are using Sass variables and mixins to create your layout, you probably do not need the grid classes described in this recipe. The `$enable-grid-classes` option enables you to set whether the grid classes should be compiled in your CSS code or not.

See also

You can find out which browsers support the Flexible box layout at `http://caniuse.com/#feat=flexbox`.

Making custom buttons

In the *Customizing Bootstrap with variables* recipe in this chapter, you can read how to change Bootstrap's buttons by setting the brand color variables. In this recipe, you will learn how to extend Bootstrap with one or more custom buttons by leveraging Sass.

Getting ready

First, read the *Downloading and installing Bootstrap* recipe of this chapter to find out how to download and install Bootstrap, enabling you to recompile the Bootstrap CSS code. You can edit the Bootstrap source files with a text editor.

How to do it...

Learn how to extend Bootstrap with custom buttons:

1. First, install Bootstrap as described in the *Downloading and installing Bootstrap* recipe of this chapter.

2. Open the `scss/bootstrap.scss` file and write the following lines of SCSS code at the end of this file:

   ```
   .btn-custom {
    @include button-variant(white, darkblue, green);
   }
   ```

3. After that, recompile Bootstrap's CSS by running the following command in your console:

   ```
   grunt dist
   ```

4. Now, you can include the newly generated CSS code into an HTML file with the following line of code:

   ```
   <link rel="stylesheet" type="text/css" href="dist/css/bootstrap.css">
   ```

5. The HTML file should also contain the following snippet of HTML code:

   ```
   <button class="btn btn-custom">Custom button</button>
   ```

6. Finally, load the HTML file from Step 4 into your browser and you will find that it looks like that shown in the following figure:

   Custom button

How it works...

Bootstrap's buttons have two CSS classes: a base class that sets the default button properties, and a second class that provides button styles, such as colors.

To add a custom button, you can generate a new style class with the `button-variant()` mixin and reuse the base class. The `button-variant()` mixin has three arguments. The first argument defines the font color, the second argument defines the background color, and the third argument defines the border color.

Bootstrap prefers the usage of base classes over the `[class^="btn-"]`, `[class*="btn-"]` attribute selectors because of performance issues in some browsers.

There's more...

In addition to the already mentioned base and style classes, Bootstrap provides size classes for the button. You can add the `.btn-lg`, `.btn-sm` or `.btn-xs` classes to your HTML code to give your button the desired size.

To use the Bootstrap button in your non-Bootstrap projects, you can use the following SCCS code:

```
@import 'variables';
@import 'mixins';
@import 'buttons';

.btn-custom {
  @extend .btn;
  @extend .btn-lg;
  @include button-variant(white, darkblue, green);
}
```

If you compile the preceding code with the Ruby Sass compiler, the autoprefixer does not run. You can save the code in the `bootstrap.scss` file and run Bootstrap's Grunt build tool to make sure the compiled CSS code supports the same browsers as Bootstrap does. In the *Implementing semantic layouts with Bootstrap* recipe of this chapter you can read how to compile only the grid classes in a separate CSS file.

Notice that the CSS code for the custom button contains lot of unused CSS code due to the `@extend` directive usages without placeholders. Read the *Using placeholder selectors with the @extend directive* and *Using the @extend directive with care* recipes of *Chapter 4, Nested Selectors and Modular CSS* to understand why the preceding happens.

And, finally, in the *Extending components using @extend* recipe of this chapter, you can find some use cases of using the `@extend` directive to extend Bootstrap.

Read the *SASS Placeholders Versus Mixins and Extends* article by Miguel Camba to learn more about writing reusable Sass code and DRY coding. Camba's article can be found at `http://miguelcamba.com/blog/2013/07/11/sass-placeholders-versus-mixins-and-extends/`.

Making custom cards

Bootstrap provides you with many CSS components to build your design. In the *Making custom buttons* recipe, you can read about the button component. In this recipe, you will learn how to use and reuse the cards component. Cards are a brand new component to Bootstrap in version 4. Cards replace **wells**, **panels**, and **thumbnails** used in earlier versions of Bootstrap.

A card is a flexible and extensible content container. It includes options for headers and footers, a wide variety of content, contextual background colors, and powerful display options.

Getting ready

First, read the *Downloading and installing Bootstrap* recipe of this chapter to find out how to download and install Bootstrap, enabling you to recompile the Bootstrap CSS code. You can edit the Bootstrap source files with a text editor.

How to do it...

Learn how to customize Bootstrap's Card component with Sass:

1. Install Bootstrap as described in the *Downloading and installing Bootstrap* recipe of this chapter.

2. Then, open the `scss/bootstrap.scss` file and write the following lines of SCSS code at the end of this file:

```
.card {
  max-width: 20rem;
}
```

3. Next, recompile Bootstrap's CSS by running the following command in your console:

```
grunt dist
```

4. Now, you can include the newly generated CSS code into an HTML file with the following line of code:

```
<link rel="stylesheet" type="text/css" href="dist/css/bootstrap.css">
```

5. The HTML file should also contain the following snippet of HTML code:

```
<div class="card text-center card-success">
  <div class="card-header">
    Featured
  </div>
  <div class="card-block">
    <h4 class="card-title">Special title treatment</h4>
    <p class="card-text">With supporting text below as a natural
lead-in to additional content.</p>
    <a href="#" class="btn btn-primary">Go somewhere</a>
  </div>
  <div class="card-footer text-muted">
    2 days ago
  </div>
</div>
```

6. Finally, load the HTML file from Steps 4 and 5 into your browser and you will find that your custom panel looks like what is shown in the following screenshot:

How it works...

The card module contains a lot of CSS classes to style your cards. The example card in this recipe shows you that you can easily add headers and footers to your cards. The content of the card can hold any HTML such as text, buttons, and images. Notice that card images take the full width of your card by default. You can make the card images fluid/responsive by adding the `.img-fluid` class to the images in your HTML. Read the *Extending components using @extend* recipe of this chapter to learn more about fluid and responsive images in bootstrap. Newer releases of Bootstrap 4 will possibly have fluid images for cards by default.

Cards include a class for quickly toggling the text color. By default, cards use dark text and assume a light background. Add the `.card-inverse` class in your HTML for white text and specify the `background-color` and `border-color` properties to go with it.

In the recipe, the `.card-success` class had been used to set the `background-color` and `border-color` properties. In accordance with Bootstrap's default colors, predefined classes for different contextual states of your cards are predefined. To create a custom state, you can simply use the following SCSS code and choose whether or not to use the `.card-inverse` class:

```scss
$variant-color: pink;

.card-#{"" + $variant-color} {
  background-color: $variant-color;
  border-color: darken($variant-color, 20%);
  @extend .card-inverse;
}
```

Notice in the preceding code that the `@extend .card-inverse;` code is optional. When extending the `.card-inverse` class, you do not explicitly have to use the `.card-inverse` class in your HTML.

The code applies string interpolation, as described in the *Interpolation of variables* recipe of the *Chapter 3, Variables, Mixins, and Functions*. Notice the `"" + $variant-color` notation, which forces the string value of the variable being used, otherwise the `pink` value compiles into the `#ffc0cb` color value.

There's more...

Bootstrap also has special predefined classes to group cards. You can use the `.card-group` class to render cards as a single, attached element with equal width and height columns. Notice that the `.card-group` class uses the `display: table;` and `table-layout: fixed;` declarations to uniformly group the cards unless the optional flexbox has been enabled. You should use the `border-spacing, border-collapse` CSS properties instead of the `margin` property to create space between the cards, for instance, as follows:

```scss
.card-group {
  border-spacing: 30px;
  border-collapse: separate;
}
```

With flexbox enabled you can create space between the cards by using the `margin` property, your SCSS code may look like that shown in the following:

```scss
.card-group {
  @if $enable-flex {
    padding: 15px;
    .card {
      margin: 15px;
    }
  }
  @else {
    border-spacing: 30px;
    border-collapse: separate;
  }
}
```

Instead of the previous code to create space between the cards, you can also use the `.card-deck-wrapper` and `.card-deck` classes in your HTML. These classes already group cards with equal width and height that are not attached to one another.

Finally, the `.card-columns` class can be used to group cards into Masonry-like columns. The Masonry structure only needs CSS and does not require any JavaScript.

See also

▸ A complete list of Bootstrap's components can be found at `http://getbootstrap.com/components/`

▸ Read more about Masonry layouts at `http://masonry.desandro.com/`

Making custom navbars

The navigation bar, or navbar for short, is an important component used in many Bootstrap projects. In this recipe, you can read how to modify the navbar leveraging Sass.

Getting ready

First, read the *Downloading and installing Bootstrap* recipe of this chapter to find out how to download and install Bootstrap, enabling you to recompile the Bootstrap CSS code. You can edit the Bootstrap source files with a text editor.

How to do it...

The navbar component is an important part of Bootstrap used in many situation. The following steps will help you to customize it for your own needs and requirements:

1. First, install Bootstrap as described in the *Downloading and installing Bootstrap* recipe of this chapter.

2. Then, create an `index.html` file that contains the HTML code like that shown in the following:

```html
<!doctype html>
<html lang="en">
<head>
  <meta charset="utf-8">

  <title>Making Custom Navbars</title>
  <meta name="description" content="Making Custom Navbars">
  <meta name="author" content="Bass Jobsen">
  <link rel="stylesheet" type="text/css" href="bootstrap-4/dist/css/bootstrap.css">
  <script src="https://ajax.googleapis.com/ajax/libs/jquery/2.1.4/jquery.min.js"></script>
  <script src="bootstrap-4/dist/js/bootstrap.js"></script>
</head>
<body>

<nav class="navbar navbar-dark bg-faded">
  <a class="navbar-brand" href="#">Navbar</a>
  <ul class="nav navbar-nav">
    <li class="nav-item active">
      <a class="nav-link" href="#">Home <span class="sr-only">(current)</span></a>
    </li>
    <li class="nav-item">
      <a class="nav-link" href="#">Features</a>
    </li>
    <li class="nav-item">
      <a class="nav-link" href="#">Pricing</a>
    </li>
    <li class="nav-item">
      <a class="nav-link" href="#">About</a>
    </li>
  </ul>
```

```
<form class="form-inline navbar-form pull-right">
  <input class="form-control" type="text" placeholder="Search">
  <button class="btn btn-success-outline" type="submit">Search</
button>
  </form>
</nav>

</body>
</html>
```

3. Open the `scss/bootstrap.scss` file and write the following lines of SCSS code at the end of this file:

    ```
    .navbar {
      background-color: black;
    }
    ```

4. Then, recompile Bootstrap's CSS by running the following command in your console:

    grunt dist

5. Finally, open the `index.html` file in your browser and find that your navbar looks like that shown in the following screenshot:

How it works...

You can set the color of your navbar by using Bootstrap's contextual backgrounds or otherwise simply set the `background-color` property.

To ensure that the color of the background has enough contrast with the color of the navigation links and text, you can add the CSS `.navbar-dark` or `.navbar-light` class to your HTML.

You can also use a gradient background by using the SCSS code like that shown in the following:

```
.navbar {
  @include gradient-vertical-three-colors;
}
```

There's more...

The navbar can act responsive too, meaning it can have stacked links for small screens and horizontal links for wider screens. You can use the following HTML code with predefined CSS classes to create a responsive navbar:

```html
<nav class="navbar navbar-light bg-faded">
  <button class="navbar-toggler hidden-sm-up" type="button" data-
toggle="collapse" data-target="#exCollapsingNavbar2">
    &#9776;
  </button>
  <div class="collapse navbar-toggleable-xs" id="exCollapsingNavbar2">
    <a class="navbar-brand" href="#">Responsive navbar</a>
    <ul class="nav navbar-nav">
      <li class="nav-item active">
        <a class="nav-link" href="#">Home <span class="sr-
only">(current)</span></a>
      </li>
      <li class="nav-item">
        <a class="nav-link" href="#">Features</a>
      </li>
      <li class="nav-item">
        <a class="nav-link" href="#">Pricing</a>
      </li>
      <li class="nav-item">
        <a class="nav-link" href="#">About</a>
      </li>
    </ul>
  </div>
</nav>
```

The toggle button is hidden for screens wider than the `xs` breakpoint at 544 pixels by the `.hidden-sm-up` class. The breakpoint for the navbar itself is set by the `.navbar-toggleable-xs` class. Collapsing of the navbar requires the JavaScript Collapse plugin.

Responsive breakpoints are also available via Sass mixins. The following mixin can be used to write CSS rules, which are only available for screens wider than the `xs` breakpoint:

```scss
@include media-breakpoint-up(xs) { ... }
```

Use the following Sass mixin for the other direction:

```scss
@include media-breakpoint-down(xs) { ... }
```

The `.hidden-sm-up` class is part of Bootstrap's responsive utility classes. You can use these classes for showing and hiding content by device via media queries. Sass mixins for the responsive utility classes are not available yet. You can use the mixins for responsive breakpoints together with other utility mixins to do the same. The styles of the `.hidden-sm-up` can also be produced with the following SCSS code:

```
@include media-breakpoint-up(sm) {
  .hidden-sm-up {
    visibility: hidden;
  }
}
```

Notice that in the previous toggle, only the `visibility` of an element, meaning the `display` property, is not modified and the element can still affect the flow of the document.

You cannot `@extend` the `.invisible` class in the preceding code because you may not `@extend` an outer selector from within `@media`.

See also

▸ Read more about Bootstrap's navbar component at `http://getbootstrap.com/components/navbar/`

▸ Bootstrap's responsive breakpoints are described at `http://getbootstrap.com/layout/overview/#responsive-breakpoints/`

▸ Finally, read more about Bootstrap's responsive utility classes at `http://getbootstrap.com/layout/responsive-utilities/`

Extending components using @extend

You can read more about the `@extend` directive in the *Utilizing the @extend directive* recipe of *Chapter 4, Nested Selectors and Modular CSS*. In this recipe, you will see how to use this directive to make all images in your Bootstrap project responsive by default.

Getting ready

You can edit the Bootstrap source Sass files with a text editor. You also have to install Bootstrap and learn how to recompile it. Read the *Downloading and installing Bootstrap* recipe of this chapter to find out how to install Bootstrap and recompile the Bootstrap CSS code.

How to do it...

In Bootstrap 4, images can be made responsive by adding the `.img-fluid` to the `img` tag in your HTML. You can use the following steps to make your images responsive by default:

1. Before you start, install Bootstrap as described in the *Downloading and installing Bootstrap* recipe of this chapter.

2. Then, open the `scss/bootstrap.scss` file and write the following lines of SCSS code at the end of this file:

    ```scss
    img {
      @extend .img-fluid;
    }
    ```

3. Recompile Bootstrap by running the following command in the console:

    ```
    grunt dist
    ```

4. The compiled CSS code for the `img` selector will look like that shown in the following:

    ```css
    .img-fluid, .figure > img, .carousel-inner > .carousel-item > img,
    .carousel-inner > .carousel-item > a > img, img {
      display: block;
      max-width: 100%;
      height: auto;
    }
    ```

How it works...

Bootstrap has got a special class that makes images responsive. Responsive in this case means that you set the width property of the image to 100%. All images will get the size of their parent. The max-width property is set to 100% too; this prevents small images scaling up to a larger size than the original size. The `.img-fluid` class can easily be applied on the `img` selector leveraging the `@extend` directive. You can read more about extending selectors in the *Utilizing the @extend directive* recipe of *Chapter 4, Nested Selectors and Modular CSS*.

When inspecting the preceding compiled CSS, you will find that the `display` property of the `img` selector has been set to `block`. Block-level elements occupy the entire space of its parent element, which seems the desired behavior for responsive images. When you wrap your images inside the p elements, where `display: inline-block` seems to fit better, you should consider making your image not responsive by default at all, or try the following SCSS code:

```scss
p img {
display: inline-block;
}
```

There's more...

In the *Making Custom Cards* recipe of this chapter, you can read how to make the card images responsive by adding the `.img-fluid` class in your HTML code.

Now you will understand that you can make the card images responsive by default by adding the following SCSS code at the end of Bootstrap's SCSS code:

```
.card > img {
    @extend .img-fluid;
}
```

Instead of the `@extend` directive, you can also use the `img-fluid` mixin. When using the `img-fluid` mixin, your SCSS should look like that shown in the following:

```
.card > img {
    @include img-fluid();
}
```

Using mixins instead of extends will generate more CSS code in most cases, but will keep the code better organized. For small mixins, which set a small number of properties, the extra generated code will be limited.

> *"@extend can be messy. My advice would be to avoid it when possible and use mixins instead, because at the end of the day, it makes absolutely no difference."*

> – *Hugo Giraudel*

Both previous examples use the child > selector. Bootstrap tries to avoid the > child selectors for simpler styling via un-nested classes.

Finally, you will have noticed that you cannot easily extend all Bootstrap components. Bootstrap components are intended to use with CSS classes in your HTML code.

Consider the SCSS code that is shown here:

```
.parent .btn {
  color: white;
}

.btn {
  color: blue;
}

button {
    @extend .btn;
}
```

When compiling the preceding SCSS code into CSS code, you will find that it will contain the following selector:

```
.parent .btn, .parent button {
  color: white; }
```

In most cases, your custom HTML will not have defined the .parent .button structure. Also, read the *Utilizing the @extend directive* recipe of *Chapter 4, Nested Selectors and Modular CSS,* to learn more about how to use the @extend directive.

Using the @extend directive does not require the class to be compiled already. Try to compile the code like that shown in the following:

```
.class2 {
@extend .class1;
}
.class1 {
property: extended;
}
.class3 {
@extend .class1;
}
```

The preceding SCSS code compiles into the CSS code like that shown in the following. As you can see, the .class2 class can extend the .class1 class, though the .class2 class has been declared before the .class1 class:

```
.class1, .class2, .class3 {
  property: extended; }
```

See also

- ▶ Read Hugo Giraudel's article about avoiding Sass @extend. You can find this article at http://www.sitepoint.com/avoid-sass-extend/
- ▶ You can read more about inline versus block level in HTML at https://developer.mozilla.org/en-US/docs/Web/HTML/Inline_elemente#Inline_vs._block-level
- ▶ W3C recommendations for the content of the p HTML element can be found at http://www.w3.org/TR/html-markup/p.html

Using Bootstrap mixins and classes

Although Bootstrap is a complete CSS framework, you can use some of its components for other non-Bootstrap projects. In this recipe, you will see how to reuse Bootstrap's pagination.

Other examples of reusing Bootstrap's code can be found in other recipes of this book. In the *There's more...* section of this recipe, you can read how to create a clearfix. The mixin for this clearfix can be found in the `mixins/_clearfix.scss` file, which is included in Bootstrap's source files.

Both the *There's more...* section of the *Creating grids with semantic.gs* recipe in *Chapter 9, Building Layouts with Sass* and the *Implementing semantic layouts with Bootstrap* recipe of this chapter describe how to use Bootstrap's grid mixins to build a semantic grid. Also, other recipes in this chapter describe how to use the grid, button, or card components of Bootstrap for your projects.

Getting ready

Of course, you should read the *Downloading and installing Bootstrap* recipe of this chapter first. In this recipe, you will edit the files of Bootstrap's Grunt build system. You can edit these files with any text editor.

How to do it...

Before you start, install Bootstrap as described in the *Downloading and installing Bootstrap* recipe of this chapter:

1. Create a new `scss/bootstrap-pagination.scss` file and write the following lines of SCSS code at the end of this file:

   ```scss
   // Core variables and mixins
   @import "variables";
   @import "mixins";
   @import "pagination";

   footer > ul {
     @extend .pagination;
     @include pagination-size(10px, 10px, 3em, 10px, 5px);
   }
   ```

2. Open the `Gruntfile.js` file and change the sass-compile task so that it will also compile the files of the `sass::extra` subtask, as follows:

   ```js
   grunt.registerTask('sass-compile', ['sass:core', 'sass:extras',
   'sass:docs']);
   ```

3. After that, open the `grunt/bs-sass-compile/libsass.js` file, or the `sass.js` file if you are using Ruby Sass. Add the file from Step 2 to the `sass::extra` subtask, it should look like that shown in the following:

```
extras: {
        files: {
            'dist/css/<%= pkg.name %>-flex.css': 'scss/<%= pkg.name
%>-flex.scss',
            'dist/css/<%= pkg.name %>-grid.css': 'scss/<%= pkg.name
%>-grid.scss',
            'dist/css/<%= pkg.name %>-reboot.css': 'scss/<%= pkg.
name %>-reboot.scss',
            'dist/css/<%= pkg.name %>-pagination.css': 'scss/<%=
pkg.name %>-pagination.scss'
        }
    }
```

4. Now build Bootstrap by running the following command in the console:

   grunt dist

5. Step 4 will also create a new `dist/css/bootstrap-pagnation.css` CSS file. Load this CSS file in an `index.html` file, using the following line of HTML code:

```
<link rel="stylesheet" type="text/css" href="bootstrap-4/dist/css/
bootstrap-pagination.css">
```

6. The `index.html` file from Step 5 should contain the HTML code like that shown in the following:

```
<footer>
    <ul class="pagination">
        <li><a href="#">&laquo;</a></li>
        <li><a href="#">1</a></li>
        <li><a href="#">2</a></li>
        <li><a href="#">3</a></li>
        <li><a href="#">4</a></li>
        <li><a href="#">5</a></li>
        <li><a href="#">&raquo;</a></li>
    </ul>
</footer>
```

7. Finally, load the `index.html` file in your browser and you will find that the results will look like that shown in the following figure:

How it works...

Bootstrap uses the files in the `scss` directory to compile the CSS classes for the framework. The mixins to build these classes can be found in the `scss/mixins` directory. The `_mixins.scss file` includes the mixins into the project. When building a custom version of Bootstrap, you can comment out the mixins you do not use in the `_mixins.scss` file. Not all Bootstrap mixins are suitable for reuse without the corresponding CSS classes.

In this recipe, you used the `pagination-size()` mixin, which can be found in the `scss/mixins/pagination.scss` file. Without the `.pagination` class, the `pagination-size()` mixin makes no sense. On the other hand, you can use the `.pagination` class without the `pagination-size()` mixin. In this recipe, you combined both the `.pagination` class and the `pagination-size()` mixin into the `footer > ul` selector. Notice that the `.pagination` class has been extended with the `@extend` directive as also described in the *Extending components using @extend* recipe.

The `pagination-size()` mixin has to be called with five parameters: the first two parameters set the padding, the third parameter sets the font size, the fourth parameter sets the line height, and the fifth parameter sets the border radius of the first and last element of the navigation.

The SCSS code used for this recipe imports the `mixins.scss` file, and so all files in the `scss/mixins` directory, where you expected that only importing the `scss/mixins/_pagination.scss` would be sufficient. The `pagination-size()` mixin also makes use of the `border-left-radius()` and `border-right-radius()` mixins, which are defined in the `mixinins/_border-radius.scss` file. Importing all these files from the `mixins` folder guarantees that the mixins from other files are also available. Mixins do not generate output in the compiled CSS till they are called.

Also, the complete `_variables.scss` file was imported. The variables in this file gave default colors to Bootstrap's pagination. If you inspect the Sass code in the `_variables.scss` file, you will find that all the colors for the pagination are prefixed with `$pagination`, as can also be seen in the following SCSS code from the `_variables.scss` file:

```
// Pagination

$pagination-padding-x:          .75rem !default;
$pagination-padding-y:          .5rem !default;
$pagination-padding-x-sm:       .75rem !default;
$pagination-padding-y-sm:       .275rem !default;
$pagination-padding-x-lg:       1.5rem !default;
$pagination-padding-y-lg:       .75rem !default;
```

```
$pagination-color:                    $link-color !default;
$pagination-bg:                       #fff !default;
$pagination-border:                   #ddd !default;

$pagination-hover-color:              $link-hover-color !default;
$pagination-hover-bg:                 $gray-lighter !default;
$pagination-hover-border:             #ddd !default;

$pagination-active-color:             #fff !default;
$pagination-active-bg:                $brand-primary !default;
$pagination-active-border:            $brand-primary !default;

$pagination-disabled-color:           $gray-light !default;
$pagination-disabled-bg:              #fff !default;
$pagination-disabled-border:          #ddd !default;
```

You can change these variables or declare them at the beginning of the `bootstrap-pagination.scss`, so that they fit your needs.

There's more...

A `clearfix` method is a way for HTML elements to automatically clear themselves without additional markup. The clearfix properties are frequently used in layouts with floated elements. Bootstrap uses the micro clearfix hack by Nicolas Gallagh.

Bootstrap's Sass code enables you to use the clearfix code in two different ways. Firstly, the clearfix code is used as a mixin in Sass to clearfix elements of your layout. The code that compiles the `.row` class of the grid uses the `clearfix()` mixin as follows:

```
@mixin make-row($gutter: $grid-gutter-width) {
  @if $enable-flex {
    display: flex;
    flex-wrap: wrap;
  } @else {
    @include clearfix();
  }
  margin-left:  ($gutter / -2);
  margin-right: ($gutter / -2);
}
```

Secondly, a .clearfix class is compiled into the CSS code, which enables you to add a class="clearfix" attribute to your HTML elements. Notice also that the clearfix class is compiled by using the clearfix() mixin. The SCSS code for the .clearfix class, in the _utilities.scss partial file, looks like that shown in the following:

```scss
.clearfix {
  @include clearfix();
}
```

Bootstrap prefers to use mixins instead of extends for more portable code. The preceding SCSS code can also be written as follows:

```scss
.clearfix {
  @extend .clearfix;
}
```

The previous code will only work if the .clearfix class has been compiled already.

When you are using the flexbox layout with enabled, see also the *Configuring Bootstrap using variables* recipe of this chapter, you do not need a clearfix at all.

See also

▸ Read about how to configure tasks for your project using a Grunt file at http://gruntjs.com/configuring-tasks

▸ More information about Nicolas Gallagher's Micro clearfix can be found at http://nicolasgallagher.com/micro-clearfix-hack/

Extending the mixins with your own mixins

You can easily extend Bootstrap with your own mixins. In this recipe, you will see how to do this.

Getting ready

Install Bootstrap as described the *Downloading and installing Bootstrap* recipe of this chapter. You can use a text editor to edit the SCSS code. In the *There's more...* section of this recipe, the Sass version of Dan Eden's Animate.css will be used.

How to do it...

Perform the following steps:

1. Before you start, install Bootstrap as described in the *Downloading and installing Bootstrap* recipe of this chapter.

2. Create a Sass partial file called `_figures.scss` and write the following SCSS code into this file:

```scss
@mixin figures() {
  article {
    figure {
      @include center-block();
      > img {
        @include img-fluid();
      }

      @include media-breakpoint-up(md) {
        max-width:50%;
        @include pull-right();
      }
    }
    @include clearfix();
  }
}

#maincontent {
  @include figures();
}
```

3. Then, open the `scss/bootstrap.scss` file and add the following line of code at the end of this file:

```scss
@import "figures";
```

4. Now, recompile Bootstrap by running the following command in your console:

`grunt dist`

5. Create an `index.html` file that loads the compiled stylesheet from the `/dist/css/boostrap.css` file and contains the following snippet of HTML code:

```html
<div id="maincontent">
    <article>
        <figure><img src="http://dummyimage.com/16:9x1080"></figure>
        <p>Lorem ipsum dolor sit amet, consectetuer adipiscing elit.
```

```
        Aenean commodo ligula eget dolor. Aenean massa. Cum sociis
    natoque
        penatibus et magnis dis</p>
    </article>
</div>
```

6. Finally, load the `index.html` file into your browser to inspect the results. Resize your browser window to see the effect of the media query.

How it works...

In this recipe, you wrote your own mixins, which leverage Bootstrap's variables and mixins. If you change the `$grid-breakpoints` variable for the project, not only does the behavior of the Bootstrap code change, but the effect of the custom `figures()` mixin is also adopted.

The `$grid-breakpoints` variable is declared in the file as follows:

```
$grid-breakpoints: (
  // Extra small screen / phone
  xs: 0,
  // Small screen / phone
  sm: 544px,
  // Medium screen / tablet
  md: 768px,
  // Large screen / desktop
  lg: 992px,
  // Extra large screen / wide desktop
  xl: 1200px
) !default;
```

The previous `$grid-breakpoints` variable is used by the `media-breakpoint-up()` mixin.

Also, the `center-block()`, `img-fluid()` and `clearfix()` mixins of Bootstrap are reused in the custom code.

There's more...

Instead of using your own custom mixins, you can also extend Bootstrap with mixins of other libraries. **Animate.css** is a bunch of cool, fun, and cross-browser animations for you to use in your projects written by Dan Eden.

You can download a Sass version of Animate.css at `https://github.com/tgdev/animate-sass`. Or install with bower by running the following command:

```
bower install animate-sass
```

Simply import into your main Sass stylesheet (the `scss/bootstrap.scss` file), as follows:

```
@import "animate-sass/animate";
```

Now you can recompile you CSS code and use, for instance, the following HTML snippet in your project:

```
<div class="animated fadeIn">
        <p>Watch me fade in!</p>
</div>
```

You can also use the helper mixins of **animate-scss** as follows:

```
body {
    -webkit-backface-visibility: hidden; // Addresses a small issue in
webkit: http://bit.ly/NEdoDq
}
.animated {
    @include animate-prefixer(animation-duration, $base-duration);
    @include animate-prefixer(animation-fill-mode, both);

    &.hinge {
        @include animate-prefixer(animation-duration, $base-duration *
2);
    }
}
```

Notice that the `animate-prefixer()` mixin call also adds a vendor prefixer, while the autoprefixer of Bootstrap's build chain does the same. For the reason given previously, you can consider rewriting the `animate-prefixer()` mixin, found in the `/helpers/_mixins.scss` file, as follows, and use the autoprefixer to set the required prefixes according to Bootstrap's defaults:

```
@mixin animate-prefixer($property, $value...) {
    #{$property}: unquote('#{$value}');
}
```

See also

▸ Read more about Bootstrap's responsive breakpoints at `http://getbootstrap.com/layout/overview/#responsive-breakpoints/`

▸ You can find Animate.css at `http://daneden.github.io/animate.css/`

Implementing semantic layouts with Bootstrap

Bootstrap 4 has a 12-column grid and predefined grid classes by default. You can also use the grid mixins to apply the grid on selectors without predefined classes to generate more semantic CSS for individual grid columns. In this recipe you will learn how to use these grid mixins.

Getting ready

In this recipe, you will rebuild the layout from the *Applying the grid on your design* recipe of *Chapter 9, Building Layouts with Sass*, using Bootstrap 4. Other ways to implement the same layout with Sass can be found in the *Mobile first and responsive grids* recipe of *Chapter 10, Building Grid-based Layouts with Susy and Sass*, the *Creating semantic grids with Foundation* recipe of *Chapter 11, Foundation and Sass*, and the *Semantic grids with Neat* recipe of *Chapter 13, Meeting The Bourbon Family*.

Read the *Downloading and installing Bootstrap* recipe of this chapter; you will need it for the first step of this recipe.

How to do it...

For this recipe you should perform the following steps:

1. Install Bootstrap as described in the *Downloading and installing Bootstrap* recipe of this chapter.

2. Edit the `bootstrap.scss` file and write down the following SCSS code at the end of it:

    ```scss
    // colors
    $header-background-color: black;
    $header-font-color: white;
    $blocks-background-color: darkgreen;
    $blocks-font-color: white;

    header {
      @include make-row;
      @include make-col;
      @include make-col-span(12);
      background-color: $header-background-color;
      color: $header-font-color;
    }
    ```

```
#main {
  @include make-row;
  section {
    @include make-col;
    @include make-col-span(9);
  }

  aside {
    @include make-col;
    @include make-col-span(3);
  }
}
```

3. Recompile Bootstrap by running the following command in your console:

    grunt dist

4. The index.html file of your project should contain the following HTML code:

```
<div class="container">
    <header>
    <h1>Powered by Bootstrap 4</h1>
    </header>


    <!-- Main Body -->
    <div id="main">
        <section>
        <ul class="blocks">
        <li>1</li>
        <li>2</li>
        <li>3</li>
        <li>4</li>
        <li>5</li>
        <li>6</li>
        <li>7</li>
        <li>8</li>
        <li>9</li>
        </ul>
        </section>

        <aside>
        <h2>Sidebar</h2>
        <nav>
        <ul>
        <li>Item 1</li>
```

```
            <li>Item 2</li>
            <li>Item 3</li>
            </ul>
            </nav>
            </aside>
        </div>

    </div>
```

5. Load the `index.html` file from Step 4 in your browser and you will find that it should look like that shown in the following screenshot:

6. As can be seen in the figure in Step 5, the list in the main section is still unstyled. Open the `bootstrap.scss` file again and write down the following SCSS code at the end of it:

```scss
.blocks {
  @include make-row;
  padding: 0;
  li {
    @include make-col;
    @include make-col-span(4);
    background-color: $blocks-background-color;
    border: 2px solid;
    color: $blocks-font-color;
    font-size: 3em;
    height: 75px;
    list-style-type: none;
    padding: 10px;
  }
}
```

7. After recompiling your CSS and reloading the `index.html` file, the result should look like that shown in the following screenshot:

How it works...

In this recipe, you use the grid mixins of Bootstrap to build a semantic grid. Notice that the semantic layout still requires the `.container` wrapper. Containers are the most basic layout element in Bootstrap. The `.container` class sets the `max-width` property, which changes for each breakpoint. You can also with the `.container-fluid` class for a `100%` width all the time. Bootstrap allows you to nest `.container` classes.

Sass mixins for the container are available too. Take a look at the following SCSS code:

```scss
.container {
  @include make-container();
  @include make-container-max-widths();
}
```

The `make-container()` mixin creates a fluid container and the `make-container-max-widths()` mixin overrides it and sets the `max-width` properties for each breakpoint.

Bootstrap also supports an optional flexbox grid. You can simply enable the flexbox grid by setting the `$enable-flex` variable to `true`, as described in the *Configuring Bootstrap using variables* recipe of this chapter. You do not have to change your HTML code when switching between the default and flexbox grids.

There's more...

Whoever uses Bootstrap's Sass grid mixins for creating layouts does not need the predefined grid classes. The `$enable-grid-classes` variable enables you to compile Bootstrap's CSS code without predefined grid classes.

The source code of Bootstrap also contains a `scss/bootstrap-grid.scss` file; you can compile this file to create the CSS code for only the grid. You can use this CSS code in any project. Notice that Bootstrap requires the `box-sizing` property or CSS Box model set to the border-box model. Read more about the CSS Box model in the *Building a grid with grid classes* recipe of *Chapter 9, Building Layouts with Sass*. You can also use Bootstrap Reboot to set the CSS Box model to the border-box model. Reboot is an HTML reset module based on **Normalize.css**. It gives you more resets, including `box-sizing: border-box` and margin tweaks. You can create your own copy of Reboot by compiling the `scss/bootstrap-reboot.scss` file. Also read the *Using a CSS Reset* recipe of *Chapter 9, Building Layouts with Sass*, to learn more about CSS Resets.

See also

Read more about the Sass mixins for the grid at `http://getbootstrap.com/layout/grid/#sass-mixins`.

Using WordPress with Bootstrap and Sass

WordPress is one of the most popular Content Management Systems (CMS) on the web. Although it is originally a blog system, more than 60 million websites are driven by WordPress now. In this recipe, you will learn how to use WordPress together with Bootstrap and Sass.

Getting ready

You will need a running webserver with PHP and MySQL to run WordPress. WampServer is a Windows web development environment, which can be found at `http://www.wampserver.com/en/`. Or try AMPPS for Windows, OS and Linux; you can find it at `http://ampps.com/`. Also read the *Using the Sass-gulp plugin with Gulp* recipe of *Chapter 1, Getting Started with Sass,* to learn how to install Node.js, which includes npm, on your system. The JBST4 theme used in this recipe is a fork of the JointsWP theme discussed in the *Using Foundation 6 with WordPress and Sass* recipe of *Chapter 11, Foundation and Sass*.

How to do it...

The following steps will show you how to set up a WordPress theme with Bootstrap 4:

1. Download the JBST4 theme at `https://github.com/bassjobsen/jbst-4-sass/archive/master.zip` and unzip it in the `wordpress/wp-contents/themes` folder of your WordPress installation.
2. Activate the theme in the WordPress Dashboard.

3. Navigate to the `wordpress/wp-contents/themes/jbst-4-sass-master` folder and run the following commands in your console to compile the CSS code for the theme:

```
npm install
```

```
gulp
```

4. Now your WordPress website should look like that shown in the following image:

5. Now you can edit both the `_main.scss` and `_variables.scss` files to create new and modified style rules with Sass (SCSS) for your WordPress site. Run the `gulp` command after your changes.

How it works...

The Bootstrap source files are installed with Bower. The file imports the Bootstrap SCSS code from the `bower` folder. All Bootstrap variables are declared with `!default` in a single file. Because the local `_variables.scss` file was imported before Bootstrap's code, you can easily overwrite Bootstrap's variables in it.

Bootstrap 4 got an optional flexbox grid; you can enable it by setting the `$enable-flex` variable to `true` in the local `_variables.scss` file. The Gulp build process also runs the autoprefixer to add the required vendor prefixes. The autoprefixer is required to compile Bootstrap's CSS code. Read more about the autoprefixer in the *Automatically prefixing your code with Grunt* recipe of *Chapter 16, Setting up a Build Chain with Grunt*.

Bootstrap also requires JavaScript. The Gulp build process of theme compiles and loads Bootstrap's JavaScript modules into the theme too.

There's more...

Both Bootstrap and WordPress use many predefined CSS classes for styling. The preceding means that you will have to change the output of WordPress to fit Bootstrap CSS classes or use Bootstrap's SCSS code to compile CSS classes for WordPress.

The theme applies to both strategies mentioned previously. The HTML code navigation bar of the theme contains Bootstrap's CSS classes of the navbar component. The file in the theme folder contains PHP code, which extends and overwrites WordPress PHP classes for navigation. The PHP implementation is beyond the scope of this book.

To use Bootstrap's SCSS code to compile CSS classes for WordPress, you should reuse Bootstrap's mixins or extend its classes by using the Sass @extend feature as described in the *Utilizing the @extend directive* recipe of *Chapter 4, Nested Selectors and Modular CSS*.

Read the *Using Bootstrap mixins and classes* recipe of this chapter to find out how to reuse Bootstrap's mixins. The _main.scss file will give you some examples of extending Bootstrap classes to fit the WordPress HTML code.

The following SCSS code shows you how to apply the buttons styling of Bootstrap on the HTML buttons in the theme using the @extend directive:

```scss
// form buttons
.form-submit {
    .button {
        @extend .btn;
        @extend .btn-primary;
    }
}
```

Notice that Bootstrap does not have a mixin to create the button styles, so you will have to use the @extend feature. Using the @extend directive means that the compiled CSS code contains some unused CSS classes. Also read the *Extending components using @extend* recipe of this chapter.

See also

- ▶ The *Famous 5-Minute Install* for WordPress can be found at https://codex.wordpress.org/Installing_WordPress#Famous_5-Minute_Install

- ▶ Read more about theme development for WordPress at https://codex.wordpress.org/Theme_Development

- ▶ Also read my blog post about Bootstrap 4 and WordPress at http://bassjobsen.weblogs.fm/bootstrap-4-and-wordpress

13
Meeting the Bourbon Family

In this chapter, you will learn the following topics:

- ▶ Bourbon mixins for prefixing
- ▶ Creating visual triangles
- ▶ Using modular scales for typefacing
- ▶ Semantic grids with Neat
- ▶ Creating buttons with Bitters
- ▶ Using the page navigation component from Refills

Introduction

Bourbon is a simple and lightweight mixin library for Sass; it helps you to write CSS faster and easier, without the need for using vendor prefixes. Bourbon is maintained by the design team at Thoughtbot. From the same team, there's also Neat. Neat is a lightweight semantic grid framework for Sass with Bourbon. Finally, there are components and patterns built with Bourbon and Neat called Bitters. They can be used to scaffold styles, variables, and structure for Bourbon projects. In this chapter, you will learn how to use these libraries of the Bourbon family for your Sass projects.

Some example code in the recipes in this chapter import a CSS Reset, as described in the *Using a CSS Reset* recipe of *Chapter 9, Building Layouts with Sass*. The following declaration in SCSS code is used to do this:

```scss
@import 'base/normalize';
```

Bourbon mixins for prefixing

The **Bourbon** mixin library for Sass helps you to code faster without vendor prefixes. This recipe will show you how to use this library. This recipe will show you how to use Bourbon to create **CSS animations**. These animations make it possible to animate transitions from one CSS style configuration to another. Animations consist of two components: a style describing the CSS animation, and a set of keyframes that indicate the start and end states of the animation's style, as well as possible intermediate waypoints. The W3C CSS specifications for CSS animations has not stabilized till now, so you will have to use vendor prefixes for full browser support. Also, read the *Using vendor prefixes* recipe of *Chapter 7, Cross Browser CSS3 Mixins* to understand why vendor prefixes are needed.

Getting ready

You will have to install Bourbon. You can use the Bourbon Ruby gem as described here; alternatively, you can download the SCSS from GitHub. Using Ruby gems also requires having Ruby installed on your system; read the *Installing Sass for command line usage* recipe of *Chapter 1, Getting Started with Sass* to learn more about Ruby and Ruby gems.

Run the following command in your console to install Bourbon:

```
gem install bourbon
```

The preceding code installs the Ruby Gem for Bourbon. The Ruby Gem sets up a Ruby script, which can run as an executable from the command line.

Now you can install the Bourbon library into the current directory by running the following command in your console:

```
bourbon install
```

How to do it...

Learn how to prefix your CSS code with Bourbon by performing the following steps:

1. Install Bourbon as described in the preceding section and create the file and directory structure as shown in the following screenshot:

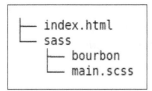

2. The `sass/main.scss` file should contain the SCSS code as shown in the following:

```scss
@import ''bourbon/bourbon'';

$circle-color: #8fdce5;
$circle-color-light: lighten($circle-color, 20%);
$circle-color-dark: darken($circle-color, 20%);

.box {
  @include background-image(linear-gradient($circle-color-light,
$circle-color-dark));
  border: 1px solid $circle-color;
  border-radius: 40px;
  box-shadow: inset 0 1px 0 rgba(255, 255, 255, .45);
  height: 40px;
  width: 40px;

  section:hover & {
    // Animation shorthand works the same as the CSS3 animation
shorthand
    @include animation(scale 2s ease infinite, slide 2s ease
infinite);
    position: relative;
  }
}

@include keyframes(scale) {
  0%, 100% {
    @include transform(scale(1));
  }

  50% {
    @include transform(scale(2));
  }
}

@include keyframes(slide) {
  0%, 100% {
    left: 0;
  }

  50% {
    left: 100px;
  }
}
```

3. Then run the following command in your console:

```
sass sass/main.scss main.css
```

4. Finally, create a index.html file, which contains the following HTML code, and inspect the results in your browser:

```
<section>
    <div class=""box""></"div>
</section>
```

How it works...

In the CSS code of this recipe, you will find some mixin calls instead of property declaration. These mixins output the properties, including all vendor prefixes. The background-image() mixins also automatically sets a fall back color. Note that lineair-gradient() is a function and not a mixin.

Instead of the animation() shorthand mixin, you can also use the independent and granular mixins, as shown in the SCSS code here:

```
@include animation-name(scale, slide);
@include animation-duration(2s);
@include animation-timing-function(ease);
@include animation-iteration-count(infinite);
```

You can also nest the animation mixins, as can be seen in the declarations for the keyframes of the scale animation. These declarations look as follows:

```
@include keyframes(scale) {
  0%, 100% {
    @include transform(scale(1));
  }

  50% {
    @include transform(scale(2));
  }
}
```

The nesting of the section:hover & {} selector definition in the .box class selector uses the parent reference to revert the selector order, as described in the *Using the & operator to change the selector order* recipe of *Chapter 4, Nested Selectors and Modular CSS*.

There's more

One of the big cons of the Bourbon library is the ability to write a single-line declaration for properties that requires vendor prefixes. Bourbon supports a fixed set of browsers and other methods for auto prefixing, such as Compass, as described in *Chapter 6, Using Compass*, and **autoprefixer**, as described in the *Automatically prefixing your code with Grunt* recipe in *Chapter 16, Setting up a Build Chain with Grunt*, do have more options to customize which browsers to support. Bourbon allows you to disable some prefixes by setting variables to false at the top of your style sheet. These variables can be found in the list here:

```
$prefix-for-webkit:     true;
$prefix-for-mozilla:    true;
$prefix-for-microsoft:  true;
$prefix-for-opera:      true;
$prefix-for-spec:       true;
```

The preceding variables enable vendor prefixes for all mixins. When disabling a vendor prefix, you cannot be sure which browser version will be affected, because the need of a prefix depends on the property and not the browser version. Using all possible prefixes, on the other hand, means that your code contains some unused prefixes and more bytes than needed.

Not all Bourbon mixins are for only vendor prefixing. Consider, for instance, the Border Radius (Shorthand) mixins; these mixins provide a shorthand syntax to target and add border radii to both corners on one side of a box. See the following SCSS code:

```
.element {
@include border-top-radius(5px);
}
```

The preceding code compiles into the CSS code, as shown here:

```
.element {
  border-top-left-radius: 5px;
  border-top-right-radius: 5px;
}
```

Another example of a Bourbon mixin not for prefixing can be found in the *Creating visual triangles* recipe of this chapter.

To integrate Bourbon into your build chain with `node-sass`, you have to set the `includePath` option, as described in the *Integrating Bourbon in the build chain* recipe of *Chapter 16, Setting up a Build Chain with Grunt*.

See also

▸ Thoughtbot is a group of expert designers and developers. They design, build, and grow products for iOS, Android, and the web. The official website of Thoughtbot can be found at `https://thoughtbot.com`.

▸ Read more about using CSS animations at `https://developer.mozilla.org/en-US/docs/Web/CSS/CSS_Animations/Using_CSS_animations`.

Creating visual triangles

You can create triangles with pure CSS, and you can use these triangles to create a triangular pointer for tooltips or other components of your project. In this recipe, you will learn how to use Bourbon to create tooltips with triangular pointers for your projects.

Getting ready

Make sure that you have installed Bourbon already, as described in the *Bourbon mixins for prefixing* recipe of this chapter.

How to do it...

The following steps help you to understand how to create pure CSS triangles with the Bourbon library:

1. After installing Bourbon, you should create the file and directory structure as shown in the following screenshot:

```
├── index.html
└── sass
    ├── bourbon
    └── main.scss
```

2. The `sass/main.scss` file should contain the SCSS code, as shown here:

```scss
@import 'bourbon/bourbon';

$tooltip-backgroundcolor: #ffffa5;
$tooltip-color: #000;
$tooltip-height: 4em;
$tooltip-width: 8em;
```

```scss
.tooltip {
  background-color: $tooltip-backgroundcolor;
  height: $tooltip-height;
  position: relative;
  width: $tooltip-width;

  h2 {
    color: $tooltip-color;
    line-height: $tooltip-height / 2;
    padding: .2em .5em;
  }

  &::after {
    @include triangle($tooltip-height ($tooltip-height / 2),
$tooltip-backgroundcolor, right);
    content: '';
    display: block;
    left: $tooltip-width;
    position: absolute;
    top: 0;
  }
}
```

3. Then, run the following command in your console:

   sass sass/main.scss main.css

4. Finally, create an `index.html` file, which contains the following HTML code, and inspect the results in your browser:

   ```html
   <div class="tooltip"><h2>Tooltip</h2></div>
   ```

When inspecting the results in your browser, you will find something that will look like the following image:

Tooltip

How it works...

CSS triangles are created by HTML elements having borders and no content. When the border thickness is half the size of the element, an element with four borders may appear as shown in the following screenshot:

Now, give only one border background color and set the `background-color` of the other three borders to `transparent`. This results in a triangle, as shown in the following screenshot:

The triangle mixin helps you to generate the CSS code for the preceding step based on parameters. The triangle mixin accepts three arguments: `$size`, `$color`, and `$direction`. Both the `$size` and `$color` arguments may have two values. The `$size` element can take a width and height value, and the `$color` argument can take a value for the foreground and background colors. The `$direction` can be set to `up`, `down`, `left`, `right`, `up-right`, `up-left`, `down-right`, or `down-left`.

There's more

In this recipe, the `::after` pseudo element had been used to display the triangle. The `::before` and `::after` pseudo elements are often used to add additional content to an element using the `content` property. The `content` property is inline by default. Using the pseudo element to create the CSS triangle with the Bourbon mixins is not required. You can also apply the `triangle()` mixin on element selector, but doing that requires extra HTML elements in your HTML documents too.

- An animation to explain CSS triangles can be found at `http://codepen.io/chriscoyier/pen/lotjh`.

- The `::before` pseudo element has been explained in a clear manner at `https://developer.mozilla.org/en-US/docs/Web/CSS/%3A%3Abefore`.

Using modular scales for typefacing

The term **modular scale** refers to a series of harmonious values that relate to one another in a meaningful way. A modular scale helps you to create visual harmony in the whole design. A number of the scales are used to set font sizes, line heights, margins, and even grid sizes in your design. In this recipe, you will learn how to apply a modular scale for your designs using Bourbon.

Getting ready

In this recipe, you will create a modular scale with the modular scale function of Bourbon. To use this function, you should install Bourbon first. The *Bourbon mixins for prefixing* recipe of this chapter describes how to install Bourbon. You can read more about Sass functions in *Chapter 5, Built-in Functions*, of this book. Of course, you should also have Sass installed as described in *Chapter 1, Getting Started with Sass*.

How to do it...

Learn more about modular scales for your designs when performing the following steps:

1. Firstly, install Bourbon and create a file and directory structure like that shown here:

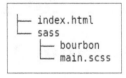

```
├── index.html
└── sass
    ├── bourbon
    └── main.scss
```

2. Now, open the `sass/main.scss` file with your text editor and write the following SCSS code into it:

```scss
@import 'bourbon/bourbon';

h1 {
  font-size: modular-scale(4, 1em 6.250em, $golden);
}
```

```
h2 {
  font-size: modular-scale(3, 1em 6.250em, $golden);
}


h3 {
  font-size: modular-scale(2, 1em 6.250em, $golden);
}


h4 {
  font-size: modular-scale(1, 1em 6.250em, $golden);
}


p {
  font-size: modular-scale(0, 1em 6.250em, $golden);
}
```

3. Then, edit the `index.html` file. This HTML file should contain the following snippet. of HTML code:

```
<h1>Heading 1</h1>
<h2>Heading 2</h2>
<h3>Heading 3</h3>
<h4>Heading 4</h4>
<p>Paragraph</p>
```

4. Compile your Sass code by running the following command in your console:

    `sass sass/main.scss main.css`

5. Finally, open the `index.html` file in your browser, and you will find that the result looks like the following figure:

Heading 1

Heading 2

Heading 3

Heading 4

Paragraph

How it works...

The `modular-scale()` function of Bourbon increments up or down a defined scale, then returns an adjusted value. It accepts three arguments: the first argument sets the increment number, the second argument sets the base value, and the third argument sets the scale.

In this recipe, the scale has been set with the golden ratio, which is approximately `1.618`. When building a scale with the golden ratio for a base value of `1em` (the equivalent of `16px`), you will get the values shown in the table, as follows:

```
1em
1em * 1.618 = 1.618em
1.618em * 1.618 = 2.618em
2.618em * 1.618 = 4.236em
4.236em * 1.618 = 6.854em
```

Using the preceding values, your SCSS code could be shown as the following:

```
h1 {font-size: 6.854em; }
h2 {font-size: 4.236em; }
h3 {font-size: 2.618em; }
h4 {font-size: 1.618em; }
p {font-size: 1em;}
```

As you can see, the size of the `h1` seems to be too large due to the scale. You can solve this option by adding a second base value (dimension) to the scale. In the recipe, a second base value of `6.250em` (equivalent of `100px`) has been used. With a base value of `6.250em` and the golden ration, you can construct a scale like the one shown, as follows:

```
6.250em / 1.618 = 3.863em
3.863em / 1.618 = 2.387em
2.387em / 1.618 = 1.476em
1.476em / 1.618 = 0.912em
```

Now, you can combine both scales to get a double-stranded scale. Using the double-stranded scale, your SCSS code should look as shown here:

```
h1 {font-size: 2.618em;    }
h2 {font-size:  2.387em; }
h3 {font-size: 1.618em; }
h4 {font-size: 1.476em; }
p {font-size: 1em;}
```

There's more

The golden ratio, which is approximately `1.618`, has a special meaning because it describes the ratio between the sides of a golden rectangle. The golden rectangle is considered aesthetically pleasing.

The following figure and text is from Wikipedia:

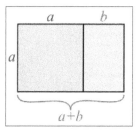

A golden rectangle (the smallest rectangle in the preceding figure, with longer side a and shorter side b) when placed adjacent to a square with sides of length a, will produce a similar golden rectangle with longer side a + b and shorter side a. This illustrates the relationship:

$$\frac{a+b}{a} = \frac{a}{b} \equiv 1.618$$

The golden ratio should play an important role in aesthetics, architecture, painting, book design, design, and nature.

You do not have to use the golden ratio for your scales. Bourbon ships with a list of predefined variables for scales.

See also

▶ A calculator to build modular scales can be found at `http://www.modularscale.com/`

▶ Read more about the golden rectangle and ratio at Wikipedia. Visit `https://en.wikipedia.org/wiki/Golden_rectangle`

Semantic grids with Neat

Neat is an open source semantic grid framework built on top of Sass and Bourbon. In this recipe, you will discover how to build semantic layouts with Neat.

Getting ready

To start, you will have to install Neat. It requires both Sass and Bourbon. In *Chapter 1, Getting Started with Sass* of this book, you can read how to install Sass, and installing Bourbon has been described in the *Bourbon mixins for prefixing* recipe of this chapter already. After installing Sass and Bourbon, you can install Neat by running the following command in your console:

```
gem install neat
```

Finally, run the following command in your project's `sass` directory to copy the Neat files into the `neat` directory:

```
neat install
```

In this recipe, you will rebuild the layout you have built already in the *Applying the grid on your design* recipe of *Chapter 9, Building Layouts with Sass*, and the *Defining containers and columns* recipe of *Chapter 10, Building Grid-Based Layouts with Susy and Sass*, and the *Implementing semantic layouts* recipe of *Chapter 12, Bootstrap and Sass*.

How to do it...

Neat can help you to create semantic grids. Perform the following steps to find out how to do this:

1. First, install Neat and Bourbon and create the file and directory structure as shown in the following screenshot:

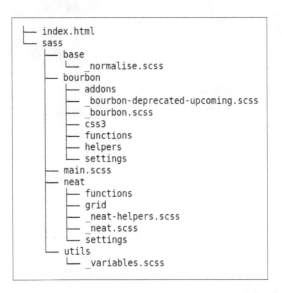

2. Then write down the following SCSS code in the `main.scss` file:

```scss
@import 'utils/variables';
@import 'base/normalize'';
@import 'bourbon/bourbon';
@import 'neat/neat';

body {
  @include outer-container;
}

header {
  @include span-columns(12);
  background-color: $header-background-color;
  color: $header-font-color;
}

section {
  @include span-columns(9);
}

aside {
  @include span-columns(3);
}
```

3. After that, you should create the `index.html` file, which contains the HTML code for your design. This file should contain the HTML markup code, as shown here:

```html
<header>
<h1>Powered by Neat</h1>
</header>

<!-- Main Body -->
    <section>
        <ul class="blocks">
            <li>1</li>
            <li>2</li>
            <li>3</li>
            <li>4</li>
            <li>5</li>
            <li>6</li>
            <li>7</li>
            <li>8</li>
            <li>9</li>
        </ul>
    </section>

    <aside>
```

```
<h2>Sidebar</h2>
<nav>
    <ul>
        <li>Item 1</li>
        <li>Item 2</li>
        <li>Item 3</li>
    </ul>
</nav>
</aside>
```

4. Now, you should compile the Sass code into CSS by running the following command in your console:

   sass sass/main.scss main.css

5. Make sure that the `index.html` file from step 4 links the `main.css` file you created in the previous step. The `head` section should contain the following line of HTML code:

   ```
   <link rel="stylesheet" type="text/css" href="main.css" />
   ```

6. Finally, load the `index.html` file and the result should look as shown in the following screenshot:

How it works...

In this recipe, the `outer-container` mixin was applied on the `body` element of your HTML code, which means your HTML does not have to contain a unnecessary element to hold your grid.

In the `main.scss` file, the columns span for the HTML elements of your layout is set by calling the `span-columns()` mixin. The `span-columns()` mixin is called with the number of columns the element should span.

The element should span 3 of 12 columns, so the SCSS code should be as shown here:

```
aside {
  @include span-columns(3);
}
```

There's more

When you compare the result of the recipe with that from the *Applying the grid on your design* recipe of *Chapter 9, Building Layouts with Sass*, you will find that the list in the main content area is not styled.

The following steps show you how to style the list element in the main content area so that it looks like the blocks from the *Applying the grid on your design* recipe.

First, create a file called `elements/_blocks.scss`. This file should contain the following SCSS code:

```scss
.blocks {
  padding: 0;

  li {
    @include span-columns(3 of 9);
    @include omega(3n);
    background-color: $blocks-background-color;
    border: 2px solid;
    color: $blocks-font-color;
    font-size: 3em;
    height: 100px;
    list-style-type: none;
    padding: 10px;
  }
}
```

Finally, add the `elements/_block.scss` file to the `@import` declaration at the beginning of the `main.scss` file. You should import the `_block.scss` file after importing Bourbon and Neat.

Recompile your CSS code and find that the result in your browser looks as shown in the following screenshot:

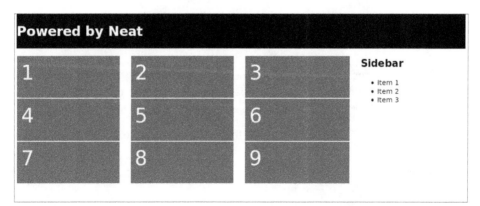

Because the block elements are nested inside the main section elements, which span nine columns of the grid, each block element should span three of the available nine columns. In Neat, you can do this using the mixins again, as follows:

```
@include span-columns(3 of 9);
```

The preceding means that each block element spans 3 of 9 columns of the 12 column grid. The Neat grid has gutters constructed with a right margin; the last column got no margin. When changing the number of columns, you can remove the gutter of the last element with the omega() mixin. It removes the element's gutter margin, regardless of its position in the grid hierarchy or display property. You can use nth-child selectors as a parameter for the omega() mixin. In the preceding code, the margin of every third element is removed using the following mixin call:

```
@include omega(3n);
```

See also

▶ More about Neat can be found at http://neat.bourbon.io/.

▶ Also, check out the example page, which explains the grid mixins in a clear manner. You can find this example page at http://neat.bourbon.io/examples.

▶ More information about nth-child selectors can be found at https://css-tricks.com/how-nth-child-works/.

Creating buttons with Bitters

Bitters scaffolds styles, variables, and structure for Bourbon projects. In this recipe, you will see how to use Bitters to style the buttons for your Bourbon projects.

Getting ready

Of course, you will have to install Ruby Sass as described in *Chapter 1, Getting started with Sass,* of this book. You also have to install Bourbon and Bitters. Run the following commands in your console to install Bourbon and Bitters:

gem install bourbon

gem install bitters

Note that *Chapter 1, Getting Started with Sass,* of this book also describes how to install Ruby and Ruby gems.

How to do it...

Perform the following steps to style your buttons with Bitters:

1. Create the file and directory structure, as shown in the following:

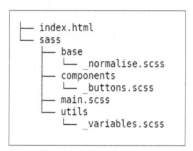

2. Navigate to the `sass` directory and run the following commands to copy the Bourbon and Bitters files:

```
bourbon install
bitters install --path=bitters
```

3. Now, edit the `sass/main.scss` file and write down the following SCSS code in it:

```
''
@import ''base/normalize'';
@import ''bourbon/bourbon'';
@import ''bitters/base/variables'';
@import ''bitters/base/buttons'';
```

4. You should compile the Sass code into CSS by running the following command in your console:

`sass sass/main.scss main.css`

5. Then, add the following HTML snippet into the `index.html` file:

```
<button>Button</button>
<input type=""submit"" value=""Submit"">
```

6. Finally, load `index.html` in your browser, and your buttons should look as shown in the following figure:

How it works...

You can find the Sass code for the styling of the buttons in the `bitters/base/_buttons.scss` partial file. The styles are wrapped in the following selector:

```
#{$all-buttons} {}
```

The preceding code creates a list of selectors using variable interpolation as described in the *Interpolation of variables* recipe of *Chapter 3, Variables, mixins, and functions*. The `$all-buttons` variable has been declared in the `bourbon/addons/_buttons.scss` partial file as follows:

```
$buttons-list:  'button',
                'input[type="button"]',
                'input[type="reset"]',
                'input[type="submit"]';

$all-buttons:         assign-inputs($buttons-list);
```

The color of the buttons is set by the `$action-color` variable, and it has been declared in the `bitters/base/_variables.scss` partial file. With the preceding information, you should understand that the order of the imports in the third step does matter.

Also note the `--path=bitters` option had been set when installing Bitters. It copies the files into the `base` directory by default. The structure created in the first step does already contain a `base` directory, so you have to install the Bitter files into a different directory.

There's more...

As you have already read, you can change the color of your buttons by changing or redeclaring the `$action-color` variable. Changing this variable will change the color of all your buttons. Some of your projects possibly require buttons of different colors. Also, refer to the *Making custom buttons* recipe of *Chapter 12, Bootstrap and Sass*, which shows you how to create button variants with Bootstrap.

To create button variants with Bitters, you can create a new `components/_buttons.scss` partial file, which contains the following SCSS code:

```
@mixin button-variant($color, $font-color: #fff) {
  background-color: $color;
  color: $font-color;

  &:hover,
  &:focus {
    background-color: shade($color, 20%);
    color: $font-color;
```

```scss
    }

    &:disabled {
      &:hover {
        background-color: $color;
      }
    }
  }

  .button-red {
    @include button-variant(#f00);
  }
  .button-green {
    @include button-variant(#0f0, #000);
  }
  .button-blue {
    @include button-variant(#00f);
  }
```

Import the `components/_buttons.scss` partial file after Bitters in your `sass/main.scss` project file and recompile your CSS code.

Now you can use the HTML code as shown beneath:

```html
<button class="button-red">Button</button>
<button class="button-green">Button</button>
<button class="button-blue">Button</button>
```

In your browser, the buttons should look as shown in the following figure:

See also

Read more about Bitters at `http://bitters.bourbon.io/`.

Using the page navigation component from Refills

Bourbon Refills are the components and patterns built with Bourbon and Neat. You can use these components and patterns by simply copying and pasting them from the Refills website into your Sass code.

Getting ready

Install Ruby Sass as described in *Chapter 1, Getting Started with Sass*, of this book. Then install Bourbon and Neat by running the following commands in your console:

```
gem install bourbon
```

```
gem install neat
```

Note that *Chapter 1, Getting started with Sass*, of this book also describes how to install Ruby and Ruby gems.

How to do it...

Most websites require a page navigation. The following steps will show you how to build a page navigation with ease by using the pattern from the Refills website:

1. Create the file and directory structure as shown in the following diagram:

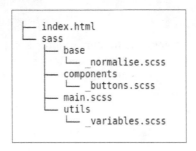

```
├── index.html
└── sass
    ├── base
    │   └── _normalise.scss
    ├── components
    │   └── _buttons.scss
    ├── main.scss
    └── utils
        └── _variables.scss
```

2. Navigate to the `sass` directory and run the following commands to copy the Bourbon and Neat files into your stylesheets directory:

```
bourbon install
```

```
neat install
```

3. Now, edit the `sass/main.scss` so that it contains the following SCSS code:

```
@import 'utils/variables';
@import 'base/normalise';
@import 'bourbon/bourbon';
@import 'neat/neat';
@import 'components/pagination';
```

4. Navigate your browser to `http://refills.bourbon.io/components/` and find the pagination component. Then, click on **Show Code** under the component and copy paste the code.

5. Copy paste the SCSS code from the fourth step into the `components/_pagination.scss` partial file.

6. Copy-paste the HTML code from the fourth step into the `index.html` file.

7. Compile your SCSS code by running the following command in your console:

```
sass sass/main.scss main.css
```

8. Finally, load the `index.html` in your browser and you will find that you have a page navigation now, which looks as shown in the following screenshot:

How it works...

The Refills website contains code snippets for components and patterns built with Bourbon and Neat, which you can simply copy paste into your Sass projects. The snippets require both Bourbon and Neat. Some components require **jQuery** too. You can download or load jQuery from **content delivery network** (**CDN**).

There's more

When using Bourbon and Neat in a Ruby on Rails app, you can also add components and patterns via Rake tasks. Read more about Ruby on Rails and Sass in *Chapter 14, Ruby on Rails and Sass* of this book.

See also

▶ The Refills website can be found at `http://refills.bourbon.io/`.

▶ You can find jQuery at `http://jquery.com/`. It is a fast, small, and feature-rich JavaScript library.

14

Ruby on Rails and Sass

In this chapter, you will learn the following topics:

- ▶ Hello world with Ruby on Rails
- ▶ Explaining the `main.css.scss` file
- ▶ Adding Compass to your Ruby on Rails setup
- ▶ Using Susy with Ruby on Rails
- ▶ Using Bourbon inside Rails
- ▶ Integrating Bootstrap
- ▶ Creating an RoR app with Foundation 6

Introduction

Ruby on Rails, or simply Rails, is a web application framework written in Ruby under MIT license. Rails 3.1 introduced Sass as the standard CSS preprocessor. In this chapter, you will learn how to build web applications with Rails and Sass. You do not have to create all your Sass (SCSS) from scratch because you can integrate other frameworks and libraries into your work flow.

In this chapter, you can read how to add Compass, Bourbon, Bootstrap, Susy, and Foundation on your Rails setup.

You can perform the recipes in the chapter without having any prior experience with Rails.

In this chapter, Ruby Gems are used to integrate CSS and mixins frameworks into your Ruby on Rails applications. These Gems can also be used with Compass; also read the *Maintaining your applications with Compass* and *Using Bootstrap with Compass* recipes of *Chapter 6, Using Compass*. You require the library in your `config.rb` file as follows:

```
require '{library}';
```

Hello world with Ruby on Rails

In this recipe, you will learn how to create a simple web application using **Ruby on Rails** (**RoR**). You can repeat the instruction in this recipe when building the other recipes in this chapter.

Getting ready

Rails is a web application development framework written in the Ruby language. So, you need to have some prerequisites installed; you should install both the Ruby language and the **RubyGems** packaging system. Read the *Installing Sass for command line usage* recipe of *Chapter 1, Getting started with Sass* or visit `https://www.ruby-lang.org/en/documentation/installation/` to find out how to install Ruby and RubyGems.

How to do it...

Learn how to set up a Ruby on Rails app by performing the following steps:

1. After installing Ruby and RubyGems, you can run the following command in your console to install Rails:

   ```
   gem install rails
   ```

2. Now, you create a new RoR web application by running the following command in your console:

   ```
   rails new recipe1
   ```

3. The command from the previous step installs all required files, including the Rails tools to run your application. After changing to the `recipe1` directory, you can start a web server on your developing machine to view your application by running the following command:

   ```
   bin/rails server
   ```

4. The preceding command not only compiles your Sass and JavaScript code but also starts a web server on port `3000`. Point your browser to `http://localhost:3000/` to find your application up and running. Now, your application should look like the following screenshot:

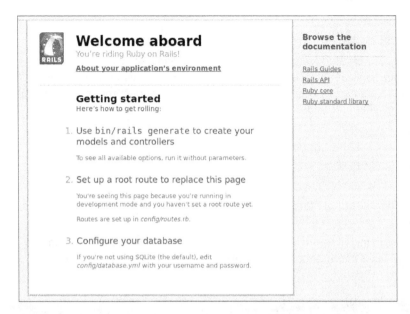

5. You will need to run the `controller` generator in order to create a new controller and tell it that you want a controller called `welcome` with an action called `index`, with the following command:

```
bin/rails generate controller welcome index
```

6. Now, you can change the view by editing the file located at `app/views/welcome/index.html.erb`. Write the following HTML code into it:

```
<h1>Hello World!!</h1>
<p>Find me in app/views/welcome/index.html.erb</p>
```

7. Point your browser to `http://localhost:3000/welcome/index.html` and you will find that the page should look like that shown in the screenshot here:

Hello World!!

Find me in app/views/welcome/index.html.erb

How it works...

When you created the controller and view in the fifth step, `app/assets/stylesheets/welcome.scss` was also automatically generated. When you add some SCSS into this file, it will be compiled into `../css/welcome.css` and included in your `index` action. Read the *Explaining the main.css.scss file* recipe of this chapter for a better understanding of using Sass in your RoR applications.

There's more...

In this recipe, you created a controller and view; you can also use this view for the root (home) of your application. Open the `config/routes.rb` file in your text editor and add the following line of domain-specific language to this file to connect the root of your site to the `welcome` controller and `index` action:

```
root 'welcome#index'
```

See also

  ▶ Read the *Getting Started with Rails* guide at `http://guides.rubyonrails.org/getting_started.html`

  ▶ You can install **Rack::LiveReload** to enable Live reload when developing your RoR app. More information can be found at `https://github.com/johnbintz/rack-livereload`

Explaining the main.css.scss file

The Ruby on Rails setup compiles all the `.scss` files into CSS by default. In this recipe, you will learn how to organize your Sass files for code reuse and meeting the **Don't Repeat Yourself** (**DRY**) methodology.

Getting ready

Read the *Hello world with Ruby on Rails* recipe of this chapter to find out how to setup a Ruby on Rails web application.

How to do it...

The following step demonstrate you how to organize the Sass files of your RoR app to develop your CSS code DRY:

1. Repeat all the steps of the *Hello world with Ruby on Rails* recipe or copy the `recipe1` folder to the `recipe2` folder.

2. Then rename the `app/assets/stylesheets/application.css` file to `app/assets/stylesheets/application.scss`.

3. Remove the content of the `app/assets/stylesheets/application.scss` file and write the following line of SCSS code into it:

    ```scss
    @import 'headers';
    ```

4. Create a new partial file called `app/assets/stylesheets/_headers.scss` and write down the SCSS code shown here into it:

```
h1 {
  color: #f00; //red;
}
```

5. Now, start the web server by running the command and you will find that the `Hello World` text is colored red.

How it works...

When you start a new Rails application by running the rails new command, an `app/assets/stylesheets/application.css` file is created by default. Other files with the `.scss` extension in the `app/assets/stylesheets/` folder are compiled into CSS and imported in the `application.css` file. RoR does not use the Sass `@import` directive to import the Sass files. Files are included in the main file after running the Sass compiler. The preceding means that the reuse of variables and mixins is not possible by default. Note that RoR also compiles your partials into CSS and ignores the "_" prefix.

When you rename the `application.css` file as `application.scss` and remove the lines shown in that file, it will cause only the other files include in the compiled CSS, to be compiled into CSS.

Start with an empty `application.scss` file and use the `@import` directive to import Sass code from other files. Read the *Working with partials* recipe of *Chapter 1, Getting started with Sass* and the *Applying the OOCSS, SMACSS, and BEM methodologies* recipe of *Chapter 4, Nested Selectors and Modular CSS*, to read more about **OOCSS**, **SMACSS**, **BEM**, and other strategies and methodologies to help you to create modular, reusable, and maintainable CSS code.

There's more...

RubyGems for frameworks such as Compass and Bootstrap are available. When you install these gems, you can also `@import` the framework's SCSS code. Read the other recipes of this chapter to find out how to employ these gems for your RoR projects.

See also

Read *7 must have Development Gems to install on every project* at `http://www.rubyonrails365.com/7-must-have-gems-to-install-on-any-project/`.

Adding Compass to your Ruby on Rails setup

Compass is a Sass library with prebuilt functions and mixins. In this recipe, you will learn how to use Compass for your RoR applications.

Getting ready

Read *Chapter 6, Using Compass*, of this book to learn more about Compass and also read the *Hello world with Ruby on Rails* recipe of this chapter to find out how to set up a RoR web application.

How to do it...

Learn how to add Compass to your RoR set up:

1. Create a new Rails app by running the following command in your console:

   ```
   rails new recipe3
   ```

2. Run, as already described in the *Hello world with Ruby on Rails* recipe, the `controller` generator and tell it that you want a controller called `welcome` with an action called `index`, using the following command:

   ```
   bin/rails generate controller welcome index
   ```

3. Then add the `compass-rails` gem line to your application's Gemfile, as follows:

   ```
   gem 'compass-rails'
   ```

4. Don't forget to run the `bundle` command in your console after the previous step.

5. Change your `application.css` file to `application.scss`, as described in the *Explaining the main.css.scss file* recipe of this chapter, and write down the following SCSS code from the Compass gradient example into it:

   ```scss
   @import "compass";

   .ex {
     width: 48%;
     margin-right: 2%;
     float: left;
     @include clearfix;
     p {
       padding-top: 10px;
     }
   }

   .gradient-example {
     width: 80px;
   ```

```
    height: 80px;
    background: red;
    float: left;
    margin: 1em 1em 0 0;
}


// This will yield a radial gradient with an apparent specular
highlight
#radial-gradient {
    @include background-image(radial-gradient(45px 45px, cyan 10px,
dodgerblue 30px));
}
```

6. Finally, write the following HTML code into the `app/views/welcome/index.html.erb` file:

```
<div class='ex'>
    <div class='gradient-example' id='radial-gradient'></div>
    <p>
        This will yield a radial gradient with an apparent specular
highlight
    </p>
</div>
```

7. Start a web server by running the `bin/rails server` command in your console and point your browser to `http://localhost:3000/welcome/index.html`. The result should look like the following screenshot:

 This will yield a radial gradient with an apparent specular highlight

How it works...

You can `@import` the Compass function and mixins into your main `application.scss` file due to the compass-rails Gem.

There's more...

Other frameworks such as Susy may require Compass. Read the *Using Susy with Ruby on Rails* recipe of this chapter to find out how to use both Susy and Compass in your RoR applications.

Compass adds vendor prefixes to the compiled CSS code by default, read the *Tuning vendor prefixes from Compass stylesheets* recipe of *Chapter 6, Using Compass* to learn how to configure Compass cross browser by Sass.

See also

▶ Compass rails is an adapter for the Compass Stylesheet Authoring Framework for Ruby on Rails. You can read more about the Gem at `https://github.com/Compass/compass-rails`

▶ You can find the Compass background gradient examples at `http://compass-style.org/examples/compass/css3/gradient/`

Using Susy with Ruby on Rails

Susy is a Sass add-on for grids recommended by Compass. You can read more about Susy in *Chapter 10, Building grid-based layouts with Susy and Sass* chapter of this book.

Getting ready

To demonstrate the Susy grid in the RoR app, the SCSS and HTML code of the *Defining containers and columns* recipe of *Chapter 10, Building grid-based layouts with Susy and Sass*, will be used again.

 Rails 4.1 and below include a version of sass-rails, which does not support Sass 3.3 by default. Susy 2 requires `Sass >= 3.3`. So in order to use Susy 2 with Rails, you must update your Gem file to use `sass-rails ~> 5.0.0`.

How to do it...

After performing the followings step you will know how to use the Susy add-on for Compass to create a grid-based layout for your RoR app:

1. Create a new Rails app by running the following command in your console:

   `rails new recipe4`

2. Run, as already described in the *Hello world with Ruby on Rails* recipe, the "controller" generator and tell it that you want a controller called "welcome" with an action called "index", just like this:

   `bin/rails generate controller welcome index`

3. Then, add the compass-rails gem line to your application's Gemfile as follows and run the he `bundle` command afterwards:

   `gem 'susy'`

4. Remove the `app/assets/stylesheets/application.css` file.

5. Copy the Sass files from the `sass` folder of the *Defining containers and columns* recipe of *Chapter 10, Building Grid-Based Layouts with Susy and Sass*, into the `app/assets/stylesheets/Rails` folder.

6. Rename the `app/assets/stylesheets/main.scss` file to `app/assets/stylesheets/application.scss`.

7. You should end up with the following file and folder structure:

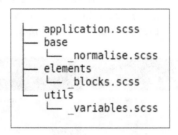

```
├── application.scss
├── base
│   └── _normalise.scss
├── elements
│   └── _blocks.scss
└── utils
    └── _variables.scss
```

8. No change to the preceding files is required.

9. Now, you can edit the `views/welcome/index.html.erb` file created in the second step. Write the following HTML into this file:

```
<header>
<h1>Powered by Susy</h1>
</header>

<!-- Main Body -->
    <section>
        <ul class="blocks">
            <li>1</li>
            <li>2</li>
            <li>3</li>
            <li>4</li>
            <li>5</li>
            <li>6</li>
            <li>7</li>
            <li>8</li>
            <li>9</li>
        </ul>
    </section>

    <aside>
    <h2>Sidebar</h2>
    <nav>
        <ul>
```

```
            <li>Item 1</li>
            <li>Item 2</li>
            <li>Item 3</li>
        </ul>
    </nav>
    </aside>
```

10. Start a web server by running the `bin/rails server` command in your console; point your browser to `http://localhost:3000/welcome/index.html` and you will find that the result looks like the following screenshot:

How it works...

As you can see, using Susy in your RoR app is really simple. In the *Installing and configuring Susy* recipe of *Chapter 10, Building grid-based layouts with Susy and Sass*, you can read more about Susy's Sass settings declared in the `utils/_variables.scss` file; note that you should import this partial file before Susy. The imports in the `application.scss` file should look like the following:

```
@import 'utils/variables';
@import 'base/normalise';
@import 'susy';
@import 'elements/blocks';
```

There's more...

You can use Susy together with Compass by adding the following gem line to your Gemfile and running the `bundle` command:

```
gem 'compass-rails'
```

Susy's mixins already add vendor prefixes for modern browsers; you cannot configure these prefixes.

See also

▶ Susy is a toolkit for building layouts of all types with a simple, natural syntax. You can find the Susy Ruby Gem at `https://rubygems.org/gems/susy/versions/2.2.5`

▶ Learn more about Susy at `http://susy.oddbird.net/`

Using Bourbon inside Rails

Bourbon is a lightweight mixin library for Sass. You can read more about Bourbon in *Chapter 13, Meeting the Bourbon family* of this book, this chapter also explains the other members of the Bourbon family. Neat is a lightweight semantic grid framework for Sass and Bourbon. Bitters can be used to declare variables and structure for your Bourbon projects. Finally, Refills is a library with prebuilt patterns and components built with Bourbon, Neat, and Bitters. In this recipe, you will learn how to use the Bourbon family to develop RoR web applications.

Getting ready

First read *Chapter 13, Meeting the Bourbon family*, of this book to learn more about the Bourbon family. Also read the *Hello world with Ruby on Rails* recipe to understand how to setup a new RoR web application.

How to do it...

The following steps demonstrate how to use Bourbon inside Rails:

1. Create a new Rails app by running the following command in your console:

   ```
   rails new recipe5
   ```

2. Change directory to the new `recipe5` directory. Run, as already described in the *Hello world with Ruby on Rails* recipe, the `controller` generator and tell it you want a controller called `welcome` with an action called `index`, just like this:

   ```
   bin/rails generate controller welcome index
   ```

3. Then add the Bourbon gems to your application's Gemfile as follows and run the `bundle` command afterwards:

   ```
   gem 'bourbon'
   gem 'neat'
   gem 'refills', group: :development
   ```

4. Now, you can install the Refill-centered navigation snippet by running the following command in your console:

```
rails generate refills:import centered-navigation
```

5. The command in the previous step creates the three files here:

```
app/views/refills/_centered_navigation.html.erb
app/assets/stylesheets/refills/_centered-navigation.scss
app/assets/javascripts/refills/centered_navigation.js
```

6. Then, rename the `app/assets/stylesheets/application.css` file to `app/assets/stylesheets/application.scss` and write down the SCSS code shown here:

```
@import 'bourbon';
@import 'neat';
@import 'refills/centered-navigation';
```

7. You also will have to edit your view. Open the `app/views/welcome/index.html.erb` file with your favorite text editor. Write down the following code snippet into it:

```
<%= render partial: "refills/centered_navigation" %>
```

8. Finally, run the `bin/rails server` command in your console, point your browser to `http://localhost:3000/welcome/index.html`, and you will find that the page contains the centered navigation which look like that shown in the following screenshot:

How it works...

The refills Gem enables you to automatically generate the partials for the code snippets. It generates not only the Sass code but also HTML partials and the required JavaScript code. You have to integrate the partials into your app structure as described in the recipe.

The following command lists all available snippets in your console:

```
rails generate refills:list
```

Of course, you can also use the snippets from the Refills website and not use the Refills Gem at all, as already described in the *Using the page navigation component from Refills* recipe of *Chapter 13*, *Meeting The Bourbon family*.

Each Refills snippet contains some variables for easy configuration. You can find these variables at the beginning of the file `app/assets/stylesheets/refills/_centered-navigation.scss`. Note that not all these variables are declared with the `!default` value; see also the *Declaring variables with !default* recipe of *Chapter 3*, *Variables, Mixins, and Functions*, so you cannot overwrite them in the `application.scss` file. You will have to edit these variables in the `_centered-navigation.scss` file directly.

There's more...

The `app/assets/javascripts/refills/centered_navigation.js` file is automatically included in the HTML page by Rails.

See also

- ▶ The Refills Gem can be found at `https://github.com/thoughtbot/refills`
- ▶ The Refills website can be found at `http://refills.bourbon.io/`
- ▶ Read more about using HTML templates or partials in Ruby on Rails at `http://guides.rubyonrails.org/layouts_and_rendering.html#using-partials`

Integrating Bootstrap

Bootstrap is an HTML, CSS, and JS framework for developing responsive, mobile-first projects on the web. Bootstrap 4 is built with Sass. In this recipe, you will learn how to use Bootstrap when developing Ruby on Rails web applications.

Getting ready

You can read more about Bootstrap 4 in *Chapter 12*, *Bootstrap and Sass*, of this book. Note that the code in this recipe uses the alpha release of Bootstrap 4. You should not use alpha or beta releases for production. The final release of Bootstrap 4 may differ from the alpha release.

How to do it...

Integrate Bootstrap into your RoR app by performing the following steps:

1. Repeat the steps of the *Hello world with Ruby on Rails* recipe of this chapter to create a new RoR app; also, create a controller called `welcome` with an action called `index`.

2. Then, add the Bootstrap and Autoprefixer gems to your application's Gemfile as follows and run the `bundle` command afterwards:

```
gem 'bootstrap', '~> 4.0.0.alpha3'
gem "autoprefixer-rails"
```

3. Rename the `app/assets/stylesheets/application.css` file to `app/assets/stylesheets/application.scss` and write down the SCSS code as shown here:

```scss
@import "bootstrap";
/* Move down content because we have a fixed navbar that is 50px
tall */
body {
  padding-bottom: 2rem;
}
.navbar {
  border-radius: 0;
}
```

4. Write the following HTML code into the `views/welcome/index.html.erb` file:

```html
<nav class="navbar navbar-static-top navbar-dark bg-inverse">
    <a class="navbar-brand" href="#">Project name</a>
    <ul class="nav navbar-nav">
      <li class="nav-item active">
        <a class="nav-link" href="#">Home <span class="sr-only">(current)</span></a>
      </li>
      <li class="nav-item">
        <a class="nav-link" href="#">About</a>
      </li>
      <li class="nav-item">
        <a class="nav-link" href="#">Contact</a>
      </li>
    </ul>
</nav>

    <!-- Main jumbotron for a primary marketing message or call to
action -->
    <div class="jumbotron">
      <div class="container">
        <h1 class="display-3">Hello, world!</h1>
```

```
        <p>This is a template for a simple marketing or
informational website. It includes a large callout called a
jumbotron and three supporting pieces of content. Use it as a
starting point to create something more unique.</p>
        <p><a class="btn btn-primary btn-lg" href="#"
role="button">Learn more &raquo;</a></p>
      </div>
    </div>

    <div class="container">
      <!-- Example row of columns -->
      <div class="row">
        <div class="col-md-4">
          <h2>Heading</h2>
          <p>Donec id elit non mi porta gravida at eget metus.
Fusce dapibus, tellus ac cursus commodo, tortor mauris condimentum
nibh, ut fermentum massa justo sit amet risus. Etiam porta sem
malesuada magna mollis euismod. Donec sed odio dui. </p>
          <p><a class="btn btn-secondary" href="#"
role="button">View details &raquo;</a></p>
        </div>
        <div class="col-md-4">
          <h2>Heading</h2>
          <p>Donec id elit non mi porta gravida at eget metus.
Fusce dapibus, tellus ac cursus commodo, tortor mauris condimentum
nibh, ut fermentum massa justo sit amet risus. Etiam porta sem
malesuada magna mollis euismod. Donec sed odio dui. </p>
          <p><a class="btn btn-secondary" href="#"
role="button">View details &raquo;</a></p>
        </div>
        <div class="col-md-4">
          <h2>Heading</h2>
          <p>Donec sed odio dui. Cras justo odio, dapibus ac
facilisis in, egestas eget quam. Vestibulum id ligula porta
felis euismod semper. Fusce dapibus, tellus ac cursus commodo,
tortor mauris condimentum nibh, ut fermentum massa justo sit amet
risus.</p>
          <p><a class="btn btn-secondary" href="#"
role="button">View details &raquo;</a></p>
        </div>
      </div>

      <hr>

      <footer>
        <p>&copy; Company 2016</p>
      </footer>
    </div> <!-- /container -->
```

5. Finally, run the `bin/rails server` command in your console, point your browser to `http://localhost:3000/welcome/index.html`, and you will find that the page will look like the following screenshot:

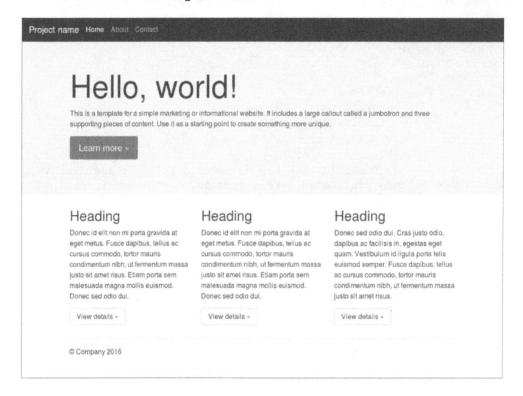

How it works...

The Bootstrap 4 ruby gem for Ruby on Rails makes Bootstrap's SCSS code available for direct import with the Sass `@import` directive; see also the *Explaining the main.css.scss file* recipe of this chapter.

Bootstrap also requires some JavaScript plugins. You can require Bootstrap JavaScript in `app/assets/javascripts/application.js` by adding the following lines of code:

```
//= require jquery
//= require bootstrap
```

Both the tooltips and pop-over plugins depend on tether for positioning. If you use them, add tether to the Gemfile as follows:

```
source 'https://rails-assets.org' do
  gem 'rails-assets-tether', '>= 1.1.0'
end
```

Of course, you then should add tether in the `app/assets/javascripts/application.js` file too:

```
//= require tether
```

There's more...

As already described in *Chapter 12, Bootstrap and Sass*, Bootstrap requires the autoprefixer postprocessor to run to add the vendor prefixes to the compiled CSS code for cross-browser support. In the second step of the recipe, you have already added the **autoprefixer-rails** gem. To set the target browsers for the autoprefixer plugin, you can add a new file called `browserslist` to your `app/assets/stylesheets` folder. This `browserslist` file should contain the lines of code as shown here:

```
Chrome >= 35
Firefox >= 38
Edge >= 12
Explorer >= 9
iOS >= 8
Safari >= 8
Android 2.3
Android >= 4
Opera >= 12
```

The preceding list may change for new versions of Bootstrap 4. You can always check your browser targets with the latest version of Bootstrap's source code at Github.

See also

Read more about the Bootstrap 4 ruby gem for Ruby on Rails (Sprockets) and Compass at `https://github.com/twbs/bootstrap-rubygem`.

Creating a RoR app with Foundation 6

You can read more about Foundation for Sites 6 in *Chapter 11, Foundation and Sass*. Foundation for Sites 6 is a CSS and JavaScript Framework build with Sass have been designed to get your project from prototype to production more efficiently than ever before. In this recipe, you can read how to use Foundation for Sites 6 for your RoR projects.

How to do it...

Learn how to create a RoR app with Foundation 6 yourself:

1. Create a new Rails app by running the following command in your console:

    ```
    rails new recipe7
    ```

2. Run, as already described in the *Hello world with Ruby on Rails* recipe, the *controller* generator and tell it that you want a controller called *welcome* with an action called *index*, as follows:

    ```
    bin/rails generate controller welcome index
    ```

3. Then, add the Foundation 6 gem to your application's Gemfile as follows and run the `bundle` command afterwards:

    ```
    gem 'foundation-rails'
    ```

4. Now, you can add Foundation to your Rails setup by simply running the following command in your console:

    ```
    rails g foundation:install
    ```

5. Choose to overwrite all, when running the preceding command.

6. Download the Foundation Zurb template at `https://github.com/zurb/foundation-zurb-template/archive/master.zip`. Unzip this file and copy the `foundation-zurb-template-master/src/pages/index.html` file to `app/views/welcome/index.html.erb`.

7. Finally, run the `bin/rails server` command in your console, point your browser to `http://localhost:3000/welcome/index.html`, and you will find that the page will look like the following screenshot:

Welcome to Foundation for Sites

We're stoked you want to try Foundation!

To get going, this file (index.html) includes some basic styles you can modify, play around with, or totally destroy to get going.

Once you've exhausted the fun in this document, you should check out:

Foundation Documentation

Everything you need to know about using the framework.

Foundation Code Skills

These online courses offer you a chance to better understand how Foundation works and how you can master it to create awesome projects.

Foundation Forum

Join the Foundation community to ask a question or show off your knowlege.

Foundation on Github

Latest code, issue reports, feature requests and more.

@zurbfoundation

Ping us on Twitter if you have questions. When you build something with this we'd love to see it (and send you a totally boss sticker).

Here's your basic grid:

This is a twelve column section in a row. Each of these includes a div.callout element so you can see where the columns are - it's not required at all for the grid.

Six columns

Six columns

Four columns

Four columns

Four columns

Try one of these buttons:

Simple Button

Success Btn

Alert Btn

Secondary Btn

So many components, girl!

A whole kitchen sink of goodies comes with Foundation. Check out the docs to see them all, along with details on making them your own.

Go to Foundation Docs

We bet you'll need a form somewhere:

Input Label

large-12.columns

Input Label

large-4.columns

Input Label

large-4.columns

Input Label

input-group   .com

Select Box

Husker

Choose Your Favorite
○ Radio 1   ○ Radio 2

Check these out
☐ Checkbox 1   ☐ Checkbox 2

Textarea Label

small-12.columns

How it works...

The `rails g foundation:install` command in the fourth step of this recipe creates and modifies all files to use Foundation in your RoR app. A `_setttings.scss` file has also been created, you can use this file, which is imported in the `_foundation_and_overrides.scss` file; to configure Foundations. Read the *Installing Foundation CLI* recipe of *Chapter 11*, *Foundation and Sass*, to find out how to configure Foundation by changing the variables in the `_setttings.scss` file.

Foundation's Sass code does not include vendor prefixes. So, to compile the CSS code of Foundation, the Autoprefixer is required. Read the *There's more* section of the *Integrating of Bootstrap* recipe of this chapter to learn how to add the `rails-autoprefixer` gem in your RoR application.

There's more...

During the installation process, you used the `rails g foundation:install` command to install Foundation. You can also perform a manual installation, which requires among others the renaming of the `application.css` file as described in the *Explaining the main.css.scss file* recipe of this chapter. Rename `application.css` to `application.scss`. That file should then look as follows:

```
@import "foundation_and_overrides";
/* Add imports of custom sass/scss files here */
```

You also have to create the `_foundation_and_overrides.scss` yourself. This file should contain the following lines of SCSS code:

```
@import "foundation";
```

Add your custom settings (Sass variables) before the `@import` statement in the above code. Also see the *Installing Foundation CLI* recipe of *Chapter 11*, *Foundation and Sass*, to find out how to configure Foundation using the variables in the `_settings.scss` file.

Note that you also have to change your application layout to fit foundation and add Foundation's JavaScript code. You can add the JavaScript plugins to your application by appending the following lines to your `app/assets/javascripts/application.js` file:

```
//= require foundation
$(document).foundation();
```

See also

▶ Foundation for Rails can be found at `https://github.com/zurb/foundation-rails`

▶ Read more about the starter project templates for Foundation for sites 6 at `http://foundation.zurb.com/sites/docs/starter-projects.html`

▶ Read the *Foundation 6, Prototype to Production* blog by Brandon Arnold at `http://zurb.com/article/1403/foundation-6-prototype-to-production`

15

Building Mobile Apps

In this chapter, you will learn the following topics:

- ▶ Installing the Ionic framework
- ▶ Starting a new Ionic project using Sass
- ▶ Customizing the buttons of your Ionic project
- ▶ Setting up a Foundation App project
- ▶ Using mixins to customize your Foundation App project

Introduction

Most of the content of this book is about using Sass to create CSS code for your web apps and responsive website. In this chapter, you will learn how to style your mobile apps with Sass. In this chapter, both the Ionic and Foundation for apps frameworks are discussed.

Because this book is about Sass, you will learn about mobile apps using web technologies, such as HTML, CSS, and JavaScript. Topics focus mainly on the look and feel of mobile apps using Sass. Discussing **PhoneGap** (or **Apache Cordova**) and other JavaScript Frameworks for building **cross-platform mobile apps** is out of the scope of this book.

jQuery Mobile is another popular framework to build your web apps. Although jQuery Mobile is built with Sass and Compass, it's advised to use the **ThemeRoller** to build your themes. The ThemeRoller can be found at `https://themeroller.jquerymobile.com/`. Because no Sass build processes for jQuery Mobile are available yet, it is not discussed in this chapter.

Also, other frameworks, such as **Rachet** (`http://goratchet.com/`) and **Gumby Framework** (`http://www.gumbyframework.com/`), are left out of this chapter, as the community and/or maintainers seem to have dropped support.

Installing the Ionic framework

The Ionic Framework offers you a library of mobile-optimized HTML, CSS, and JS CSS components, gestures, and tools for building highly interactive apps. You can use Ionic for free; it is open source and released under the MIT license. Of course, Ionic is built with Sass.

Getting ready

The easiest way to get the Ionic CLI is through npm. npm is the package manager for Node.js. Read the *Installing Grunt* recipe of *Chapter 16*, *Setting up a Build Chain with Grunt*, to learn more about installing Node.js and npm.

How to do it...

Learn how to set up the Ionic CLI trough npm by doing the following steps:

1. After installing Node.js and npm, run the following command in your console to install the Ionic Framework:

    ```
    npm install -g ionic
    ```

2. Notice the usage of the -g (global) flag in the preceding command; it ensures that Ionic is installed globally and can be use from anywhere on your system. Global installation requires administrator rights on most of the systems.

3. Now, you can start a new Ionic by running the following command in your console:

    ```
    ionic start recipe1
    ```

4. Navigate to the new `recipe1` folder and run the following command to develop your project in the browser with LiveReload:

    ```
    ionic serve
    ```

5. Then, point your browser to http://localhost:8000. You will find that your project looks like that shown in the following screenshot:

How it works...

You probably might have noticed that you have not used Sass in this recipe. In the next *Starting a new Ionic project using Sass* recipe, you will learn how to set up your project to use Sass.

As you can see, your project already contains some example code. By default, the `start` command creates a project using the tab layout. Use the following command to create a blank project:

```
ionic start {new} blank
```

There's more...

The HTML template files of your project can be found in the `www/templates` folder; one file for each tab. Ionic creates an **Apache Cordova** project by default; this is why your files are in the `www` folder, which becomes the root of your Cordova project.

> Apache Cordova is an open source mobile development framework. It allows you to use standard web technologies, such as HTML5, CSS3, and JavaScript for cross-platform development, thus avoiding each mobile platform's native development language. Applications execute within wrappers targeted at each platform, and rely on standards-compliant API bindings to access each device's sensors, data, and network status.

By using Ionic with Cordova, you can build your projects for both Android and iOS. Notice that iOS development requires OS X currently.

See also

- ▶ More layouts for your Ionic project can be found at `http://market.ionic.io/`
- ▶ Check out Ionic's official website for full documentation at `http://ionicframework.com/`
- ▶ Learn more about Apache Cordova at `https://cordova.apache.org/`

Starting a new Ionic project using Sass

In this recipe, you will learn how to build and maintain your Ionic projects using Sass.

Getting ready

Read the *Installing the Ionic Framework* recipe of this chapter to find out how to set up a new Ionic project.

How to do it...

In the Installing the Ionic Framework recipe you have learn how to set up the CLI tool, now will learn how to use Sass in your Ionic projects:

1. Start a new Ionic by running the following command in your console:

   ```
   ionic start recipe2
   ```

2. Then, navigation to the `recipe2` folder and run the following command in your console to set up Sass:

   ```
   ionic setup sass
   ```

3. Now, start your Ionic app by running the following command in your console:

   ```
   ionic serve
   ```

4. Open the `scss/ionic.app.scss` file in your text editor and edit the `$positive` variable as follows:

   ```
   $positive: #f00 !default; //red
   ```

5. After saving the `scss/ionic.app.scss` file, you will find that your browser automatically reloads. The hyperlinks and other elements are colored red now.

How it works...

Before you ran the `ionic setup sass` command, your project folder already contained a `scss` sub folder. The `scss` folder contains the Sass code to compile the CSS code for your Ionic project.

The `ionic setup sass` command installs Gulp and some subtasks, including gulp-sass. Gulp is a JavaScript task runner for Node.js. Gulp is similar to Grunt, as described in *Chapter 16, Setting up a Build Chain with Grunt,* of this book. The command also adds a watch task to the `ionic serve` command. The watch task watches the `scss/ionic.app.scss` file for changes. When you save the `scss/ionic.app.scss` file, the watch task triggers the Sass compiler and reloads your application. Ionic uses LiveReload to reload your application in the browser. Also, see the *Getting grunt watch for sass, and LiveReload to work* recipe of *Chapter 16, Setting up a Build Chain with Grunt.* Notice that the changes in the templates in the www/ `template` folder trigger a page reload.

You can also read the *Using the sass-gulp plugin with Gulp* recipe of *Chapter 1, Getting Started with Sass,* to find out how to set up Gulp to compile your Sass code with `ssass-node` yourself.

The `scss/ionic.app.scss` file already contains a list of variables for the default colors of Ionic. You can modify these variables to redesign an app by simply changing the default colors.

There's more...

The Sass code for Ionic contains many more variables. A complete list of variables to change the style rules of your application can be found in the `www/lib/ionic/scss/_variables.scss` file.

Other custom Sass codes for your app can be written in the `scss/ionic.app.scss` file, as also described in the *Customizing the buttons of your Ionic project* recipe of this chapter.

See also

- You can also manually set up Sass for Ionic; read the instructions at `http://ionicframework.com/docs/cli/sass.html` to find out how to do this

- The official website of Gulp can be found at `http://gulpjs.com/`

- Finally, read more about LiveReload at `http://livereload.com/`

Customizing the buttons of your Ionic project

The compiled CSS code already contains many components and styles to build your mobile apps. The SCSS code compiles into predefined CSS classes for easy styling. Advanced Sass coders can also extend the code with custom code for more flexibility. In this recipe, you will learn how to create a custom button for your app.

Getting ready

Before starting, read the preceding *Installing the Ionic Framework* and *Starting a new Ionic project using Sass* recipes of this chapter first.

How to do it...

Use Sass to customize the button of your Ionic project by performing the following steps:

1. Create a new Ionic app, as described in the *Installing the Ionic Framework* recipe of this chapter, by running the following command:

   `ionic start recipe3`

2. The preceding command creates a new `recipe2` folder in this directory. Then, run the following command in your console to set up Sass; also see the *Starting a new Ionic project using Sass* recipe of this chapter:

   `ionic setup sass`

3. Now, open the `scss/ionic.app.scss` file in your favorite text editor and write the following SCSS at the end of this file:

```
$button-custom-bg:                  tomato !default;
$button-custom-text:                #fff !default;
$button-custom-border:              darken($royal, 8%) !default;
$button-custom-active-bg:           darken($royal, 8%) !default;
$button-custom-active-border:       darken($royal, 8%) !default;


.button {
  &.button-custom {
    @include button-style($button-custom-bg, $button-custom-
border, $button-custom-active-bg, $button-custom-active-border,
$button-custom-text);
    @include button-clear($button-custom-bg);
    @include button-outline($button-custom-bg);
  }
}
```

4. After recompiling your CSS code, you can use the `button-custom` CSS class in your HTML for tomato-colored buttons. You can add, for instance, the following HTML code to the `www/templates/tab-dash.html` file:

```
<button class="button button-block button-custom">
    Block Button
</button>
<button class="button button-outline button-custom">
    Outlined Button
</button>
```

5. The buttons from the preceding step will look like that shown in the following screenshot:

How it works...

The complete SCSS code for the CSS styles of the buttons can be found in the `www/lib/ionic/scss/_buttons.scss` file. This file contains SCSS code to generate CSS classes for each color, and mixins are called to generate different button types.

There's more...

You might possibly wonder why Ionic does not have a single mixin to generate the button styles. Sass does not support interpolation on variables and mixins. This means that you cannot call the mixins in another mixin with the variable parameter.

You can try to use Sass maps to solve the problem described previously. You can read more about Sass maps in the *Map functions* recipe of *Chapter 5, Built-in Functions*. Now consider the following list of variables:

$light:	**#fff !default;**
$stable:	**#f8f8f8 !default;**
$positive:	**#f00 !default;**

You can replace the preceding variables with Sass maps, which should look as follows:

```
$colors: (
  light: #fff,
  stable: #f8f8f8,
  positive: #f00
);
```

Now, in this Sass map, you can write the following SCSS code:

```
@mixin setcolor($color) {
  color: $color;
}

@mixin button($state, $color) {
  .btn-#{$state} {
    @include setcolor($color);
  }
}

@each $state, $color in $colors {
  @include button( $state, $color );
}
```

The preceding SCSS code compiles in CSS code as follows:

```
.btn-light {
  color: #fff; }

.btn-stable {
  color: #f8f8f8; }

.btn-positive {
  color: #f00; }
```

Setting up a Foundation App project

In this recipe, you will use the Foundation CLI tools to set up a Foundation for Apps project. You should note that Foundation for Apps was built for making responsive web apps. Using Foundation for App to create native-hybrid apps with wrappers, such as Cordova, is not trivial.

Getting ready

This recipe uses the same CLI tool as the one used in the *Installing Foundation CLI* recipe of *Chapter 11, Foundation and Sass*. So, reading the *Installing Foundation CLI* recipe before starting is recommended.

How to do it...

Learn how to set up a Foundation App project:

1. Install Foundation CLI, as described in the *Installing Foundation CLI* recipe of *Chapter 11, Foundation and Sass*.

2. Run the following command in your console to start a new Foundation project:

   ```
   foundation new
   ```

3. Choose the `A web app (Foundation for Apps)` option. The output in your console should look as follows:

```
$ foundation new
? What are you building today? A web app (Foundation for Apps)
? What's the project called? recipe4

          /|
       | | /| ,
   .  /\|  \/ I/I
   |\/        |        Thanks for using ZURB Foundation for Apps!
   ||\__/\___/||       --------------------------------------------
  _||  ======= ||_     Let's set up a new project.
 /__||  o   o  ||__\   It shouldn't take more than a minute.
   ||   ____,  ||
  /|          |\
  /_/\\/\  /\/\_\
     \/\\//\/
       \/

Downloading the project template...
Done downloading!
```

4. The preceding step installs the files for Foundation for Apps in a new folder called `recipe4`.

5. Now, run `foundation watch` while inside the `recipe4` folder.

6. The command in the previous step starts a web server running on `http://localhost:8079`. Open this URL in your browser to preview your app.

7. Now, you can modify both the `client/assets/scss/_settings.scss` and `client/index.html` files and directly see the effects of your modifications in your browser.

8. Finally, you can add your custom Sass code in the `client/assets/scss/app.scss` file.

How it works...

The command installs and downloads all the files needed to start your Foundation for Apps project. The source files of Foundation for Apps are installed with bower. You can update these files without undoing your modifications, because a copy of the `_settings.scss` file is installed in the `client/assets/scss/` folder. This folder also contains an `app.scss` file for your other custom Sass code.

There's more...

Besides many components, the source code of Foundation also contains some functions and mixins to build your own components and CSS classes. For instance, the `css-triangle` mixin helps you create pure CSS triangles, as described in the *Creating visual triangles* recipe of *Chapter 13, Meeting the Bourbon Family*.

The following SCSS code creates a CSS triangle; you can add this code to the file too:

```
.component {
  &::after {
    @include css-triangle(
    $triangle-size: 10px, // Size of the triangle
    $triangle-color: red, // Color of the triangle
    $triangle-direction: top // Orientation of the triangle; can be
  top, right, bottom, or left
    );
  }
}
```

In the *Using mixins to customize your Foundation App project* recipe of this chapter, you can read how to use Foundation for Apps mixins for components to create your own CSS classes.

Finally, notice that compiling the SCSS code of Foundation for Apps requires the Autoprefixer to automatically add vendor prefixes to the compiled CSS code. Read more about the Autoprefixer in the *Using vendor prefixes* recipe of *Chapter 7, Cross-Browser CSS3 mixins* and the *Automatically prefixing your code with Grunt* recipe of *Chapter 16, Setting up a Build Chain with Grunt*.

See also

The full documentation of Foundation for Apps can be found at `http://foundation.zurb.com/apps/docs/`.

Using mixins to customize your Foundation App project

By default, Foundation for Apps comes with lot of predefined CSS classes. You can use these classes in your HTML. You can also define your own classes with Foundation for Apps functions and mixins. Mixins are available for each component. In this recipe, you will learn how to use these mixins to create your own CSS class structure. In this recipe, the Title bar component is used to demonstrate how to reuse Foundation's mixins.

Getting ready

Read the *Setting up a Foundation App project* recipe of this chapter before you start finding out how to install Foundation for Apps.

How to do it...

1. Create a new Foundation for Apps project by running the following command in your console, as described in the *Setting up a Foundation App project* recipe of this chapter:

   foundation new

2. Run the `foundation watch` command in your console and open the app in your browser at `http://localhost:8079`.

3. Now, edit the `client/index.html` file and write down the following HTML in the `body` section:

   ```html
   <div class="primary title-bar">
   <div class="center title">Center</div>
   <span class="left"><a href="#">Left</a></span>
   <span class="right"><a href="#">Right</a></span>
   </div>
   ```

4. Without any changes in the SCSS code, the preceding HTML will look like that shown in the following screenshot:

5. Now, edit the `client/assets/scss/app.scss` file and write down the following SCSS code at the end of it:

```
.custom-title-bar {
// Extend the base selector to get core structural styles
@extend %title-bar;
// Add visual styles with this mixin
@include title-bar-style(
$background: orange, // Background color
$color: #000, // Text color
$border: 1px solid #000,
$padding: 1rem
);
}
```

6. Replace the `primary` and `title-bar` CSS classes in your HTML with the `custom-title-bar` class. You will find that your title bar is orange now.

How it works...

The SCSS code for the title bar is built with a placeholder and can be extended with the `@extend` syntax. The placeholder ensures that the compiled CSS code does not contain the placeholder itself; you can read more about extending with placeholders in Sass in the *Using placeholder selectors with the @extend directive* recipe of the *Chapter 4, Nested selectors and modular CSS*

The placeholder also contains a call to the `title-bar-style()` mixin, which will set the colors for your title bar.

There's more...

The %title-bar placeholder also generates the nested left, right, and center.title CSS classes. You can use the $variable to change the names of these classes. By default, the $titlebar-item-classes variable in the _settings.scss file looks as follows:

```scss
$titlebar-item-classes: (
center: 'center',
left: 'left',
right: 'right',
title: 'title',
);
```

You can use the $titlebar-item-classes variable only to set CSS class names and cannot use it to set CSS selectors. This means that the items of your title bar should always have a CSS class, and creating a semantic title bar without additional CSS classes is not possible with the SCSS code of Foundation.

Creating CSS code for a more semantic solution is possible. Consider the HTML shown here:

```html
<nav>
    <h1 class="center title">Center</h1>
    <a class="left" href="#">Left</a>
    <a class="right"href="#">Right</a>
</nav>
```

You can use the following SCSS code to create the style rules for the preceding HTML code. The title bars should look like a normal Foundation title bar now:

```scss
body nav:first-of-type {
  // Extend the base selector to get core structural styles
  @extend %title-bar;
  // Add visual styles with this mixin
  h1,
  a {
    color: #fff; // Text color
    font-weight: normal;
    font-style: normal;
    font-size: 100%;
    line-height: 1;
    margin-bottom: 0;
  }
```

```
@include title-bar-style(
  $background: tomato, // Background color
  $color: #fff, // Text color
  $border: 1px solid #fff,
  $padding: 1rem
);
}
```

See also

- ▸ An overview of Foundation for Apps' components can be found at `http://foundation.zurb.com/apps/docs/#!/`.

- ▸ **AngularJS** or **Angular 2** is a JavaScript Framework, which extends HTML attributes with directives and binds data to HTML with expressions. Foundation uses AngularJS for dynamic routing to component directives. Read more about Foundation's Angular integration at `http://foundation.zurb.com/apps/docs/#!/angular`.

- ▸ The official website of Angular2 can be found at `https://angular.io/`.

16
Setting up a Build Chain with Grunt

In this chapter, you will learn the following topics:

- ▶ Installing Grunt
- ▶ Installing Grunt plugins
- ▶ Utilizing the Gruntfile.js file
- ▶ Adding a configuration definition for a plugin
- ▶ Adding the Sass compiler task
- ▶ Integrating Compass in the build chain
- ▶ Installing Bourbon in the build chain
- ▶ Automatically prefixing your code with Grunt
- ▶ Getting Grunt watch for Sass, and LiveReload to work
- ▶ Utilizing Yeoman

Introduction

This chapter introduces you to the **Grunt Task Runner** and the features it offers to make your development workflow a delight. Grunt is a JavaScript Task Runner that is installed and managed via **npm**, the **Node.js** package manager. You will learn how to take advantage of its plugins to set up your own flexible and productive workflow, which will enable you to compile your Sass code. Although there are many applications available for compiling Sass, Grunt is a more flexible, versatile, and cross-platform tool that will allow you to automate many development tasks, including Sass compilation. It can not only automate the Sass compilation tasks, but also wrap any other mundane jobs, such as linting and minifying and cleaning your code, into tasks and run them automatically for you. By the end of this chapter, you will be comfortable using Grunt and its plugins to establish a flexible workflow when working with Sass. Using Grunt in your workflow is vital. You will then be shown how to combine Grunt's plugins to establish a workflow for compiling Sass in real time. Grunt becomes a tool to automate integration testing, deployments, builds, and development.

Finally, by understanding the automation process, you will also learn how to use alternative tools, such as **Gulp**. Gulp is a JavaScript task runner for Node.js and relatively new in comparison to Grunt, so Grunt has more plugins and a wider community support. Currently, the Gulp community is growing fast. The biggest difference between Grunt and Gulp is that Gulp does not save intermediary files, but pipes these files' content in memory to the next stream. A stream enables you to pass some data through a function, which will modify the data and then pass the modified data to the next function. In many situations, Gulp requires less configuration settings, so some people find Gulp more intuitive and easier to learn. In this book, Grunt has been chosen to demonstrate how to run a task runner; this choice does not mean that you will have to prefer the usage of Grunt in your own project. Both the task runners can run all the tasks described in this chapter. Simply choose the task runner that suits you best. This recipe demonstrates shortly how to compile your Sass code with Gulp. In the *Using sass-gulp with Gulp* recipe of *Chapter 1, Getting Started with Sass* of this book, you can read in brief about how to compile your Sass code with Gulp and gulp-sass.

In this chapter, you should enter your commands in the command prompt. Linux users should open a terminal, while Mac users should run `Terminal.app` and Windows users should use the `cmd` command for command line usage.

Installing Grunt

Grunt is essentially a Node.js module; therefore, it requires Node.js to be installed. The goal of this recipe is to show you how to install Grunt on your system and set up your project.

Getting ready

Installing Grunt requires both Node.js and npm. Node.js is a platform built on Chrome's JavaScript runtime for easily building fast, scalable network applications, and npm is a package manager for Node.js. You can download the Node.js source code or a prebuilt installer for your platform at `https://nodejs.org/en/download/`. Notice that npm is bundled with Node. Also, read the instructions at `https://github.com/npm/npm#super-easy-install`.

How to do it...

After installing Node.js and npm, installing Grunt is as simple as running a single command, regardless of the operating system that you are using. Just open the command line or the Terminal and execute the following command:

```
npm install -g grunt-cli
```

That's it! This command will install Grunt globally and make it accessible anywhere on your system. Run the `grunt --version` command in the command prompt in order to confirm that Grunt has been successfully installed. If the installation is successful, you should see the version of Grunt in the Terminal's output:

```
grunt --version
grunt-cli v0.1.11
```

After installing Grunt, the next step is to set it up for your project:

1. Make a folder on your desktop and call it workflow. Then, navigate to it and run the `npm init` command to initialize the setup process:

    ```
    mkdir workflow && cd $_ && npm init
    ```

2. Press *Enter* for all the questions and accept the defaults. You can change these settings later. This should create a file called `package.json` that will contain some information about the project and the project's dependencies. In order to add Grunt as a dependency, install the Grunt package as follows:

    ```
    npm install grunt --save-dev
    ```

3. Now, if you look at the `package.json` file, you should see that Grunt is added to the list of dependencies:

    ```
    ..."devDependencies": {"grunt": "~0.4.5"
    }
    ```

In addition, you should see an extra folder created. Called `node_modules`, it will contain Grunt and other modules that you will install later in this chapter.

How it works...

In the preceding section, you installed Grunt (`grunt-cli`) with the `-g` option. The `-g` option installs Grunt globally on your system. Global installation requires superuser or administrator rights on most systems. You need to run only the globally installed packages from the command line. Everything that you will use with the `require()` function in your programs should be installed locally in the root of your project. Local installation makes it possible to solve your project's specific dependencies. More information about global versus local installation of npm modules can be found at `https://www.npmjs.org/doc/faq.html`.

There's more...

Node package managers are available for a wide range of operation systems, including Windows, OS X, Linux, SunOS, and FreeBSD. A complete list of package managers can be found at `https://github.com/joyent/node/wiki/Installing-Node.js-via-package-manager`. Notice that these package managers are not maintained by the Node.js core team. Instead, each package manager has its own maintainer.

See also

► The npm Registry is a public collection of packages of open source code for Node.js, frontend web apps, mobile apps, robots, routers, and countless other needs of the JavaScript community. You can find the npm Registry at `https://www.npmjs.org/`.

► Also, notice that you do not have to use Task Runners to create build chains. Keith Cirkel wrote about how to use npm as a build tool at `http://blog.keithcirkel.co.uk/how-to-use-npm-as-a-build-tool/`.

Installing Grunt plugins

Grunt plugins are the heart of Grunt. Every plugin serves a specific purpose and can also work together with other plugins. In order to use Grunt to set up your Sass workflow, you need to install several plugins. You can find more information about these plugins in this recipe's *How it works...* section.

Getting ready

Before you install the plugins, you should first create some basic files and folders for the project. You should install Grunt and create a `package.json` file for your project. Also, create an `index.html` file to inspect the results in your browser. Two empty folders should be created too. The `scss` folder contains your Sass code and the `css` folder contains the compiled CSS code.

Navigate to the root of the project, repeat the steps from the *Installing Grunt* recipe of this chapter, and create some additional files and directories that you are going to work with throughout the chapter. In the end, you should end up with the following folder and file structure:

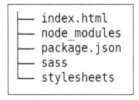

```
├── index.html
├── node_modules
├── package.json
├── sass
└── stylesheets
```

How to do it...

Grunt plugins are essentially Node.js modules that can be installed and added to the `package.json` file in the list of dependencies using npm. To do this, follow the ensuing steps:

1. Navigate to the root of the project and run the following command, as described in the *Installing Grunt* recipe of this chapter:

   npm init

2. Install the modules using npm, as follows:

   **npm install **

   **grunt-contrib-sass **

   **load-grunt-tasks **

   **grunt-postcss **

   --save-dev

> Notice the single space before the backslash in each line. For example, on the second line, `grunt-contrib-sass \`, there is a space before the backslash at the end of the line. The space characters are necessary because they act as separators. The backslash at the end is used to continue the commands on the next line.

The `npm install` command will download all the plugins and place them in the node_ modules folder in addition to including them in the `package.json` file. The next step is to include these plugins in the `Gruntfile.js` file.

How it works...

Grunt plugins can be installed and added to the `package.json` file using the `npm install` command followed by the name of the plugins separated by a space, and the `--save-dev` flag:

```
npm install nameOfPlugin1 nameOfPlugin2 --save-dev
```

The `--save-dev` flag adds the plugin names and a tilde version range to the list of dependencies in the `package.json` file so that the next time you need to install the plugins, all you need to do is run the `npm install` command. This command looks for the `package.json` file in the directory from which it was called, and will automatically download all the specified plugins. This makes porting workflows very easy; all it takes is copying the `package.json` file and running the `npm install` command. Finally, the `package.json` file contains a **JSON** object with metadata. It is also worth explaining the long command that you have used to install the plugins in this recipe. This command installs the plugins that are continued on to the next line by the backslash. It is essentially equivalent to the following:

```
npm install grunt-contrib-sass --save-dev
npm install load-grunt-tasks --save-dev
npm install grunt-postcss --save-dev
```

As you can see, it is very repetitive. However, both yield the same results; it is up to you to choose the one that you feel more comfortable with. The `node_modules` folder contains all the plugins that you install with npm. Every time you run `npm install name-of-plugin`, the plugin is downloaded and placed in the folder.

If you need to port your workflow, you do not need to copy all the contents of the folder. In addition, if you are using a version control system, such as Git, you should add the node_ modules folder to the .gitignore file so that the folder and its subdirectories are ignored.

There's more...

Each Grunt plugin also has its own metadata set in a `package.json` file, so plugins can have different dependencies. For instance, the `grunt-contrib-sass` plugin, as described in the *Adding the Sass compiler task* recipe, has set its dependencies as follows:

```
"dependencies": {
    "async": "^0.9.0",
    "chalk": "^0.5.1",
    "cross-spawn": "^0.2.3",
    "dargs": "^4.0.0",
    "which": "^1.0.5"
}
```

Besides the dependencies described previously, this task also requires you to have Ruby and Sass installed. In the *Installing Sass for command line usage* recipe of *Chapter 1, Getting Started with Sass*, you can read how to install Ruby Sass. You should use the grunt-sass plugin to compile Sass into CSS with node-sass.

In the following list, you will find the plugins used in this chapter, followed by a brief description:

▸ `load-grunt-tasks`: This loads all the plugins listed in the `package.json` file

▸ `grunt-contrib-sass`: This compiles Sass files into CSS code

▸ `grunt-postcss`: This enables you to apply one or more postprocessors to your compiled CSS code

CSS postprocessors enable you to change your CSS code after compilation. In the *Automatically prefixing your code with Grunt* recipe of this chapter, you will learn how to use the Node autoprefixer module together with the grunt-postcss plugin to parse CSS code and add vendor-prefixed CSS properties using the **Can I use database**. CSSnano, which minifies your CSS code, is an other example of a postprocessor.

In addition to installing plugins, you can remove them as well. You can remove a plugin using the `npm uninstall name-of-plugin` command, where `name-of-plugin` is the name of the plugin that you wish to remove. For example, if a line in the list of dependencies of your `package.json` file contains `grunt-concurrent": "~0.4.2",`, then you can remove it using the following command:

```
npm uninstall grunt-concurrent
```

Then, you just need to make sure to remove the name of the plugin from your `package.json` file so that it is not loaded by the load-grunt-tasks plugin the next time you run a Grunt task. Running the `npm prune` command after removing the items from the `package.json` file will also remove the plugins. The `prune` command removes *extraneous* packages that are not listed in the parent package's dependencies list.

See also

▸ More information on the npm version's syntax can be found at `https://www.npmjs.org/doc/misc/semver.html`

▸ Also, see `http://caniuse.com/` for more information on the Can I Use database

Utilizing the Gruntfile.js file

The `Gruntfile.js` file is the main configuration file for Grunt that handles all the tasks and task configurations. All the tasks and plugins are loaded using this file. In this recipe, you will create this file and will learn how to load Grunt plugins using it.

Getting ready

First, you need to install Node and Grunt, as described in the *Installing Grunt* recipe of this chapter. You will also have to install some Grunt plugins, as described in the *Installing Grunt plugins* recipe of this chapter.

How to do it...

Once you have installed Node and Grunt, follow these steps:

1. In your Grunt project directory (the folder that contains the `package.json` file), create a new file, save it as `Gruntfile.js`, and add the following lines to it:

```
module.exports = function(grunt) {
  grunt.initConfig({
    pkg: grunt.file.readJSON('package.json'),

    //Add the Tasks configurations here.
  });
// Define Tasks here
};
```

2. This is the simplest form of the `Gruntfile.js` file that only contains two information variables.

3. The next step is to load the plugins that you installed in the *Installing Grunt plugins* recipe. Add the following lines at the end of your `Gruntfile.js` file:

```
grunt.loadNpmTasks('grunt-sass');
```

4. In the preceding line of code, grunt-sass is the name of the plugin you want to load.

That is all it takes to load all the necessary plugins. The next step is to add the configurations for each task to the `Gruntfile.js` file.

How it works...

Any Grunt plugin can be loaded by adding a line of JavaScript to the `Gruntfile.js` file, as follows:

`grunt.loadNpmTasks('name-of-module');`

This line should be added every time a new plugin is installed so that Grunt can access the plugin's functions. However, it is tedious to load every single plugin that you install. In addition, you will soon notice that, as your project grows, the number of configuration lines will increase as well. As described in the *Loading the Grunt tasks* recipe of this chapter, you can also use the `load-grunt-tasks` plugin to load your plugins automatically based on the information in your `package.json` file.

The `Gruntfile.js` file should be written in JavaScript or **CoffeeScript**. Grunt tasks rely on configuration data defined in a **JSON object** passed to the `grunt.initConfig` method. JavaScript Object Notation (JSON) is an alternative for **XML** and used for data exchange. JSON describes name-value pairs written as `"name": "value"`. All the JSON data is separated by commas with JSON objects written inside curly brackets and JSON arrays inside square brackets. Each object can hold more than one name/value pair with each array holding one or more objects.

> You can also group tasks into one task. Your alias groups of tasks using the following line of code: `grunt.registerTask('alias', ['task1', 'task2']);`

There's more...

Instead of loading all the required Grunt plugins one by one, you can load them automatically with the load-grunt-tasks plugin. You can install this by using the following command in the root of your project:

`npm install load-grunt-tasks --save-dev`

Then, add the following line at the very beginning of your `Gruntfile.js` file after `module.exports`:

`require('load-grunt-tasks')(grunt);`

Now, your Gruntfile.js file should look like this:

```
module.exports = function(grunt) {
  require('load-grunt-tasks')(grunt);
  grunt.initConfig({
    pkg: grunt.file.readJSON('package.json'),
```

```
        //Add the Tasks configurations here.
    });
// Define Tasks here
};
```

The load-grunt-tasks plugin loads all the plugins specified in the `package.json` file. It simply loads the plugins that begin with the `grunt-` prefix or any pattern that you specify. This plugin will also read `dependencies`, `devDependencies`, and `peerDependencies` in your `package.json` file and load the Grunt tasks that match the provided patterns.

A pattern to load specifically chosen plugins can be added as a second parameter. You can load, for instance, all the `grunt-contrib` tasks with the following code in your `Gruntfile.js` file:

```
require('load-grunt-tasks')(grunt, {pattern: 'grunt-contrib-*'});
```

See also

Read more about the load-grunt-tasks module at `https://github.com/sindresorhus/load-grunt-task`

Adding a configuration definition for a plugin

Any Grunt task needs a configuration definition. The configuration definitions are usually added to the `Gruntfile.js` file itself and are very easy to set up. In addition, it is very convenient to define and work with them because they are all written in the JSON format. This makes it very easy to spot the configurations in the plugin's documentation examples and add them to your `Gruntfile.js` file.

In this recipe, you will learn how to add the configuration for a Grunt task.

Getting ready

For this recipe, you will first need to create a basic `Gruntfile.js` file and install the plugin you want to configure. If you want to install the grunt-example plugin, you can install it using the following command in the root of your project:

```
npm install grunt-example --save-dev
```

How to do it...

Once you have created the basic `Gruntfile.js` file (also refer to the *Utilizing the Gruntfile.js file* recipe of this chapter), follow this step:

1. A simple form of the task configuration is shown in the following code. Start by adding it to your `Gruntfile.js` file wrapped inside `grunt.initConfig{}`:

```
example: {
  subtask: {
    files: {
      "stylesheets/main.css": "sass/main.scss"
    }
  }
}
```

How it works...

If you look closely at the task configuration, you will notice the `files` field that specifies what files are going to be operated on. The `files` field is a very standard field that appears in almost all the Grunt plugins simply due to the fact that many tasks require some or many file manipulations.

There's more...

The **Don't Repeat Yourself** (**DRY**) principle can be applied to your Grunt configuration too.

First, define the name and the path added to the beginning of the `Gruntfile.js` file as follows:

```
app {
  dev : "app/dev"
}
```

Using the templates is a key in order to avoid hard coded values and inflexible configurations. In addition, you should have noticed that the template has been used using the `<%= %>` delimiter to expand the value of the development directory:

```
"<%= app.dev %>/css/main.css": "<%= app.dev %>/scss/main.scss"
```

The `<%= %>` delimiter essentially executes inline JavaScript and replaces values, as you can see in the following code:

```
"app/dev/css/main.css": "app/dev/scss/main.scss"
```

So, put simply, the value defined in the `app` object at the top of the `Gruntfile.js` file is evaluated and replaced.

If you decide to change the name of your development directory, for example, all you need to do is change the app's variable that is defined at the top of your `Gruntfile.js` file.

Finally, it is also worth mentioning that the value for the template does not necessarily have to be a string and can be a JavaScript literal.

See also

You can read more about templates in the Templates section of Grunt's documentation at `http://gruntjs.com/configuring- tasks#templates`

Adding the Sass compiler task

The Sass tasks are the core task that you will need for your Sass development. It has several features and options, but at the heart of it is the Sass compiler that can compile your Sass files into CSS. By the end of this recipe, you will have a good understanding of this plugin, how to add it to your `Gruntfile.js` file, and how to take advantage of it.

In this recipe, the `grunt-contrib-sass` plugin will be used. This plugin compiles your Sass code by using Ruby Sass. You should use the grunt-sass plugin to compile Sass into CSS with node-sass (LibSass). In *Chapter 1, Getting Started with Sass*, of this book, you can read about the difference between Ruby Sass and LibSass and how to install Ruby Sass.

Getting ready

The only requirement for this recipe is to have the grunt-contrib-sass plugin installed and loaded in your `Gruntfile.js` file. If you have not installed this plugin in the *Installing Grunt Plugins* recipe of this chapter, you can do this using the following command in the root of your project:

```
npm install grunt-contrib-sass --save-dev
```

You should also install grunt locally by running the following command:

```
npm install grunt --save-dev
```

Finally, your project should have the file and directory, as described in the *Installing Grunt plugins* recipe of this chapter. The SCSS code of this recipe has been copied from the *Browser support* recipe of *Chapter 7, Cross-Browser CSS3 Mixins*.

How to do it...

Add the Sass compiler task to your Grunt set up by doing the following steps:

1. An example of the Sass task configuration is shown in the following code. Start by adding it to your `Gruntfile.js` file wrapped inside the `grunt.initConfig({})` code.

2. Now, your `Gruntfile.js` file should look as follows:

```
module.exports = function(grunt) {
  grunt.initConfig({
    //Add the Tasks configurations here.
    sass: {
      dist: {
        options: {
          style: 'expanded'
        },
        files: {
          'stylesheets/main.css': 'sass/main.scss'  'source'
        }
      }
    }
  });

  grunt.loadNpmTasks('grunt-contrib-sass');

  // Define Tasks here
  grunt.registerTask('default', ['sass']);
}
```

3. Then, run the following command in your console:

    grunt sass

4. The preceding command will create a new `stylesheets/main.css` file. Also, notice that the `stylesheets/main.css.map` file has also been automatically created. The Sass compiler task creates **CSS sourcemaps** to debug your code by default.

How it works...

In addition to setting up the task configuration, you should run the Grunt command to test the Sass task. When you run the `grunt sass` command, Grunt will look for a configuration called Sass in the `Gruntfile.js` file. Once it finds it, it will run the task with some default options if they are not explicitly defined. Successful tasks will end with the following message:

```
Done, without errors.
```

There's more...

There are several other options that you can include in the Sass task. An option can also be set at the global Sass task level, so the option will be applied in all the subtasks of Sass.

In addition to options, Grunt also provides targets for every task to allow you to set different configurations for the same task. In other words, if, for example, you need to have two different versions of the Sass task with different source and destination folders, you could easily use two different targets. Adding and executing targets are very easy. Adding more builds just follows the JSON notation, as shown here:

```
sass: {                                          // Task
  dev: {                                         // Target
    options: {                                   // Target options
      style: 'expanded'
    },
    files: {                                     // Dictionary of
files
      'stylesheets/main.css': 'sass/main.scss' // 'destination':
'source'
    }
  },
  dist: {
    options: {
      style: 'expanded',
      sourcemap: 'none'
    },
    files: {
      'stylesheets/main.min.css': 'sass/main.scss'
    }
  }
}
```

In the preceding example, two builds are defined. The first one is named `dev`, and the second is called `dist`. Each of these targets belongs to the Sass task, but they use different options and different folders for the source and the compiled Sass code.

Moreover, you can run a particular target using `grunt sass:nameOfTarget`, where `nameOfTarge` is the name of the target that you are trying to use. So, for example, if you need to run the `dist` target, you will have to run the `grunt sass:dist` command in your console. However, if you need to run both the targets, you could simply run `grunt sass` and it would run both the targets sequentially.

As already mentioned, the grunt-contrib-sass plugin compiles your Sass code by using Ruby Sass, and you should use the grunt-sass plugin to compile Sass to CSS with node-sass (LibSass).

To switch to the grunt-sass plugin, you will have to install it locally first by running the following command in your console:

```
npm install grunt-sass
```

Then, replace `grunt.loadNpmTasks('grunt-contrib-sass');` with `grunt.loadNpmTasks('grunt-sass');` in the `Gruntfile.js` file; the basic options for grunt-contrib-sass and grunt-sass are very similar, so you have to change the options for the Sass task when switching to grunt-sass.

Finally, notice that grunt-contrib-sass also has an option to turn Compass on. In the *Integrating Compass in the build chain* recipe of this chapter, we discussed the integration of Compass into the build process in more detail.

See also

▶ Please refer to Grunt's documentation for a full list of options, which is available at `https://gruntjs/grunt-contrib-sass#options`

▶ Also, read Grunt's documentation for more details about configuring your tasks and targets at `http://gruntjs.com/configuring-tasks#task-configuration-and-targets github.com/`

Integrating Compass in the build chain

In *Chapter 6, Using Compass*, of this book, you can read more about Compass. Compass is an open source CSS Authoring Framework. In this recipe, you will learn how to integrate Compass in your build chain.

Getting ready

In this recipe, you will use the same directory and file structure as the one used before, in the *Creating a vertical rhythm for your website* recipe of *Chapter 8, Advanced Sass Coding*. This structure should look like the following image:

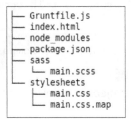

```
├── Gruntfile.js
├── index.html
├── node_modules
├── package.json
├── sass
│   └── main.scss
└── stylesheets
    ├── main.css
    └── main.css.map
```

Notice that the Sass code in `main.scss` requires Compass. It imports Compass using the following line of SCSS code:

```
@import 'compass/typography/vertical_rhythm';
```

In this recipe, you will install the `grunt-contrib-compass` plugin. This plugin requires you to have Ruby, Sass, and Compass >=1.0.1 installed. You can read how to install these tools in *Chapter 1, Getting Started with Sass*, of this book.

How to do it...

You should perform the following steps to integrate Compass in your build process:

1. Copy the files from the *Creating a vertical rhythm for your website* recipe of *Chapter 8, Advanced Sass Coding*, into your working directory.

2. Run the following command in your console to create the `package.json` file for your project:

   npm init

3. Then, locally install grunt and the plugin by running the following command:

   npm install grunt grunt-contrib-compass --save-dev

4. Create a Gruntfile.js file that will contain code like that shown here:

```
module.exports = function(grunt) {
  grunt.initConfig({
    //Add the Tasks configurations here.
    compass: {                             // Task
      dist: {                              // Target
        options: {                         // Target options
          sassDir: 'sass',
          cssDir: 'stylesheets',
          force: true,
          environment: 'production'
        },
      }
    }
  });

  grunt.loadNpmTasks('grunt-contrib-compass');

  // Define Tasks here
  grunt.registerTask('default', ['compass']);
}
```

5. Now, you can compile your project by running the following command in your console:

   grunt

How it works...

The Compass task in this recipe replaces the Sass task, as used in the *Adding the Sass compiler task* recipe of this chapter. The grunt-contrib-compass plugin comes with some options, which are similar to the options of Compass, as described in *Chapter 6, Using Compass*, of this book.

To debug your code, you will have to set the `environment` option to `development`. In the development mode, the Compass task does not generate compressed CSS code and includes CSS `sourcemaps` for debugging by default.

The grunt-contrib-compass plugin does not use the `files` field to set the paths for your destination and sources files. Instead of the commonly used `files` field, you will have to explicitly set the `sassDir` and `cssDir` options.

There's more...

Instead of the `grunt-contrib-compass` plugin, you can also use the `grunt-contrib-sass` plugin with the compass option set to `true`, as described in the *Adding the Sass compiler task* recipe of this Chapter. To compile the SCSS used in this recipe with `grunt-contrib-sass`, the Javascript code in your Gruntfile.js file should look like that shown here:

```javascript
module.exports = function(grunt) {
  grunt.initConfig({
    //Add the Tasks configurations here.
    sass: {                                     // Task
      dist: {                                   // Target
        options: {                              // Target options
          style: 'expanded',
          compass: true
        },
        files: {                                // Dictionary of
files
          'stylesheets/main.css': 'sass/main.scss' // 'destination':
'source'
        }
      }
    }
  });

  grunt.loadNpmTasks('grunt-contrib-sass');

  // Define Tasks here
  grunt.registerTask('default', ['sass']);
}
```

The `grunt-sass` plugin, which uses LibSass, cannot be used to compile your SCSS code for compass. LibSass does not support Compass due to the usage of Ruby Sass internals. Those who prefer LibSass over Ruby Sass should look for alternatives to Compass. **Eyeglass** is one such alternative for Compass. Eyeglass was created as the JavaScript-based successor to Compass; it brings the power of node modules to your Sass files. Eyeglass is very modular and has no CSS3 module.

Bourbon, as described in *Chapter 13, Meeting the Bourbon Family*, of this book, can be used with both grunt-sass and grunt-contrib-sass. It provides conveniently mixins and helpers. Read the *Using Bourbon with Grunt* recipe to find out how to use Bourbon with Grunt. Vendor prefixing can be done with the `autoprefixer` plugin, as described in the *Automatically prefixing your code with Grunt* recipe.

See also

- Read more about the grunt-contrib-compass plugin at `https://github.com/gruntjs/grunt-contrib-compass`
- The official website of Compass can be found at `http://compass-style.org/`
- Learn more about Eyeglass at `https://github.com/sass-eyeglass`

Installing Bourbon in the build chain

Chapter 13, Meeting the Bourbon Family, of this book describes, among others, how to build a semantic layout with the Bourbon and Neat Sass libraries. In this recipe, you will learn how to integrate the code of the *Semantic grids with Neat* recipe of *Chapter 13, Meeting the Bourbon Family*, into your Grunt build chain.

Getting ready

Install Grunt, as described in the *Installing Grunt* recipe of this chapter.

How to do it...

Perform the following steps to compile your code with Grunt and use the Bourbon and Neat Sass libraries:

1. Copy the files from the *Semantic grids with Neat* recipe of *Chapter 13, Meeting the Bourbon Family*, into your working directory. Remove the `sass/bourbon` and `sass/neat` folders.

2. Then, change the import paths for Bourbon and Neat in the file. These paths should look like that shown here:

```
@import 'bourbon';
@import 'neat';
```

3. Run the following command in your console to create the package.json file for your project:

```
npm init
```

4. Then, locally install grunt and the required plugins by running the following commands in your console:

```
npm install grunt node-bourbon node-neat --save-dev
```

5. Create a new Gruntfile.js that will contain a JSON code like that shown here:

```
module.exports = function(grunt) {
  grunt.initConfig({
    //Add the Tasks configurations here.
    sass: {                                    // Task
      dist: {                                  // Target
        options: {                             // Target options
          style: 'expanded',
          loadPath: require('node-neat').includePaths
        },
        files: {                               // Dictionary of
files
          'stylesheets/main.css': 'sass/main.scss' // 'destination':
'source'
        }
      }
    }
  });

  grunt.loadNpmTasks('grunt-contrib-sass');


  // Define Tasks here
  grunt.registerTask('default', ['sass']);
}
```

6. Now, you can run the following command in your console to compile your Sass code into CSS code:

```
grunt
```

How it works...

Because you have installed the node-bourbon and node-neat libraries, you do not have to install Bourbon or Neat, as described in the *Bourbon mixins for prefixing* and *Semantic grids with Neat* recipes of *Chapter 13, Meeting the Bourbon Family*. The SCSS code of the libraries should be readable for Sass; this can be done by setting the `loadPath` option for the `grunt-contrib-sass` plugin. Other sources can be concatenated to the `loadPath` option too. Because the node-neat library requires the node-bourbon library, you do not have to explicitly set the path for node-bourbon too.

Notice that you do not have to install the node-bourbon and node-neat libraries when you install both Bourbon and Neat by hand. In case you do not remove the folders, as described in the first step of this recipe, you can still compile your code with Grunt. You should also ignore the second step and leave the import paths intact.

There's more...

Notice that the `grunt-contrib-sass` plugin requires Ruby Sass installed. The node-bourbon and node-neat libraries are not tested for Ruby Sass, only for LibSass. To compile your Sass code with LibSass, you can replace the `grunt-contrib-sass` plugin with the grunt-sass plugin, as described in the *Adding the Sass compiler task* recipe of this chapter.

In *Chapter 11, Foundation and Sass*, of this book, you can read about Foundation. The Foundation 6 framework provides an extremely handy Sass package with Grunt preinstalled; even the `Gruntfile.js` file is preconfigured to compile all of Foundation's Sass files on the fly.

See also

- More information about the `node-bourbon` library can be found at `https://www.npmjs.com/package/node-bourbon`

- The `node-neat` library can be found at `https://www.npmjs.com/package/node-neat`

Automatically prefixing your code with Grunt

Browser-specific prefixes can make CSS3, and therefore, Sass code, complex and more difficult to maintain. Mixins (prebuilt), such as Compass, offer you the opportunity to write single line declarations for properties, such as gradients and shadows. The `autoprefixer` plugin can prefix your code automatically; it uses the Can I Use database (available at `http://caniuse.com/`) in order to find the prefixes that meet your requirements. In this recipe, you will not directly use the autoprefix plugin, which is depreciated now in favor of the `grunt-postcss` plugin.

Getting ready

The only requirement for this recipe is to have the `grunt-postcss` plugin installed and loaded in your `Gruntfile.js` file. If you have installed the `grunt-autoprefix` plugin in the *Installing Grunt plugins* recipe of this chapter, you can run the following commands in the root of your project:

```
npm remove grunt-autoprefixer --save-dev
```

In this recipe, you will use the CSS column layout code from the *Browser support* recipe of *Chapter 7, Cross-Browser CSS3 Mixins*, again.

How to do it...

Learn how to automatically prefix your compiled CSS code:

1. Copy the files from the *Browser support* recipe of *Chapter 7, Cross-Browser CSS3 Mixins*, into your working directory.

2. Run the following commands in your console:

    ```
    npm install grunt autoprefixer grunt-postcss --save-dev
    grunt init
    ```

3. Then, create a new `Gruntfile.js` that will contain a JSON code like that shown here:

    ```
    module.exports = function(grunt) {
      grunt.initConfig({
        //Add the Tasks configurations here.
        sass: {                                         // Task
          dist: {                                       // Target
            options: {                                  // Target options
              style: 'expanded'
            },
            files: {                                    // Dictionary of
    files
              'stylesheets/main.css': 'sass/main.scss' // 'destination':
    'source'
            }
          }
        },
        postcss: {
          options: {
            map: true,
            processors: [
              require('autoprefixer')({browsers: ['last 1 version']})
            ]
    ```

```
      },
      dist: {
        src: 'stylesheets/main.css'
      }


    }
  });


  grunt.loadNpmTasks('grunt-contrib-sass');
  grunt.loadNpmTasks('grunt-postcss');


  // Define Tasks here
  grunt.registerTask('default', ['sass','postcss:dist']);
}
```

4. The `content-columns()` mixin in the `sass/components/_columns.scss` Sass template contains only the official W3C rules to declare the properties for the CSS columns, as it can be seen in the following SCSS code:

```
@mixin content-columns($column-count, $column-gap: $grid-gutter-
width){
  column-count: $column-count;
  column-gap: $column-gap;
}
```

5. After running the `grunt` command in your console, the compiled CSS code will look like that shown here:

```
.columns {
  -webkit-column-count: 3;
     -moz-column-count: 3;
          column-count: 3;
  -webkit-column-gap: 15px;
     -moz-column-gap: 15px;
          column-gap: 15px;
}
```

6. As you can see in the preceding code, vendor prefixes are automatically added.

How it works...

The autoprefixer parses CSS and adds vendor-prefixed CSS properties using the Can I Use database. This database contains information for each browser version and also includes statistics about the current usage of the different browser versions.

With the browser options, you can set the browser you will have to support. By default, the browser option is set to an array, as follows:

```
['> 1%', 'last 2 versions', 'Firefox ESR', 'Opera 12.1']
```

Instead of using the autoprefixer directly, the `grunt-postcss` plugin has been used. Unlike the traditional approach with separate plugins, `grunt-postcss` allows you to parse and save CSS only once, applying all the postprocessors in memory and, thus, reducing your build time. PostCSS is also a simple tool for writing your own CSS postprocessors. Post processors change the compiled CSS code, so the CSS sourcemap should also be updated. The `grunt-postcss` supports both inline and separated sourcemaps.

If the sourcemap option is set to true, PostCSS will try to locate a sourcemap from Sass using an annotation comment, and create a new sourcemap based on the one found (or it will just create a new inlined sourcemap). The created sourcemap can be either a separate file or an inlined map depending on what the previous sourcemap was.

There's more...

You should not compress or minify your code before running `autoprefixer`. The `grunt-postcss` plugin enables you to run a postprocessor, which minifies your code. CSSnano is a modular minifier composed of a single responsibility PostCSS plugin. To minify your CSS code with CSSnano, you will have to install it and add it to your file, Gruntfile.js. So, you will have to run the following command in your console:

```
npm install cssnano --save-dev
```

Make sure the `postcss` task looks like that shown here:

```
        postcss: {
          options: {
            map: true,
            processors: [
              require('autoprefixer')({browsers: ['last 1 version']}),
              require('cssnano')() // minify the result
            ]
          },
          dist: {
            src: 'stylesheets/main.css'
          }
        }
```

Other minifiers, such as `grunt-contrib-cssmin`, based on `clean-css` should run in a separate task after the `autoprefixer` task.

Finally, notice that the recipe uses a mixin to set the `column-count` and `column-gap` properties for the column layout. Instead of a mixin, you can also use the column shorthand property, which enables you to set the `column-count` and `column-gap` properties at once. Doing this, your SCSS should look like that shown here:

```scss
.columns {
  columns: 3 $grid-gutter-width;
}
```

See also

▶ When using the autoprefixer task, you can define all your properties with a single declaration using the official W3C rules, described at `http://www.w3.org/Style/CSS/specs.en.html`.

▶ Read more about CSSnano at `http://cssnano.co/`.

▶ Clean-css is a fast and efficient Node.js library for minifying CSS files. You can read more about this minifier at `htps://github.com/jakubpawlowicz/clean-css`.

Getting Grunt watch for Sass, and LiveReload to work

The browser extensions from LiveReload enable you to get a live preview of your changes to your code. Currently, extensions are available for Safari, Google Chrome, and Firefox. Notice that the extension for Safari does not work when you open the files directly in your browsers by using in the file:/// protocol. In this recipe, you will learn how to integrate LiveReload into your build chain.

Getting ready

This recipe requires you to have the watch plugin (`grunt-contribe-watch`) and the Sass plugin (`grunt-contrib-sass`), as described in the *Adding the Sass compiler task* recipe, installed. You will also need Safari, Google Chrome, or Firefox, and the free LiveReload extension installed.

How to do it...

Extend your Grunt workflow by using the browser extensions LiveReload:

1. Visit `http://livereload.com/extensions/` and follow the instructions to install the required extension for your browser.

2. Copy the files from the *Browser support* recipe of *Chapter 7, Cross-Browser CSS3 mixins*, into your working directory.

3. Run the following commands in your console:

   npm install grunt grunt-contrib-sass grunt-contrib-watch --save-dev

   grunt init

4. Then, create a new `Gruntfile.js` that will contain a JSON code like that shown here:

```javascript
module.exports = function(grunt) {
  grunt.initConfig({
    //Add the Tasks configurations here.
    sass: {                                    // Task
      dist: {                                  // Target
        options: {                             // Target options
          style: 'expanded'
        },
        files: {                               // Dictionary of
files
          'stylesheets/main.css': 'sass/main.scss' // 'destination':
'source'
        }
      }
    },
    watch: {
      all: {
        files: 'index.html', // Change this if you are not
watching index.html
      },
      css: {
        files: 'sass/*.scss',
        tasks: ['sass']
      },
      options: {
        livereload: true, // Set livereload to trigger a reload
upon change
      }
    }
  });

  grunt.loadNpmTasks('grunt-contrib-sass');
  grunt.loadNpmTasks('grunt-contrib-watch');

  // Define Tasks here
  grunt.registerTask('default', ['watch']);
}
```

5. After this, you can run the following command in your console:

    `grunt`

6. The preceding command calls the watch task, and you will see the following message in your console:

    ```
     Running "watch" task
    Waiting...
    ```

7. Now, open the `index.html` file in your browser and enable LiveReload.

8. Then, open the `scss/main.scss` file in your text editor.

9. Change the number of columns in the `scss/main.scss` file and save the file. Now, you will see that your browser will automatically reload and show you the new situation. After saving the `scss/main.scss` file, the following text should also be outputted to your console:

    ```
    >> File "sass/main.scss" changed.

    Running "sass:dist" (sass) task


    Done, without errors.

    Completed in 4.737s at Thu Dec 15 2016 19:37:50 GMT+0100 (CET) -
    Waiting...
    ```

How it works...

The LiveReload browser extensions insert a Javascript (livereload.js), which listens to port 35729 by default. The `grunt-contrib-watch` plugin triggers this LiveReload script to reload the page. The `Gruntfile.js` file contains both a sass and watch task. By default, Grunt will call the watch task. The watch task has an all and CSS subtask. The CSS subtask will look like that shown here:

```
css: {
        files: 'sass/*.scss',
        tasks: ['sass']
    }
```

The preceding `files` field sets which files should be watched. When a file change of these files is detected, the plugin will run the tasks declared with the `tasks` field. So, when you edit and save `.scss`, any file in the `sass/` folder the sass compile task will run and LiveReload will be triggered afterwards.

There's more...

Since the `grunt-contrib-watch` plugin has built-in support for live reload, you do not have to install the `grunt-contrib-livereload` plugin anymore. Instead of using the LiveReload browser extensions, you can also integrate LiveReload.js directly in your HTML.

See also

▶ Read more about grunt-contrib-plug, which predefines tasks whenever watched file patterns are added, changed, or deleted at `https://github.com/gruntjs/grunt-contrib-watch`

▶ An implementation of the LiveReload server in Node.js can be found at `https://www.npmjs.com/package/livereload`

Utilizing Yeoman

Yeoman scaffolds out a new application for you. It writes Gruntfile.js and pulls in relevant build tasks. It also adds package manager dependencies for Bower and npm that you might need for your build. In this recipe, you will learn how to use Yeoman to step up an application with Bootstrap 4.

Getting ready

Yo is the scaffolding tool from Yeoman. You will have to install yo. You will also need a package manager; in this recipe, you will use Bower. Finally, the build tool used in this recipe is Grunt. Run the following command in your console to install these tools:

```
npm install -g yo grunt-cli bower
```

How to do it...

You need to perform the following steps:

1. Run the command like that shown here in your console to install the Bootstrap 4 Yeoman generator:

   ```
   npm install -g generator-bootstrap4
   ```

2. Then, run the following command in your console to generate a new project:

   ```
   yo bootstrap4
   ```

3. Now, the following output will be shown in your console. Select the icon font you want to use and choose whether you want to enable flexbox support or not:

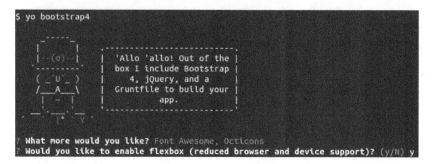

4. Now, you can run the following command to start a server and preview your app:

grunt serve

5. The server started with the command in the previous step runs on http://localhost:9000/. When your (default) browser does not automatically open this location, you can navigate to it by hand. You will find that your Bootstrap 4 app will look as follows:

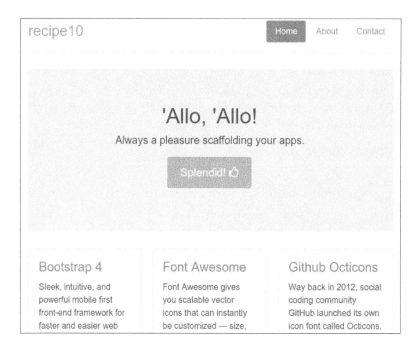

How it works...

Yeoman helps you to kickstart new projects, prescribing best practices and tools to help you stay productive. The Yeoman workflow comprises three types of tools for improving your productivity and satisfaction when building a web app: the scaffolding tool (yo), the build tool (Grunt, Gulp, and so on), and the package manager (such as Bower and npm). In the Yeoman workflow, the build tool tasks compile your Sass code into CSS code. Other recipes of this chapter describe these Grunt tasks in more detail.

Yeoman provides a generator ecosystem. A generator is basically a plugin that can be run with the yo command. Generators can scaffold complete projects. In this recipe, you used the Bootstrap 4 generator. This generator scaffolds out a frontend Bootstrap 4 web app. It also enables you to optionally integrate the flexbox grid or icon fonts into your app. In *Chapter 12*, *Bootstrap and Sass*, you can read more about Bootstrap 4.

There's more...

In the recipe, you run the grunt serve command. When running the default task, Yeoman will build your code and run several tests.

In this chapter, you can read about the differences between the Grunt and Gulp task runners. The Bootstrap 4 generator in this recipe uses the Grunt task runner. Other Yeoman generators may also use Gulp for their build process.

See also

▶ The official Bootstrap website can be found at http://getbootstrap.com

▶ More information on Node.js can be found at http://nodejs.org/

▶ Read more about Bower at http://bower.io/

▶ Finally, get information about and download jQuery at https://jquery.com/

Index

B

background gradients 71
base64 30
BEM 22, 343
Bitters
  reference link 336
  used, for creating buttons 333-336
blind text generator
  reference link 161
Block Element Modifier (BEM)
  about 84
  applying 114-118
  reference link 114
Blueprint CSS
  URL 236
Bootstrap
  about 63, 277, 351
  compiling, for project file 283
  components, URL 293
  configuring, variables used 284-287
  customizing, variables used 280-282
  downloading 278-280
  installing 278-280
  integrating 351-355
  mixins, using 301
  reference link 176
  Sass, using with 313- 315
  URL 155
  used, for implementing semantic
      layouts 309-312
  using, with Compass 154, 155
  WordPress, using with 313-315
Bootstrap 4
  and WordPress, URL 315
border-radius
  URL 149
Bourbon
  about 317, 349
  installing, in build chain 390-392
  URL 392
  using, inside Rails 349, 350
Bourbon mixins
  used, for prefixing 318-321
Bower
  reference link 265
  URL 280, 401

box-shadow 163
box-sizing property
  using, with Sass 214-216
Brackets
  about 25
  reference link 25
Breakpoint
  URL 202
  used, for writing media queries 200-202
brightness 192
browser
  Sass code, debugging 32-35
  Sass code, editing 32-35
browsers
  Sass, using 11-14
Brunch
  reference link 261
build chain
  Bourbon, installing 390-392
  Compass, integrating 387-390
  LiveReload, installing into 396, 398
buttons
  creating, Bitters used 333-336
  customizing 363-365

C

calc() CSS function
  reference link 63
Camba
  URL 290
Can I use database
  about 167, 379
  URL 147, 379
  using 167-169
cascade 205
circle
  reference link 126
classes
  using 301-305
clean-css CSS minifier
  reference link 20
clear fix
  reference link 70
clearing floats
  reference link 250